THE SOBRIETY EXPERIMENT: HOW MODERATING YOUR DRINKING CAN CHANGE YOUR LIFE

TWO WEEKS TO A HEALTHIER, HAPPIER, YOUNGER, SLIMMER YOU

CASSANDRA GAISFORD

CONTENTS

Praise for Cassandra's Sobriety Books	vii
Author's Note	xvii
How to Use This Book	1
Test Your Knowledge	3
Blame Your Brain?	6
Week One: The Call for Sobriety	9
Problem Drinking?	12
Happier Hours?	23
'Why' is the New High	31
Be Wary of What Catches Your Eye	43
Once a Liar, Always a Liar?	49
Alcohol Unmasked	56
Sweet Misery	64
Savvy Sobriety	67
Wounded Warriors	73
Control Alcohol Before It Controls You	84
The Surprising Joy of Sobriety	92
Week Two: Strategies for Sobriety	97
1. High On Believing: Wrestling With the God Thing	100
2. Be Free Where You Are: Hack Your Habits	103
3. Powerful Creativity	109
4. Pep up Your Peptides	117
5. Magic Mornings	122
6. Mindful Meditation—cultivating inner power	125
7. The Power of Now	129
8. Journal Your Way to Joyful Sobriety	132
9. Elevate Your Mindset	138
10. Face Your Demons	141
11. Get Angry	143
12. Glorious Gratitudes	149
13. Consult the Oracles	152

14. Purposeful Sobriety	155
15. Booze Busters: Look For Your Heroes	158
16. Jumping with Joy	160
17. Mind Power	162
18. Your Beautiful Minds	165
19. What's Your Truth? Do You Really Believe the Lies?	176
20. Mind Over Mojitos: Mindful Drinking	182
21. A Vision of Victory	184
22. Love is the Drug: Follow Your Passion	189
23. Move! Set your soul on fire.	193
24. Yoga	196
25. Trust Your Gut	199
26. Relationship Rehab	212
27. Prayer Therapy	217
28. Healing Hypnosis	220
29. Affirm Your Desire For Sobriety: Self-Soothe	223
30. Rational Emotive Behavioral Therapy	226
31. Book Therapy	232
32. Musicology	236
33. Massage	241
34. The Smell of Desire	244
35. Sleep	252
36. Breathe Deeply	257
37. Beat Resistance	259
38. Ride The Buzz of The Helpers High	269
39. Mood Food	272
40. Step Away	279
41. Laugh and Play	284
42. Color Your Mood	288
43. Go Low	290
44. Real Resilience	294
45. How to Party Sober	298
Free Workbook!	303
Conclusion	305
A Few Last Words	311

EXCERPT: MIND OVER MOJITOS: HOW MODERATING YOUR DRINKING CAN CHANGE YOUR LIFE

Praise for Mind Your Mojitos	317
About These Recipes	319
Giving Good Glass	321

PART I

Non-alcoholic Drinks For Spring & Summer	327
1. Virgin Island Fox	329
2. Passion Fruit Bubbly	331
3. Passion Fruit Power Punch	333
4. Blueberry and Maple Mojito	334
5. Virgin Mojito	336

EXCERPT: HOW TO FIND YOUR JOY AND PURPOSE

Praise for How to Find Your Joy and Purpose	341
Authors Note	343
Introduction	345
How to Use This Book	351
Step 1: The Call For Joy	357
1. What is Joy?	359
2. Joy For All	361
3. What Can Joy Do?	362
4. Reality Check On Joy	364
5. Comparison Robs Joy	366
Did you enjoy this excerpt?	369

Also by Cassandra Gaisford	371
Further Resources	375
Please Leave A Review	383
Stay In Touch	385
About the Author	387
Copyright	389

PRAISE FOR CASSANDRA'S SOBRIETY BOOKS

"I work with people and their whanau/families on a daily basis who have, have had or have recovered from Alcohol and Other Drug issues. The damage caused by AOD over use and abuse is enormous and has ongoing negative effects on our society and future generations mainly due to observation and learned behaviours.

I really like the approach that this book takes in not attempting to stop drinking totally. It instead explains and coaches how to manage and cope with consuming alcohol so that the damaging effects may be minimised. This is a very useful supportive book for 'drinkers' and their families.

It is a book that is very easy to read and understand. I really like the quotes, sayings and tools contained therein. This book is much bigger than just the social and familial issues with alcohol – It is in a very big way about 'Your Beautiful Mind'.

It fits very well with my style of practice and that is to start with the basics and move onwards and upwards from there. I see in the book an AHA (awakening, honesty, action) moment in the book. I really get the reference to wisdom (The smart person knows what to say, the wise person knows when to say it) and the associated learning.

I will be recommending this 'must read' book to my clients and their whanau/families and anybody else who will listen."

~ **Philipe Eyton, Counsellor, Life and Leadership Coach, BSocP, NZAC**

"I like the content of the book a lot. As an ex-drunk who quit for both mental and physical health reasons, it's very affirming. I like her comment that she's yet to meet an ex-drinker who preferred life as a drinker.

I think it will appeal to both people who are considering change and people who have made a change to their drinking and want both affirmation and some information so they can explain why to their friends.

I like its meandering style (it makes me think of sharing in a group). It's too good a message to ignore."

~ **Andrew Nicholls**

"What an incredibly informative read. I really love how Cassandra has different viewpoints that allow the reader to come to their own conclusions.

Mind Your Drink is a non-biased informative read based on various facts, research and readings and I feel it is a book that I could pick up time and time again, and that whatever is relevant to me at that time or moment in my life is what I'll be able to take away when I pick it up.

I loved that information was backed up by science and offered rhetorical questions and facts to get the reader thinking, rather than preaching or telling the reader how to do something.

I loved the perception that it is more helpful to heal the root of our cause to drink, rather than try to blindly control alcohol consumption, and that each reader will feel empowered to choose their own method for sobriety rather than feeling like they have to stick to rules. (Who likes rules anyway!?).

Very empowering, honest and thought-provoking."

~ **LW, Founder** *Soberly*

"One thing that I like about this book is that the author doesn't trash other recovery programs whether she agrees with them or not. This approach is very different (and refreshing) from other books I've read that claim to be the "real or only solution" which involves tearing down other methods in the process, but as Cassandra's book alludes—one form of recovery may work for some people and not others—it depends on the person, their physiology, background, life experience, etc.

"At first, I thought the segments about advertising would be boring but they actually really appealed to the part of me that loves science, facts, and proof. Reading the explanations led to many "Aha!" moments! I also felt so relieved to read there is a sober/not drinking movement going on. I felt relieved and hopeful. How I wish this was going on when I started my own drinking career in my early teens. I'm feeling so grateful to Cassandra for writing it. There is so much vital information packed into this book and I wish fervently that it ends up on the best seller list!"

~ **Lisa Ruggiero, 5-Star Review**

"I realised my minimal drinking habit of the past 11 months entered my life gently without any major decision and has brought to my life a feeling of relaxedness, a feeling of self-love, I didn't realise that by the act of less alcohol I have achieved the list of benefits cited in *Mind Your Drink*. This chapter allowed me to reflect on my choice and to realise that it was, and is, an act of self-love and that feels very special to me.

"This is a book for anyone who is struggling with alcohol (or even overeating/comfort eating - it can be used for several addictions) as a way to encourage the reader to look at their drinking (or other affliction) in a loving way, encouraging the reader to work with their intelligent self, on a loving level, it offers support, (you don't feel alone), it offers stories of awareness, idea's for moving beyond the clutches of alcohol and experiencing the joy of living a full, creative, and/or self-loving life."

~ **Catherine Sloan, Counselor**

"I see people that I would love to give this book recommendation to. They need this in their lives-a few of who would not consider, they have any problem with alcohol, nor have any desire to stop drinking - but I liked this book because the message is that you take control of how you steer the ship. You can choose to decrease and manage your drinking or you can choose to omit alcohol altogether from your life.

"Alcohol is abused and I know a few young people (18-25yrs) that haven't a clue of what they're drinking or the impacts on them physically, mentally or emotionally. This is huge. Yet each and every week they are returning to the bottle to find some solace in drinking or in fact getting pissed.

"I love the connection Cassandra shares with herself in this book. The Sobriety Journal she mentions and has created is a fantastic tool - and I would recommend people use conjunction with this book and your own journey- it will do wonders. It's a great reflective tool also to go back to down the track, as Cassandra has openly displayed herself.

"I am quite surprised myself about the new knowledge I gained from what I read in this book. And wondered why when I was drinking did I never stop to consider what I was drinking, what my drink was made of and how- never ever! I can remember thinking, I wonder how many calories are in this beer. Or how much sugar. But never looked it up as such, as I didn't actually want to know at the time. I was in somewhat of a denial. I just wanted to consume it anyway. I quite often was sick on the evening or the next day after a binge.

"So this information needs to be shared and is available in this book. I think that's fantastic. It's not too complex. At first, I wondered if I would see my younger relatives reading this and relating to it. And thought, maybe not. But then when momentum picked up and the diverse realities were seen and heard - I thought it would relate to many soft spots they have and I hopefully allow them to take control of themselves and their drinking.

"Loving what I read. I am seeing some home truths and common vulnerabilities which makes this book relatable to many."

~ **Jo-Maitera**

"I cold-turkey stopped imbibing alcohol and I've gained twenty years in energy. We all know we don't drink a lot but what an insidious thing nightly alcohol is."

~ **Melinda Hammond, Author**

DEDICATION

This book is dedicated to four beautiful women:
My daughter Hannah Joy,
My grandmother Molly Fairweather
songstress Amy Winehouse
and Venus, the goddess of love

...and to all the beautiful souls whose lives have been impacted by alcohol and became sober warriors, fought their way back from addiction, and inspired us all

AUTHOR'S NOTE

I won't lie to you. I used to love to drink. I loved the color, the texture, the taste. I don't agree with other sobriety authors who write how horrible alcohol tastes.

The booze barons know how to package alcohol so it ticks all the boxes: product, price, packaging, promotion and place. Commonly known as the 5 P's of marketing, alcohol manufacturers and their distributors have it down pat—and profits are soaring.

But so is consumer consciousness. As with tobacco, so increasingly with booze. Alcohol tells lies masquerading as truth.

- Happier hours? Not if you don't know when to stop.
- Increased confidence? Not if you can only find it in a glass.
- Sexual appeal? Not if you count the concealed calories.
- Skyrocketing success? Not if you count lost hours to hangovers, stress and reduced clarity.

Here's my truth:

- Insomnia
- Bloating
- Weight gain
- Vomiting
- Shame
- Anxiety
- Insecurity
- Isolation
- Depression
- Suicide idealization

Here's the truth of what has happened to those closest to me:

- Suicide
- Sexual abuse
- Alcohol-induced psychosis
- Incarceration
- Psychiatric care
- Depression
- Anxiety
- Weight-gain
- Financial ruin
- and more, much more

I once dreamt of a world where sobriety was normalized not stigmatized. And it's happening. Increasing numbers of people are embracing the joy of sobriety. Mind your drink? Yes, please.

As movie-producer and fashion icon Tom Ford said in an interview, "It doesn't hurt. I mean, can we talk about the drinking in London? The two glasses at lunch? The three vodka tonics you have in the evening at the office—cos you're there until eight? The two you have in the bath. Then you go out to dinner and they bring you more teeny-tiny drinks. So you're now up to 10 and then you go to a party and you're in your forties, drinking 12-13 glasses each day. And eating lettuce to stay slim. I spent so many days writing apology notes and sending flowers. It had to stop."

Don't panic. Sobriety does NOT mean abstinence. Although, that's how some organizations like Alcoholics Anonymous define it. And that's okay.

For others sobriety means being sober—a nice glass of wine from time-to-time—but strictly no binging, puking, or getting 'shit-faced.' However, for a great many people abstinence is truly the only path to freedom.

You don't have to be an alcoholic to have a problem with alcohol—it's one of the most addictive, legalized drugs on the planet.

Perhaps, like me, you're ready to break-up with alcohol and do a J. Lo and, flaunt your sober glow. Maybe you'd like to join the masses who are sexier, healthier, and happier alcohol-free.

Whether you're flirting with the idea of sobriety or starting out on your sober journey, or ready to give going tee-total a whirl, you'll find plenty of support in the pages that follow.

HOW TO USE THIS BOOK

Knowledge is power, which is why *The Sobriety Experiment* kicks of with truths—many of which are suppressed by the booze barons.

Why do we over-drink? The answer, neuroscientists tell us, lies not in our bellies, but in our brains. *Blame Your Brain* take a short but deep dive in the psychology, biology and physiology of why alcohol keeps us coming back for more, more, more.

With knowledge comes wisdom. Armed with the truth you'll find it easy to kick the booze habit.

WEEK ONE CHALLENGES and guides you to rethink the role of alcohol in your life (and the wider world.)

WEEK TWO OFFERS A TASTING platter of strategies to support your successful sobriety. Take a read through first and then pick 'n mix those that you think or feel are right for you. From there you can make a daily success strategy. For you, as it does for me, this may vary from week-to-week.

For example, this week, I'm embracing some of the strategies in week one, including re-reading the chapters *'Why' Is The New High* and *Alcohol Unmasked*.

From Week Two I'm arming myself with mindfulness, meditation, journalling, purposeful sobriety, strategies from the chapter *Jumping with Joy* and boosting my supplies of tasty, guilt-free non-alcoholic alternatives.

Read to the end for free chapters from *Mind Over Mojitos: Easy Alcohol-Free Recipes for Happier Hours & a Joy Filled Life*.

TEST YOUR KNOWLEDGE

"Drinking worked in the beginning: I felt wonderful, warm, and fuzzy... almost pretty...What I didn't know was that I was in a prison of my own making," says former addict Colette Baron-Reid—now a sober intuitive counselor & author.

If you're worried about your drinking or have had a heavy drinking problem for a while chances are you're well aware of the signifant health implications, and how alcohol ruins many areas of your life.

But many people aren't. They binge drink like it's a sport, scull drinks like there's no tomorrow. Ignoring the wake of devastation they leave in their path, they resist making a change for the better. Sometimes they leave it until it's too late to undo their mistakes.

If you feel that it's time to rethink the role and purpose of alcohol in your life. Test your current knowledge by answering the questions below:

- Do you know what alcohol really is?

- How is alcohol made? What process creates stronger spirits?
- Is alcohol a known cause for more than 60 different health conditions? Do you know what these are?
- Do you really understand the damage you're doing to your body when you're hung over?
- Why can a 5 percent beer can make you twice as drunk as a 4 percent version?
- What about an 8 percent craft beer? Is wine safer to drink than vodka?
- What is the definition of binge drinking? Can it kill you? Why can't you stop?
- Which country says it's fine to drink three pints a night?
- What is a unit of alcohol? What is a standard drink? Why does it matter?
- How many units of alcohol are deemed safe daily? Weekly? Why?
- Is it true that women should drink less than men?
- What are the health-effects and risk factors if you drink more than the recommended guidelines?
- Does alcohol depress the central nervous system at high doses?
- Did you know that alcohol can offer a short-term high, followed by deep lows, depression, anxiety and suicidal thoughts?
- Did you know that many alcoholic drinks include compounds called congeners that add to the taste, smell or color of the drink? Why do they increase the likelihood and intensity of suffering a hangover, and other undesirable side effects?
- Do you really know what the labelling on the bottles you buy really means?
- Do you know that lobbyists influence governments so they can maximize the sale of alcohol to minors, and society's most vulnerable people?
- Do you even care? Are you happy remaining blissfully blind?

You'll find the answer to these questions in the pages that follow.

BLAME YOUR BRAIN?

Why do we over-drink? The answer, some neuroscientists believe, lies not in our bellies, but in our brains.

A team of New Zealand scientists has recently begun a new study that aims to pinpoint a 'sensory fingerprint' behind the urge to eat for pleasure. Their findings appear to apply equally to alcohol.

"Eating (and drinking) is a multi-sensory experience, where the taste, smell, appearance and even sound of food are integrated to give pleasure," says Dr. Mei Peng, of Otago University's Department of Food Science.

Some people are particularly susceptible to eating (and drinking) for pleasure, or what's termed hedonic pleasure, says Peng. These differences are thought to be related to brain networks related to rewards. Add alcohol to the mix and this makes fighting against our desire to over-indulge a challenging task.

But we can trick our brains and stimulate the reward networks by losing the booze, and plying ourselves with all the other sensory inputs which alcohol barons know make us attracted and addicted to their products.

Things like bright, tantalizing colors; sensuously delicious smells; sparkling water bubbling over cool crystal; the warm, sultry feel of a well-rounded glass cupped in your hand, simultaneously warming your alcohol-free drink.

Plus, alcohol is basically sugar, with more kilojoules. We know how addictive sugar is, but this time we'll get a natural high with plenty of fruits and no booze—and no poisonous ethanol (the ingredient found in beer, wine and spirits that causes drunkenness and destroys your brain cells.)

Instead of pickled pretend prettiness you'll reap the benefits of mindful sobriety and beat the drug barons at their own game. Fun!

I won't bore you with bloated tales of my own alcohol-fuelled misdemeanors, but I will surprise you with some easy-peasy bright and breezy ways to spark joy, get high, and send your dopamine levels soaring—naturally.

As the physician Alfred Mercier once said, "What we learn with pleasure we never forget."

No more pickled brain?

Cheers—I'll raise a glass to that.

WEEK ONE: THE CALL FOR SOBRIETY

WEEK ONE: THE CALL FOR SOBRIETY

Knowledge is power, which is why *The Sobriety Experiment* kicks of by challenging the way we think about alcohol and its role (or not) in our life.

PROBLEM DRINKING?

"Not everyone who has a drinking problem will be able to see it," says recovering alcoholic and author of *Drink: The Intimate Relationship Between Women and Alcohol,* Anne Dowsett-Johnston.

Is your drinking already cause for concern? How do you know if you have a real problem, versus a temporary itch that you're using alcohol to scratch?

"If you want to know if you're getting into trouble, ask yourself ... are you drinking to numb? To numb feelings, to numb stress, to numb depression or anxiety?'" Dowsett Johnston says.

Alcohol makes us love life, we're told. If this is true, why aren't we a happier lot? Burnout, stress, anxiety have become worldwide epidemics—and with them alcohol and food addictions. We're either eating or drinking our way to happiness—or both.

Granted, not everyone has a problem with alcohol. Some people say there are four types of drinkers:

- Light or non

- Weekend-non binge
- Weekend drinkers who get drunk
- Heavy drinkers where every night is party night

The problem with those in the latter two categories may not be the booze, but maladaptive attempts to mask the causal factors.

Addictions and consistent alcohol abuse, in particular, are essentially attempts to escape pain. The nature and causal factors of this pain and the scale of dependency will vary in specifics and severity from person to person.

We all suffer painful experiences—but not everyone has learned to cope in a way that promotes, not depletes emotional, mental, physical and spiritual well-being, health and happiness.

Instead, too often developing and becoming dependent on unhealthy coping techniques becomes the norm—a norm that creates even more problems.

Fortunately, developing more positive ways of coping with life's inevitable ups and downs is not only possible but even enjoyable.

Changing your habits, even very deeply entrenched ones is a learned skill—and you'll find plenty of teachers when you go in search of answers.

Don't wait to hit rock bottom before you do something about your drinking or whatever's going on in your life that causes you to drink too much.

Start now. You can, and you will control your drinking. You don't always need to check in to rehab or pay mega dollars to sit on a psychologist's couch. It's totally fine if that turns out to be your sobriety solution, in full or in part.

The trouble with the 'disempowered' and 'disease' model of addiction, is that a great number of people can lead you to believe that controlling alcohol is completely beyond your reach.

Being told that if you drink too much, you have a disease, an incurable one at that, is neither helpful, truthful, nor empowering—even if it does feel better to know that it's not your fault that you drink too much.

We'll discuss the escalating rise of the disease model of addiction later in this book, but let's look at how some of the pros define addiction and substances abuse—what they focus on and what they miss.

THE MALADAPTIVE PATTERN OF RELYING ON ALCOHOL

Psychologists, psychiatrists, and many other addiction specialists predominantly focus on addiction as being a mental disorder, rather than an attempt to self-medicate or anaesthetize ones way through life. Very often a person's personal history of trauma, bullying or societal factors which aid, abet and accelerate their drinking are ignored.

The primary source used to classify problem drinking is provided by the American Psychiatric Association and their Diagnostic and Statistical Manual of Mental Disorders known as the DSM.

Over-consuming alcohol is a disease we're told. A disorder of the mind, or an inherited genetic defect. DSM followers turn a blind eye to the fact that alcohol is a self-prescribed, self-served, legalized drug of choice turned to by many as their stress, anxiety, depression, trauma or grief-numbing cure.

Granted, not a particularly robust one, but perhaps, not the 'only-able-to-be-cured-by-medical-professionals' illness we have been led to believe.

"There's an enormous sense of self-medication…. The fastest thing you can do at the cutting board is open a bottle of wine, pour yourself a glass. It's faster than going to your doctor to say 'I'm suffering from burnout,' it's faster than going to a yoga class and relaxing in a different way," says Dowsett-Johnston.

Even though Johnston knew she was getting into trouble with her drinking she says, "It took two family members and a sweetheart who confronted me, and luckily I took a sledgehammer and went to rehab and I'm in my 10th year of sobriety."

As you'll discover later in this chapter, with the passing of time alcohol has shifted from being viewed as a problem of faulty, or maladaptive behavior, to one of disease.

This has opened the route to funding, and the creation of profitable business lines by drug companies scrambling to cure the 'disease' (or what I call the dis-ease) created by the world's most popular and legalized drug.

As a result, they have created a range of pharmaceuticals and manufactured drugs promising the ultimate (and profitable) cure. I recently heard they are trying to create an alcohol vaccine. Really? When did loving alcohol too much, or using it as an upper or a sedative, equate with Swine Flu, Chicken Pox, or Aids for that matter?

What if the ultimate cure lies in your own hands—a more mindful, holistic and therapeutic approach to how much you drink and why.

We're told loving alcohol too much is something we can't cure ourselves—that total abstinence is the only remedy. In my professional and personal experience, very often people choose to quit alcohol for good because they're just so over it.

Once alcohol is unmasked for the troublemaker it is, like a shitty lover, people choose never to go back. Whether it's fear of the havoc booze creates, or love—the joy and bliss they discover in their new partnership with life being alcohol-free—people who choose abstinence know life is better, way better, sober.

"You know, I never thought I'd never drink. I loved it, but going sober has forced me to face up to who I really am. I don't always have to be the life of the party. I can just leave and it's okay. So, I've realised I'm a lot more serious than I pretended to be," said the 36-year-old Hayley Holt, former ballroom dancing queen, snowboarding legend and TV star, and the former girlfriend of ex-All Black Captain, Richie McCaw, once said.

So serious in fact in 2017 she turned her set her sober sights high and turned her focus toward Parliament and campaigned in the electorate held by former Prime Minister, Sir John Key, on behalf of The Green Party.

Actor Colin Farrell also testifies that once problem drinking is kicked not only is life infinitely better—*you* are better.

"I have yet to meet a person whose sobriety has made their life worse. I have yet to. But I am open to it. If you find someone please get in touch with me because I would love to have a chat with them and ask them a couple of questions. I have yet to meet a person whose sobriety didn't make a better father, a better friend..."

Kristin Davis, most famous for her role as Charlotte York Goldenblatt in *Sex and the City*, has been alcohol-free since 1987. "Sometimes it would be nice to just have some red wine with dinner, but it's not worth the risk. I have a great life, a great situation. Why would I want risk self-destructive behavior?"

What do these people and others have in common? Their drinking was a problem—until it wasn't.

The chances are that you don't need a book and checklists to tell you that you have a problem, but just in case you're amongst the group of people who truly don't know how out of hand your drinking is getting you may be interested to learn what the American Psychiatric Association (APA) classifies as problematic.

WHAT IS PROBLEM DRINKING?

Regardless of whether you side with alcohol being or not being a disease, the APA classifications of problem drinking include:

- Tolerance and the never decreasing requirement for more
- Withdrawal symptoms when you can't get your fix
- Difficulty in giving up
- Persistent physical, psychological, social, mental and emotional problems that are likely to have been caused or exacerbated by your alcohol

The more symptoms you have, the more urgent the need for change.

Mmmm, using this definition, it would appear 85 percent of the drinking population has a problem. Remember this when people try to shame you for not drinking with taunts such as, "Do you have a problem?" No, my friend, they have the problem.

Addiction (termed substance dependence by the American Psychiatric Association—APA) was once defined as, "a maladaptive pattern of substance use leading to clinically significant impairment or distress."

This maladaptive pattern manifests by three (or more) of the following, occurring any time in the same 12-month period, say the APA:

1. Tolerance, as defined by either of the following: (a) A need for markedly increased amounts of the substance to achieve intoxication or the desired effect or (b) Markedly diminished effect with continued use of the same amount of the substance.

2. Withdrawal, as manifested by either of the following:

(a) The characteristic withdrawal syndrome for the substance, or

(b) The same (or closely related) substance is taken to relieve or avoid withdrawal symptoms.

3. The substance is often taken in larger amounts or over a longer period than intended.

4. There is a persistent desire or unsuccessful efforts to cut down or control substance use.

5. A great deal of time is spent in activities necessary to obtain the substance, use the substance, or recover from its effects.

6. Important social, occupational, or recreational activities are given up or reduced because of substance use.

7. The substance use is continued despite knowledge of having a persistent physical or psychological problem that is likely to have been caused or exacerbated by the substance (for example, current cocaine use despite recognition of cocaine-induced depression or continued drinking despite recognition that an ulcer was made worse by alcohol consumption).

"We just liked to have a good time."

CAN you tick-off three or more of the above? I bet you never thought of yourself as being maladaptive. As the founder of *Soberly*, a movement dedicated to supporting sober warriors, Libby Wallace writes,

"I remember a lecture I went to for one of my psychology papers, around 9 years ago, and the lecturer stood at the front and did a 'drinking quiz' similar to the Ministry of Health one to find out whether or not you have a drinking problem. About 60 out of the 100 students put their hands up to say that they had rated themselves with a score that effectively meant they were an alcoholic. After discussing with a few friends after, and in the tutorial later, we thought it was funny and that because we were students, it didn't relate to us, we just liked to have a good time."

ALCOHOL USE DISORDER & THE DISEASE OF ALCOHOL

In 2000 the DSM-IV criteria for substance dependence included several specifiers, one of which outlines whether substance dependence is accompanied by physiological dependence (evidence of tolerance or withdrawal) or without physiological dependence (no evidence of tolerance or withdrawal).

In addition, remission categories are classified into four subtypes: (1) full, (2) early partial, (3) sustained, and (4) sustained partial; on the basis of whether any of the criteria for abuse or dependence have been met and over what time frame.

The remission category can also be used for patients receiving agonist therapy (such as methadone maintenance or drugs designed to control alcohol dependence) or for those living in a controlled, drug-free environment.

This definition was altered in the 5th edition of the DSM. As compared to DSM-IV, the DSM-5's chapter on addictions was changed from "Substance-Related Disorders" to "Substance-Related and Addictive Disorders" to reflect developing understandings regarding addictions.

The DSM-5 specifically lists nine types of substance addictions within this category (alcohol; caffeine; cannabis; hallucinogens; inhalants; opioids; sedatives, hypnotics, and anxiolytics; stimulants; and tobacco).

These disorders are presented in separate sections, but they are not fully distinct because all drugs taken in excess activate the brain's reward circuitry, and their co-occurrence is common.

Problem drinking that becomes severe is given the medical diagnosis of "alcohol use disorder" or AUD in the DSM-V and is defined in the DSM-5 as a chronic relapsing brain disease characterized by compulsive alcohol use, loss of control over alcohol intake, and a negative emotional state when not using. An estimated 16 million people in the United States have

AUD. Approximately 6.2 percent or 15.1 million adults in the United States ages 18 and older had AUD in 2015. This includes 9.8 million men and 5.3 million women. Adolescents can be diagnosed with AUD as well, and in 2015, an estimated 623,000 adolescents ages 12–17 had AUD.

To be diagnosed with AUD, individuals must meet certain criteria outlined in the Diagnostic and Statistical Manual of Mental Disorders (DSM). Under DSM-5, the current version of the DSM, anyone meeting **any two of the 11 criteria during the same 12-month period receives a diagnosis of AUD.** The severity of AUD—mild, moderate, or severe—is based on the number of criteria met.

HOW DO YOU MEASURE UP?

To assess whether you or loved one may have AUD, here are some questions to ask. In the past year, have you:

- Had times when you ended up drinking more, or longer than you intended?
- More than once wanted to cut down or stop drinking, or tried to, but couldn't?
- Spent a lot of time drinking? Or being sick or getting over the after effects?
- Experienced craving—a strong need, or urge, to drink?
- Found that drinking—or being sick from drinking—often interfered with taking care of your home or family? Or caused job troubles? Or school problems?
- Continued to drink even though it was causing trouble with your family or friends?
- Given up or cut back on activities that were important or interesting to you, or gave you pleasure, in order to drink?
- More than once gotten into situations while or after drinking that increased your chances of getting hurt (such as driving,

swimming, using machinery, walking in a dangerous area, or having unsafe sex)?
- Continued to drink even though it was making you feel depressed or anxious or adding to another health problem? Or after having had a memory blackout?
- Had to drink much more than you once did to get the effect you want? Or found that your usual number of drinks had much less effect than before?
- Found that when the effects of alcohol were wearing off, you had withdrawal symptoms, such as trouble sleeping, shakiness, irritability, anxiety, depression, restlessness, nausea, or sweating? Or sensed things that were not there?

REMEMBER that meeting any two of the 11 criteria during the same 12-month period means you receive a diagnosis of AUD.

IF YOU HAVE any of these symptoms, your drinking may already be a cause for concern. The more symptoms you have, the more urgent the need for change," say professionals. But you know this already—or you wouldn't be reading this book.

Remember, there is no shame in admitting you have a problem. You're in good, or is that poor company? You decide. The true tragedy is not the problem, but not seeking help.

Like cocaine and heroin, shopping for things we don't need or eating sweet sugary food is addictive and satisfies our brain's craving for dopamine until we get our next fix.

Marketing moguls have known this for a long time and target people indiscriminately. Everywhere you look you're bombarded with ads about alcohol and sugar fixes that will cure our blues and make us supposedly happier and healthier.

Even the stuff dangled as healthier often has something to hide. Loaded with essential nutrients, natural flavors? Or concealing more than double your daily sugar requirement.

It's time to get wise!

Forget about waiting for law changes, forget about lobbying governments for more enlightened regulations. Take back your power. Open your eyes. It's not easy to change but you can begin by asking yourself more empowering questions, such as:

- Do I really need that fix?
- Will it impact on my wellbeing? How?
- How does alcohol work? Can I find a healthier, cheaper, more effective way to feel better?

The answers may prove illuminating. You may discover, as I have, that a swim in the ocean, a soak in the local hot mineral pools, a night at the movies, a massage, twenty-minutes mediation, or diverting the money I'm saving by not drinking booze for treats like pedicures, delivers a far faster, friendlier fix.

HAPPIER HOURS?

Alcohol we're told, will make you happier, more successful, attractive and socially confident.

Those who stand to profit most from your drinking don't fight fair. Instead, driven by increasing their profits they do what they can to ensure you increase your consumption.

A post in the *Advertising Age* revealed what many of us rationally know, "The trick for marketers is to project the right message in their advertisements to motivate those often motionless consumers to march down to the store or bar and exchange their money for a sip of liquor."

But do we fully understanding the emotional sabotaging tactics? Do you keep knocking back the booze, or swinging by to pick up more supplies even when you vowed you won't? Do you try a new product because it promises to be sugar-free and healthy?

Society is saturated with alcohol advertising—just as cigarette advertising once was, and fast-food outlets, like McDonalds, still are.

As with all advertising, this works simply by association with positive emotional responses and maintaining the norm of drinking as a socially desirable and safe activity.

How many billboards do you see of people puking? How many magazines are 'airbrushed' with myths and powerful story-telling tactics which wash your brain with powerful conscious and subconscious triggers designed to make you drink?

How much messaging pops up everywhere you look—even in supposed safe-places like the supermarket, seducing you with color, sensory overload, positive imaging and lies.

Loads!

You may be tempted to say that all marketing manipulates. But the truth is alcohol is in a completely different bracket from marketing shoes, watches, cars or other desirable objects.

Shopping may be addictive for some, but consumption of these products is more benign. It doesn't cause harm to innocent people, nor suck valuable tax dollars in associated costs. People don't die clutching their Louis Vuitton handbag, having overdosed on the latest purchase again.

Consumer beware—check out the untruths that booze barons want you to buy.

DEADLY PERSUASION: 5 MYTHS ALCOHOL ADVERTISERS WANT YOU TO BELIEVE

1.) Drinking is harmless

Advertisements promoting happy hours encourage excessive drinking. While we were holidaying in Fiji in 2017, posters around the pool advertised images of happy couples downing beers, with the caption, "Buckets of beer—happy hour all day."

These buckets of beer, containing four bottles each, were quickly downed by many thirsty hot holiday makers in the sun. Yes—they got messy, and ill!

Ads promoting excessive consumption communicate that it's all right, indeed cool, to be obsessed by alcohol, to consume large amounts on a daily basis (as early and as often as you can) and to include it in all your activities. At the same time, all signs of trouble and any hint of addiction are repressed.

Alcohol-related problems such as injury, arguments, fights, alcohol-impaired driving, broken marriages, abused children, derailed careers, alcohol poisoning and premature death, are never even hinted at—at least not by advertisers.

2.) Problem drinking behaviors are normal

Often symptoms of alcohol, such as the need for a daily drink, are portrayed as not only normal, but desirable. A Smirnoff ad captioned "We're Open" suggested every hour is vodka hour.

Similarly, the 2011 launch of Smirnoff's "I choose Campaign," for Vodka features an image of leather-clad motorcyclist, alongside the caption, "I choose t be a hero."

Really? My understanding of a hero is someone who rescues people from car crashes—not the drunk drivers who cause many of these fatalities.

The second ad focuses on the power of freedom with "I choose to scream".

There is no ugly drunkenness, only laughter at people's high jinks and high spirits, excessive drinking—and rage.

3.) Alcohol is essential to live

The following rationale was offered by the creators of the Smirnoff Campaign, and released by *bestmediainfo.com* (emphasis added):

"The campaign has been crafted by JWT Mumbai. The agency conducted a research that "clearly indicated that the target male is somewhat aware of Smirnoff but has had very little interaction with it, either from the desire or drinking perspective."

"Incidentally, beer and whisky grab a 70 percent lion's share of the popular drinks among men in the Indian market, **while vodka had a meager 22 percent share.** Thus the brand existed positively among its target group but lacked in making any direct statement to him.

"The challenge for JWT was to make Smirnoff a part of the consumer's consideration set and increase its equity among alcohol consumers."

Commenting on the strategy behind the campaign, Dipika Narayan VP and Executive Business Director, JWT, said, **"Our target is the male who has to constantly try and achieve a balance between 'fitting in' and 'standing out'.** He is in search of what we call a 'unique social identity', one that retains his originality without alienating him."

She added further, **"We knew that if as a brand we can help him achieve this balance and validate his right to choose, his individual identity will give him a sense of pride as well as make him readily accepted by his social universe."**

Thus, the strategy was to project Smirnoff as a brand that aims to provide a platform on which the individual can express himself.

Really, do you need alcohol to do that?

The campaign has been shot by renowned Dubai-based photographer Tejal Patni, who has captured the statement of 'I Choose' as one of **self-expression and empowerment.**

Thus, the messaging is that in order to live in this world you need to blend fitting in with standing out—and the best way to achieve this is by drinking vodka.

You may not buy into this messaging when you analyze the intent rationally away from the pull of alcohol, but many people subliminally absorb it—who doesn't want to look and feel cool, stand-apart but still be part of the 'in' set.

4.) Alcohol is magic and will liberate you

"Love wins. Share the love spirit," urged Smirnoff in their limited edition Love Wins Campaign. Featuring shrink-wrapped rainbow colored bottles and same-sex and ethnically diverse couples from all walks of life, the marketing spin was all about celebrating diversity. Love comes in all shapes and forms, we're told.

The myth they'd love you to adopt is that love comes in a bottle—a bottle of Smirnoff Vodka to be precise—certainly not a competitor's product.

Again, alcohol-related problems such as domestic violence, sexual assault, rape, suicide, depression, anxiety, and near death.

Nope, no mention of Duff McKagan and the vodka addiction that nearly killed him—nor of Amy Winehouse who was found dead with vodka bottles beside her bed. None of these and other tragic stats are never even hinted at.

Unlike other known poisons and toxic products there are absolutely no health warnings at all.

Instead, we are lead to believe that vodka-fuelled love wins—but then, hey, I guess when you're drunk everyone looks better. Why didn't they come straight out and label the campaign, "Smirnoff Wins" instead of "Love Wins"? Too obvious, yeah, that'll be the reason.

Poignantly it was Amy Winehouse who so sadly sang, "love, is a loser's game."

Love vodka? Thanks, but no thanks—I won't be increasing my consumption anytime soon.

5.) Alcohol is a sport

Alcohol consumption reduces athletic performance—and in many cases either threatens or completely derails promising careers.

One of the most enduring examples of alcohol advertising in sports is the 30-year partnership between the All Blacks and Lion-produced Steinlager.

The sponsorship of a wide range of sporting events and endorsements by sports stars wrongly imply that sports and alcohol are safely complementary activities.

Both adults, children and teens look up to sports stars as heroes. A large number of research findings have confirmed that alcohol advertising predicts drinking—particularly in adolescence.

Some of the worst boozers in sports have been publicly and professionally humiliated by their alcohol-fuelled brawls, sexual and violent assaults. Hardly inspiring role-models. The better ones head to the confessional and openly share their battle with booze—people like former All-Black Norm Hewitt. Others partner up with spin-doctors to create the ultimate cover-up.

Fiji Bitter is one of the many beers manufactured by Paradise Beverages Limited, a subsidiary of Coca-Cola, and is one of Fiji's most popular beers. Billboards all around the islands and at sporting events announce, "Fiji Bitter—The Sportsman's beer."

Other ads show highly regarded rugby players encouraging, "You Deserve It."

We're also told, Fiji Bitter, is the 'real taste' of Fiji...and you'll love this—"Fiji's iconic beer since 1957. Persistent beading creates a wonderful soft foaming head releasing the flavors of malt and hops with with a long clean bitter aftertaste leaving you looking for one more."

Of course they want you to look for one more. And one more. And one more after that.

Nobody mentions Fiji's soaring alcohol abuse rates, and the harm this 'wonderful,' 'clean' beer creates. In 2017, a Fijian representative rugby player visiting New Zealand was jailed for three years and four months for attempted rape. He had been out with his team and was clearly intoxicated. Incarcerated from alcohol-related offenses, his flourishing rugby career is now at an end.

"P" IS FOR PERSON, PROBLEM, AND PAIN"

"You must begin by identifying the person you are trying to reach with your message, understanding the problem that you are solving for them, and the pain that problem causes," writes Ray Edwards is his book, *How to Write Copy That Sells: The Step-By-Step System for More Sales, to More Customers, More Often.*

"The next step is to amplify the consequences of not solving the problem, and the aspirations they hold for the future. This is really the key to making sales."

Society is over-crowded with people in pain—it's why many take drugs and drink to excess. Booze marketers not only know this, they are out to exploit it.

Depressed? Drink and you will be happier. Ostracized? Vodka will fix it. Lonely? Fall in love with spirits. Stressed? Relax with a bucket of beer.

Ray Edwards is one of the good guys in advertizing. As he writes in the introduction of his book,

"The information supplied in this book is extremely powerful. It gives you the ability to literally manipulate people's thinking and actions. The ability to write good copy is one of the most powerful psychological tools of persuasion known to man," Edwards says.

He then urges, "If you purchase this book, I hope you'll make the commitment to using these powerful persuasion tools only for the ultimate good of your customers. **Never use these techniques to manipulate or control people to act against their own best interest.**"

STOP BUYING into their marketing messages. Instead, see their ads for the phoney, baloney they really are. Have fun analyzing their ads and dissect truth from lies.

Be empowered. Don't let the booze barons use their techniques to manipulate or control you to act against your own best interests.

Empower yourself by discovering and affirming why you want to experiment with sobriety —check out a few solid and satisfying reasons in the next chapter.

'WHY' IS THE NEW HIGH

"When you are full of food and drink an ugly statue sits where your spirit should be."

~ *Rumi*

Intensify your commitment, willpower, and desire to experiencing with sobriety by clarifying 'why' you want to scale your drinking back.

Check out some common reasons below why people give up drinking:

HEALTH HAVOC OR HEALTH NIRVANA?

Your body never lies, but many people soldier on ignoring the obvious warning signs that it's time to scale back their drinking or lose the booze.

- Headaches
- Anxiety

- Depression
- Insomnia
- Aggression
- Blackouts
- Low energy and fatigue
- High blood pressure

...are just a few of many signs that it may be time to control alcohol before it controls you.

It's easy to rationalize these feelings away, but the reality is your mind, body and soul is screaming out for liberation.

Have the courage to say 'yes' to pursuing a more energizing alternative.

Your body is a great source of wisdom and counsel—one that is increasingly respected by psychologists and medical professionals. *Somatic Psychology*, a branch of traditional psychotherapy, addresses what for so long was missing in the field of talk therapy.

Soma is a Greek word meaning "the living body" and is grounded in the belief that not only are thought, emotion and bodily experience inextricably linked (creating a *bodymind*), but also that change can be brought about in one domain of experience by mindfully accessing another.

You may consider asking your body next time you feel tempted to drink or feel the first flush of alcohol hit your system, "what does this beer (or whatever you are drinking) want me to know?" This may seem weird, but stick with me!

When I tried this recently, my body told me, "This alcohol makes me feel sick. I don't want it. Don't drink any more of it."

My mind, however, was telling me a different and conflicting story as it rattled through a range of old stories and false beliefs.

In this case, as in others, I trusted my body barometer.

Very often people don't listen to their body barometers until it's too late and health havoc can set in. Leonardo da Vinci once said that people were more motivated to act by fear than they were love. I'll let you decide, but whether the joy of health nirvana or the fear of health havoc rules supreme, as long as you heed the call for change you'll always win.

HEALTH NIRVANA

Controlling alcohol consumption or quitting for good has numerous positive benefits. Everything is interconnected but let's try to categorize a few of the health benefits you can expect with sobriety:

PHYSICAL HEALTH

- Improved liver function and health
- Better sleep
- Better eating habits
- Younger, healthier looking skin, hair, and nails
- Improved vision and clearer eyes
- Weight loss or healthy weight gain
- Increased energy and vitality
- Strengthened immune system, warding off illness and disease
- Lower blood pressure
- Optimal digestive function

MENTAL HEALTH

- Increased mental clarity

- Newfound motivation and determination
- Natural resilience
- Boost self-esteem and confidence
- Greater resilience to stress
- Improved memory
- Clarity
- Heightened intuition
- Heightened brain function
- Improved productivity
- Heightened sensory skills—everything looks, feels, tastes, sounds clearer and brighter
- Heightened willpower
- More truthfulness and honesty
- Long and short-term memory improves
- Aversion to negative thinking
- Improvement of coexisting conditions (anxiety, depression, bipolar, etc.)
- A desire to help others

Emotional Health

- Persistent and lasting feelings of joy
- Authentic happiness
- Improved relationships
- Increased joy of looking and feeling healthier and better about yourself
- Increased ability to create lasting, loving relationships
- Improved interactions with people
- Feeling younger
- Feeling empowered, in control and free
- More laughter and spontaneous joy
- Improved general sense of contentment and wellbeing

- Greater self-awareness
- Higher emotional intelligence and ability to self-regulate
- Improved sleep-related benefits
- Increased interest and engagement in new activities, hobbies or learning
- Feelings of freedom, hope, self-worth, and self-empowerment

Spiritual Health

- Increased intuition
- Greater connection to the Divine
- Commitment to spiritual practices
- Feelings of peace, joy, and love

If alcohol is a known cause for more than 60 different adverse health conditions, I'm betting sobriety is a known cause of more than 60 different positive health conditions—maybe even triple that. But finding data to back me up is hard to find. It seems more money is poured into measuring harm than keeping statistics related to health.

Keep your own stats and set yourself up to succeed. To support and maintain your sobriety, really absorb all the benefits. Enjoy the anticipated positive results of sobriety at the start of your day, in the evening, or whenever you have a spare moment.

Consider finding purpose in your sobriety as Elton John, Russel Brand and others do. "It feels great to help someone else get clean," Elton John wrote in his autobiography, *Me*.

Putting the spotlight on the harm alcohol caused me, my family, my loved ones, within my community and the world at large also drives me. Negatives can be positives when seen in the right light and used constructively.

I NO LONGER FEEL LIKE the booze hag who once wrote this:

> *"Pretty much four months after I decided to say no to booze, but the little bugger has slipped into my psyche again. Last night and the night before I had two vodkas and orange—freshly squeezed. 4pm-ish. I watched myself, observed myself. The knowledge that I was tired, weary, that I needed to meditate.*
>
> ***But I wanted that quick fix.***
>
> *That nice little forgetting of alcohol. But who's paying now? 12:15 A.M. and I'm wide awake. I haven't woken like this in months. I don't feel flash either. Yesterday I was excited about my book Flight of Passion—now I feel like it's crap. It's the depressing booze, my head aches, my throat and chest burns."*

INSTEAD, IN MY JOURNAL 'SOBER ME' wrote:

> *Hello Sunday Morning! I'm so grateful for John's drunkenness last night. It's strengthened my resolve. I want nothing to with the poison of drink—unless it's with a refined meal or a celebration. I've woken up clear-headed, clear-hearted, my energy bright, looking forward to the day.*
>
> *"When you are full of food and drink an ugly statue sits where your spirit should be." ~ Rumi*
>
> *Even if people think it's no big deal to drink a glass of wine at dinner it's important to know your body's reaction to alcohol and not just go along with the crowd.*

I'd forgotten my assignment on spiritual approaches to the treatment of alcohol addiction. I must revisit it.

A blackbird rustles amongst Autumn leaves. John is at his desk. The door is shut. I walk past the front window. "Would you like an orange juice?"

No, he wouldn't.

His eyes are dead, remorseful—as though regretting his foolishness. His skin is gray, pallid, like that of a dying man.

Rumi is right....an ugly statue sits where his spirit should be.

Even the Romans once ate and drank from a lead cup. *Poison in poison.*

HEALTH HAVOC

When you pollute your body with alcohol, a known carcinogen, and neurotoxin, it's going to play havoc with your health. Big time. Perhaps not today, not tomorrow, but it will happen, and when it does, I doubt you'll be happy about it.

You may even swear and curse your stupidity, as my step-father did, when he was diagnosed with terminal lung cancer, "You bloody stupid fool," he said, sadly and stoically accepting his fate when told he had a month to live. Having enjoyed smoking for many years, I know he would have done anything to undo the wrongs of the past.

Recently someone close to me was admitted into a psychiatric ward after a potentially life threatening binge drinking session. Having drunk 3/4 of a bottle of Jack Daniels spirits, the top-selling American whiskey in the world, she was psychotically high.

An neuropsychiatric article which appeared in the US National Library of Medicine National Institute of Health cites the following:

The existence of an acute brain syndrome manifested by psychotic reaction to alcohol without regard to the amount of alcohol consumed has been well-described in the past. The acute, chaotic disruption of behavior resulting from ingestion of a small quantity of alcohol, known as "pathological intoxication", has long been recognized as a psychiatric entity.

Pathological intoxication (PI), also called alcohol idiosyncratic intoxication, was said to occur predominantly in persons with low tolerance to alcohol, but its existence as a definable syndrome is still controversial. The disease has been defined as an acute brain syndrome manifested by a marked behavioral or psychotic reaction after minimal alcohol intake in people with no preexisting mental disorder. The essential points of all the definitions of this disease were the following:

1) marked maladaptive behavioral change (usually aggressive or assaultive behavior) with minimal alcohol intake,

2) the behavior is atypical of the person when not drinking, and

3) cause not being any other physical or mental disorder according to *DSM* (*Diagnostic and Statistical Manual of Mental Disorders*.)

Scary stuff! Sometimes we need to scare ourselves sober.

ALCOHOL, as I have said, is a known cause for more than 60 different adverse health conditions, listed below are just a few:

PHYSICAL HEALTH

- Carcinogenic—causes cancer in living tissue. Strong links between cancers of the liver, breast, bowel, upper throat, mouth, esophagus and larynx

- Negatively affects brain development in young people
- Depresses your entire nervous system
- Compromises your immune system, making you less resistant to illness and disease
- Increases the risk of breast cancer in women
- Interferes with the body's ability to absorb calcium, resulting in bones that are weaker, softer, and more brittle
- Kills cells and disrupts cellular metabolic processes
- Distorts your eyesight, making it difficult to adjust to the differing light and compromising clarity
- Diminishes your ability to distinguish between sounds and perceive their direction
- Slurs your speech
- Dulls your sense of taste and smell
- Damages the lining of your throat
- Weakens your muscles
- Inhibits the production of white and red blood cells
- Destroys your stomach lining
- Poisons you and can cause death
- Disrupts your sleep cycle, reduces rapid eye movement (REM) sleep, creates insomnia
- Suppresses breathing and can precipitate sleep apnea
- Increases weight or causes unhealthy weight loss
- Strips your body of vital nutrients and causes malnutrition
- Increases the likelihood of indulging in risky, unsafe and unlawful behaviors
- Heightens suicidal thoughts and suicidal ideation

Mental Health

- Lowers the levels of serotonin in your brain—a chemical that helps to regulate your mood

- Destroy your brain cells
- Increases suicidal tendencies
- Causes anxiety and depression and other mental disorders
- Negatively impacts memory
- Causes permanent damage to your brain
- Alters your brain chemistry
- Escalates aggression
- Increases stress levels
- Triggers dormant mental illnesses (bi-polar etc.)
- Disruptions in REM sleep may cause daytime drowsiness, poor concentration, and low mood
- Depletes willpower
- Can lead to psychotic disorders

Emotional Health

- Undermines your self-esteem and self-respect
- Depletes your courage, confidence
- Undermines your relationships with your partner, family, and friends
- Contributes to depression
- Reduces self-control
- Increases the difficulty in maintaining healthy relationships, including with bosses, co-workers and, clients
- Creates financial strain, leading to more stress, worry any and anxiety

Spiritual Health

- Pollutes your energy field

- **Lower Vibrations**

A_{ND THAT'S JUST} a few of the ways alcohol plays havoc with your health. The increased risk of developing arthritis, cancer, heart disease, hyperglycemia and hypoglycemia, kidney disease, obesity, nervous disorders, and many psychological disturbances can all be attributed to alcohol abuse. And as you know, acute alcohol poisoning can cause death.

Find out more about short and long-term effects that drinking alcohol has on many different parts of your body here—https://www.alcohol.org.nz/alcohol-its-effects/body-effects.

Y_{OUR MIND} and body may seem like separate entities but when you let your body override your craving mind you find a reservoir of unbridled power. Your body barometer never lies, and as we've seen, can save your life by expelling toxins from your system.

W_{HEN YOU DRINK} alcohol or feel hungover what do you notice? How does this differ from times when you feel sober?

If you fall off the wagon and start drinking again don't be too hard on your beautiful self. Practice mindfulness and self-compassion and tune into your body barometer.

How do you feel? Have the headaches, nausea, depression, aggression or anxiety returned again?

S_{UCCESSFUL} S_{OBRIETY}

Journal your experience as I did to reinforce your awareness and to strengthen your resolve to stop drinking again.

Scare yourself sober. Post reminders of the harm alcohol can cause to you and loved ones.

SOMETIMES THE MARKETING onslaught is so unrelenting that even when armed with your reasons 'why' they lure you in with their manipulative marketing messages. Be wary of what catches your eye—something we'll suss out in the next chapter.

BE WARY OF WHAT CATCHES YOUR EYE

What do booze barons, tobacco tycoons, and butterflies have in common?

Did you know that in nature some butterflies mimic each other by adopting the same colorings to look like other butterflies? Have you ever wondered, why?

The reason that they do this is because the other butterflies are poisonous. Birds and other things won't eat them because they know if they do they will die. By mimicking the toxic butterflies the other predators take a fright flight and leave them alone.

If only we humans were so evolved. Many marketers have leveraged off nature's wisdom but used it to their own advantage. Rather than use colors, shapes and images that make their products look dangerous, they make things look like they are harmless—even healthy.

"Of course they do. That's just good business," I hear you cry. Okay, but now you know, you don't have to be booze bait.

"I have contempt for the people who fall for it because they go in with their eyes wide open." said former smoker and Emphysema victim, the late John Holmes, about people who fall for the promises made by some marketers. Holmes was once the poster boy of health used to sell more products in the Marlboro Man cigarette campaigns.

Take up Holmes call for vigilance and avoid being manipulated. Be wary of what attracts you, or, more importantly, what catches your eye.

Many of us are innately attracted to beauty, and arguably, girls and women, in particular, make a bee-line to pretty things.

What marketing does, or attempts to do is to catch our eyes, and hijack our instinctive warning mechanisms so that we consume their poisonous products—and not in little droplets either. I'm talking gallons! Hey, they'll even make it ready for you to drink. How kind. Not!

Alcohol, just like tobacco once was, and still tries to be, is a giant, cash-rich, powerful industry.

With billions of dollars of revenue at stake, they are always going to be trying to evolve and stay ahead of what certain enlightened groups are doing. They are going to try and dissuade people from flying away from their products and alighting on healthy products. No way do they want to allow profits to be siphoned from their coffers and swelling the profits of healthy industries competing for your discretionary dollar.

They want to attract you. They want to woo you. They want to entice you to drink more. Business 101!

Hence the health kick, the fruity kick, the herb kick, the zero sugar kick and all the other trends you see right now. And then there are products that are all about the color. Like a bright round ball at the checkout of my local liquor store—(orange) it looks like candy, but it's far from it—it's 60% alcohol in a tiny, 'easy to consume' shot.

Convenience is king—removing barriers to consumption is where the profits are at. And you wonder why you drink!

That's why shooters came in. They're short, sharp and you don't even have to put your booze in a shooter glass. It didn't require the IQ of a rocket-scientist for alcohol companies to figure out consumers didn't possess the right size drinking vessel. It's the same money-grabbing logic that led to the proliferation of RTDs.

Back in my day when I was a teen, we had to buy 1-liter mixers separately to blend with our liquor of choice. It was a real drag. It slowed down our drinking.

RTD's and shooters lull people into false security – you think it's one small taster. You think it's harmless because it's small—or pretty, or some other carefully curated decoy.

Take, for example, an RTD I was lured into purchasing recently. I'm smart, I even have three degrees, but I still got hooked.

"This has just been released," my liquor store owner enthused. "For all the girls who are catching on that the reason their arse has got so fat—sugar-free and healthy."

"Healthy?" My ears pricked up. I felt my eyes sparkle as my gaze was drawn to the most beautiful RTD bottles I'd seen. My doubting mind shut down as I read the promised health kick.

Collectively the font and layout and color scrambled my mind. As I assessed it all later in the sober light of true analysis, even the product name had been scrambled—the word Mojito was split down the bottom into three lines. A love of typography, or a deliberate decoy—you decide?

Mo

Ji

To

· · ·

THE TEXT WAS COLORED 'SAFE' black, nothing flashy to alert me.

My gaze focused on the joyful orange font singing the praises of 'mandarin & lime'

The top of the bottle has an image of ripe oranges still attached to a very healthy looking tree (mmmmm….healthy!)

I ignored the fine print at the bottom of the bottle, 'Premium Vodka Cocktail' followed by teeny weeny print 300ml 5% ALC/VOLL—which is 1.2 standard drinks.

Would I really sip this over an hour to ensure my liver could process all the alcohol in this sweet, innocent looking health drink?

The chances weren't high—it was summer, abnormally hot and it was packaged in a convenient 4 pack which reminded me of the old milk crates of days gone by.

Maybe, all that white packaging wasn't innocent after all? But that thought didn't cross my mind at the time.

Instead, I zeroed in on the bolder print 'NO'

'NO SUGAR. NO CARB. ALL NATURAL'

The whole bottle is painted an opaque white–think clean, healthy–perhaps even spiritual!

So again, they were making things look harmless, rather than make them look menacing.

Arguably, if they made them look dangerous, your instincts would warn you to think twice before digesting.

In fact, this seems to be the logic behind the soon-to-be-implemented move in New Zealand to introduce plain packaging of cigarettes. The selected color of choice?

Sludgy green. Nope, not exactly appetizing and a galaxy away from the sexy Marlboro Man cowboy used in tobacco advertising campaigns for Marlboro cigarettes. Even disgusting pictures of diseased gums and rotting livers didn't dissuade hardened addicts. Could it be, that a color change may?

Interestingly, but not totally off topic, while researching this chapter I came across an excerpt from a documentary called *Death in the West*. The film contains footage of some of the original Marlboro commercials, interviews with two Philip Morris executives, and interviews with six American cowboys who have either lung cancer or emphysema, alongside testimony from physicians that the conditions were caused by heavy cigarette use.

The film interviews Helmut Wakeham, vice-president for the company's USA science and technology department. The interview with Wakeham is believed to be the first recorded admission from a tobacco company representative that smoking causes health problems.

"Yeah, cigarettes are poison. So what are we to do, stop living? The best way to avoid dying is not to be born you know. And if one avoided doing all the things which are alleged to be harmful to people these days we would vegetate in a mountain cave." Helmut Wakeham (Philip Morris USA) responded after being asked if cigarettes are unhealthy.

Shortly after the film aired, Philip Morris sued Thames Television, successfully obtaining a court order to prevent the film from being shown.

Yes, there are some things people just don't want you to know.

Somewhat disturbingly, having been slaughtered by their deceit in 2003 the company rebranded as Altria, coupled with a very enticing color-drenched logo, which attempts to look like harmless children's Lego, rather than the brand of the world's leading cigarette manufacturers.

Wikipedia notes the following, "The name 'Altria' is claimed to come from the Latin word for 'high' and was part of a trend of companies rebranding to names that previously did not exist, though linguist Steven Pinker suggests that in fact, the name is an "egregious example" of phonesthesia—with the company attempting to switch its image from bad people who sell addictive carcinogens to a place or state marked by altruism and other lofty values."

The company's branding consultants, the Wirthlin Group, said: "The name change alternative offers the possibility of masking the negatives associated with the tobacco business," thus enabling the company to improve its image and raise its profile without sacrificing tobacco profits.

What do booze barons and tobacco tycoons have in common? Once a liar, always a liar. I'm being harsh, but could it be true? You be the judge See the 'hard sell' health focus here

—http://www.altria.com/Pages/default.aspx

Let's take a look at how alcohol companies are fighting back.

ONCE A LIAR, ALWAYS A LIAR?

Consumption of alcohol is on the downward slope—and with it, profits.

Alcohol companies are exponentially increasing their efforts to appeal to increasingly health-conscious, weight-conscious consumers. The rapid rise of the sobriety movement is also something they are watching with growing alarm. What to do? If you can't beat them, join them?

In New Zealand giant brands such as Lion Breweries, have responded to declining sales by investing in alcohol-free drinks and building breweries dangling all sorts of delights, included vegan goodies and fermented foods, hoping to lure the health-conscious into the brewery to sample their wares.

They're also scrambling to meet UN-sanctioned sustainability goals. Making beer requires a lot of energy and water. Cheers to sustainability? This mammoth brewer has taken it one step further, with their new project, The Fermentist.

In January 2018, Lion's sustainability manager Kat McDonald reported in the Sunday Star Times, "The Fermentist was to create transparency in how Lion produced its beer, and also to use it as a platform that educated consumers about what was behind their purchasing decisions."

Really? Will they mention the psychological tactics they used to entice you to drink more?

"The Fermentist was a play on the brewing process of the beer but also about the fermented foods that will be sold through its café," says McDonald. "The name conjures up experimentation and trying new things while at the same time a lot of fermenters are recognizing the well-being aspect of it," she says.

There's that link to lofty values and altruistic motives I identified earlier and the attempt to switch its image from bad people who sell addictive carcinogens.

Add the non-alcoholic selection (nice move) and probiotic drinks, vegetarian options and fermented foods, the sustainability (albeit forced upon them by legislation) and you have a company clearly attempting to fight back.

"As conscious consumerism grows over time, it's increasingly going to be the company or brand's job to help them understand how they can make more sustainable choices," says The Sustainable Business Council's executive director Abbie Reynolds.

HELP YOU, OR MANIPULATE YOU?

When it comes to women and drinking, sometimes a glass of wine isn't just a glass of wine, says journalist and author of *Drink: The Intimate Relationship Between Women and Alcohol*, Ann Dowsett Johnston.

Men still consume more alcohol than women, according to the Liquor and Gaming Authority of Manitoba, but Johnston has watched the Tsunami-like rise in how much women are drinking. The question is, why? You don't have to look too far.

"In Canada, we've seen a statistically sturdy increase" in women's drinking since the early 2000s, says Dowsett Johnston. She believes that one of the biggest contributing factors to the rise of drinking among women has been marketing.

There's been a "pinking" of the market since the mid-1990s, Johnston said, with the invention of "alcopop," drinks like Mike's Hard Lemonade and Smirnoff Ice that are typically marketed to women —"what I like to call 'chick beer' or 'cocktails with training wheels', an attempt to get the female gender to keep up with men."

But that kind of marketing hasn't focused only on fruity-tasting drinks for women, says Sheri Fandrey, who heads up the Addictions Foundation Manitoba's knowledge exchange services.

"Many other products besides alcohol are marketed to women by using their own insecurities," Fandrey said.

"We're being influenced and manipulated in such subtle ways that we see it more as fun and a joke, and don't realize that it is actually shifting people's behavior," says Fandrey.

As we've seen weight worry, body issues and fear of being unpopular are some of many such insecurities booze barons are manipulating our thinking so we'll believe their alcohol products offer the best cure.

In a social media campaign by Clean Collective, whose product Mojito vodka Cocktail I spoke of earlier, they're not purely targeting men but women and use weight loss influencers to lure them to their product.

One 24-year old New Zealander, who is actively promoting her journey to health, is young, and arguably naïve—perfect fodder for sophisticated booze barons to manipulate.

With her massive 92kg weight loss, her fan base on Facebook and Instagram exceeded 500,000. It didn't take long for her story to gain Media attention, with extensive coverage both nationally and internationally including publications like The Huffington Post, The Daily Mail, Elite Daily, Fashion Quarterly, the NZ Herald and TVNZ to name just a few.

The issue I have is that she is also an influencer who markets herself as a health advocate.

In a post 'liked by 4, 687 people and shared by the Clean Collective booze barons' Facebook page she says,

> "One of the biggest questions I always get asked is when I drink what is my drink of choice. I spoke about this in my Instagram story last week and the response was so huge I thought I would share my go to drink. It's definitely the mandarin and lime Mojito by @cleancollectiveofficial. It has Zero Sugar, Zero Carbs, and Zero Preservatives. It is 100% Natural and made here in New Zealand which I love. And best of all only has 86 calories!"

WHAT'S NOT CLEAR, is whether she is being incentivized or paid in any way to endorse alcohol. And they're not the only vodka product she is endorsing:

> "Treating myself to a drink tonight after a full on day of workouts and clients. I have always been a vodka girl and never even thought to branch out until I saw this Mist Wood Gin, I fell in love with the packaging (much to Trents amusement!) and just had to try it. The Gin with Grapefruit & Lime is definitely my favourite flavour. I can totally see myself enjoying this in the summer sun! #mistwoodss16#thanksmistwood

Note how she "fell in love with the packaging"!

While we're on the topic of alluring packaging my local alcohol retailer told me of the interesting rebranding by Long White Vodka to boost flagging consumption. By suggesting the health benefits, including "naturally flavored sparkling water," less than impressive sales went through the ceiling.

"Sparkling mineral water, triple distilled vodka, natural fruit flavors. That's all you'll find in Long White Vodka, where we're lovers of less," they tell us. Don't you just love the ads where the products are surrounded by fruit?

"Just bought the passion fruit....what a pity there's no passionfruit in it! It's apple juice and vodka. Misleading, false and very disappointing!!" A disgruntled consumer posted on their Facebook page. To which the Long White Vodka Company posted the following:

> "Hi Carol, thanks for your feedback. We use a variety of ingredients in our Long White Vodka for different reasons - apple juice for sweetness (rather than table sugar), carrot juice for colour, fruit juice and natural flavours for flavouring. We use natural flavours where supply is tricky for some fruits, as is the case for passionfruit. We appreciate your feedback. Cheers, Long White Vodka."

I'm told that, because they are an independent producer of alcohol unlike other liquor companies in NZ, that they are not compelled to tell consumers what's truly in their drinks. What else are they hiding? At the time of writing, they have a tab on their Facebook page headed, "Nutritional Information" but there's nothing posted.

Want more convenience? You can have a Long White Passion 10 pack delivered within the hour for a flat fee of $5.99 by MyBeerCase—one of many liquor taxis racing for your drink dollar throughout New Zealand —https://www.mybeercase.co.nz/product/long-white- passionfruit-4-5-320ml-bottles/

And you want to know why you drink! Heck, you don't even have to be a sober driver to go in search of more.

Incidentally, Mist Wood Gin, we are told on the Fresh.co.nz website (https://fresh.co.nz/2017/03/30/mist-wood-gin/) "Can also be turned into a 'gin jelly' another twist to an old classic—the traditional vodka jelly."

Jelly…hey, isn't that what we had as kids? It must be safe. Fun too—isn't that what we're being told? There's that shape-shifting butterfly again.

BIG BUSINESS, BIG BUCKS

Alcohol sales account for billions of dollars in revenue every year, and companies pour a good chunk of that money back into advertising—including paying people to endorse their products or incentivizing them (with trips overseas and other perks) for constant legendary sales.

The most common themes of those ads? That to successfully celebrate and socialize you have to drink, that alcohol is what makes life fun, and that alcohol makes you popular.

It's not true, of course, but this is why so many people experience such high levels of anxiety at the idea of going sober. Every addiction makes you fearful of what you might lose when you give up the habit.

A great book with a strong and clear message that getting sober is not a loss is Ross Perry's *The Sober Entrepreneur: Change Your Family Tree.*

Remember, to make their products more appealing marketers and producers try to make alcohol look harmless so we do consume more of it—lots more.

Swilling booze down your neck is how some of the population define 'fun' but they're a growing minority.

As we've already discussed the sobriety movement is on the rise. Seek and you shall find increasing reminders of the life-changing magic of sobriety. Yes, you can have fun, dance, be popular, look like a lunatic and not be drunk!

Remind yourself that booze barons are highly motivated in their quest to maintain and grow profitability...aren't all drug lords!

Be wary of what catches your eye and who endorses your products. Always question their intelligence and their motivation—are they committed to true health or lining their pockets? Importantly, are they worthy of your trust?

ALCOHOL UNMASKED

Booze barons do such a great job of disguising alcohol that many people don't know what it really is.

Alcohol is ethanol, also known as ethyl alcohol or grain alcohol, and is a flammable, colorless chemical compound. Yes, folks, everything can really go up in flames when you drink.

I fondly remember Christmases spent at my grandmother's and the excitement we all felt when a match was held against the rum-soaked Christmas pudding and it burst into plumes of fire.

For some reason, until researching this chapter I never made the connection that booze was a flammable substance I poured down my throat.

Ethanol fuel is also used in some countries instead of gasoline in cars and other engines. In Brazil, for example, ethanol fuel made from sugar cane provides 18 percent of the country's fuel for cars.

In short, the alcohol or ethanol found in your favorite beer, wine, and spirits is a poison, masquerading as a happy drink. It's so toxic that, when consumed too quickly or in huge quantities, your body's default position is to expel it—usually in a totally unglamorous technicolor spray of vomit. That's if you're lucky.

Alcohol poisoning can, and does, cause death—both directly and indirectly through liver disease, breast cancer, and a staggering amount of other alcohol-related diseases. We'll explore the havoc caused by booze, as well as how sobriety leads to nirvana in the chapter, Health Havoc or Health Nirvana?

Yet, despite all the risks and dire health warnings, alcohol seems such a benign substance. Perhaps it's the allure of its origins—a uniquely natural process.

Alcohol is formed when oxygen deprived yeast ferments natural sugars found in fruits, grains, and other substances. For example, wine is made from the sugar in grapes, beer from the sugar in malted barley, cider from the sugar in apples, and most vodka from the sugar in fermented grains such as sorghum, corn, rice, rye or wheat (though you can also use potatoes, fruits or even just sugar.)

Many people use alcohol as a way to self-medicate their way through life's ups and downs. Peer into the history of alcohol and you'll find that its medical origins enjoy a good pedigree. Gin mixed with tonic containing quinine, for example, was historically used to treat malaria.

"So it's totally good for you," writes one enthusiastic supporter in an alcohol forum.

Yeah, if you've got malaria perhaps, but not if you're just sick and dog-tired of living.

Alcohol is classed as a 'sedative hypnotic' drug. That definition on its own may sound just like what you're craving until you discover the true impact. Sedative-hypnotic drugs depress the central nervous system (CNS) at high doses.

Hmmm, that doesn't sound so flash, especially if you're prone to knocking back a few too many drinks. Your central nervous system controls a majority holding of the key functions of your body and mind. The CNS consists of two parts: your brain and your spinal cord.

As you know, the brain is the chief conductor of your thoughts, interpreting your external environment, and coordinating body movement and function, both consciously and unconsciously. Complex functions, including how you think and feel, and maintaining homeostasis, a relatively stable balance between all the interdependent elements in your body, are directly attributable to different parts of your brain.

Your spinal cord with its network of sensitive nerves acts as a conduit for signals between the brain and the rest of the body.

You definitely don't want to mess with the way this important duo functions. But every time you ingest alcohol you do, weakening their ability to perform like virtuosos, interfering with maintaining a healthy balance and the finely tuned harmony which is so vital to your health, performance, and effectiveness, and causing all systems in your body to play horribly off key.

Would you love to possess an outstanding ability in your field? Excel in your chosen profession? Tap into higher knowledge? Hone a much-loved or admired skill? Be universally admired? Many people think alcohol aids the fulfillment of these desires—until they realize their beliefs were deceptively wrong.

Sobriety on the other hand... now there's a different story.

At lower doses, alcohol can act as a stimulant inducing feelings of euphoria, optimism, and gregariousness. Everything looks beautiful, your belief in yourself, your talents, and your ability elevates like a seductive piece of music. Your inhibitions float away, suddenly you imagine yourself to be far better than you really feel. Shyness disappears, in its place talkativeness.

For a little while.

But pour more and more drinks down your throat, knock back liters of your favorite elixir and you'll quickly find yourself confronted by the truth. Alcohol is trouble.

Quite simply, alcohol knocks the life out of you. The more you drink, the higher the likelihood you'll become drowsy. Recall the drunk in the corner, slouched against the wall, or the once vivacious life of the party, barely able to hold her head in her hands, as she sits slumped at the bar. I've been there—it's a predictable rite of passage. In a culture that values drinking, this is normal.

Normal but definitely not glamorous, hip or cool.

But things get worse. Sometimes much, worse. Your breathing naturally slows into a state called respiratory depression. It can become exceedingly shallow or worse, stop entirely—what's truly frightening is you have absolutely no control. No one chooses to fall into an alcohol-fueled coma, but this is exactly what happens to far too many people.

Very high levels of alcohol in the body can shut down critical areas of the brain that control breathing, heart rate, and body temperature, resulting in death. And, tragically, far too many beautiful people needlessly die this way.

Can I scare you sober? It's not my agenda, but I do know this—that's exactly what happened to Amy Winehouse. And it's exactly what's happened to a great many other talented, beautiful, smart people. People who only wanted to feel high, but never intended to die.

As well as its acute and potentially lethal sedative effects at high doses, alcohol undermines every organ in the body and these effects depend on your blood alcohol concentration (BAC) over time.

We'll examine the dangers of drinking both large and small alcoholic beverages over a short period of time in the chapter, Binge Drinking Blindness.

We'll also dive deeper into what constitutes safe drinking, including analyzing what constitutes a standard drink and why health authorities want you to control your drinking—assuming you don't want to kick the alcohol habit for good.

But first, let's stop to consider, how natural is alcohol really?

WHAT'S HIDDEN IN YOUR DRINK?

Ethanol made be created via a naturally occurring process, but that's not the end of the production cycle. The other thing to be mindful of is all the other hidden dangers lurking in your drinks.

Peer a little closer and you'll find all sorts of nasty additives—not to mention toxic sprays, pesticides, fungicides, chemical fertilizers and other things that infiltrate many crops. But you won't find many of these disclosed on the labels.

Sorry to spoil the party.

Health gurus cite dangerous levels of sulfites or sulphites (as it's spelled in New Zealand) and warn of harmful side-effects, particularly for those with a low tolerance.

The term sulfites is an inclusive term for sulfur dioxide (SO_2), a preservative that's widely used in winemaking (and most food industries) for its antioxidant and antibacterial properties. SO_2 plays an important role in preventing oxidization and maintaining a wine's freshness. When used in high levels, because it's considered harmful, it must legally be disclosed on product labels.

To be fair, many foods also contain sulfites. Some people claim the preservative is nothing to be alarmed by—unless of course, you include yourself in the numbers of people who are allergic. Sulfites cause bloating and itching in sulfite-sensitive people. Does your beloved have a beer gut or sulphite bloating?

HISTAMINE HIGH?

Some studies suggest sulfites and other additives, including compounds such as histamines and tannins, are connected to the pounding headaches many of us suffer after drinking. That, and our ballooning weight.

Fermented alcoholic beverages, especially wine, champagne, and beer are histamine-rich.

As the author and psychologist Doreen Virtue explains in her excellent book, *Don't Let Anything Dull Your Sparkle,* many people binge drink when stressed, but most don't realize that some of the excess weight may be attributed to stress-hormones and neurotransmitter responses. These biochemicals, Virtue says, are triggered by the fact when you're stressed you often binge on food and drinks to which you may unknowingly be allergic to, or which are intrinsically unhealthy.

As I've mentioned, any product that undergoes fermentation contains high levels of histamine. What I didn't know was that these histamines trigger allergic reactions in our body, especially if we're under a lot of stress.

Histamines get you both ways, not only occurring in the food and alcohol you drink but also because when you're allergic to something your body releases its own histamine, says Virtue. "Stress produces histamine. We're all naturally allergic to stress," she says.

When you consume a diet that's high in histamine or histamine-inducing foods, your body becomes overwhelmed. Add a stressful lifestyle to the mix and it's no wonder you feel less than perky.

Histamines are also manufactured and released by our bodies not only when we're stressed but also when we're dehydrated. Again, alcohol, because it magnifies dehydration, makes things worse.

Virtue explains, "The trouble is that histamine produces uncomfortable symptoms such as bloating, itchy skin, profuse sweating, hot flashes, runny or stuffy nose, and feeling cold all the time, as well as low blood pressure, arrhythmia, anxiety, and depression."

Nice.

No wonder, we start to look and feel better when we lose the booze.

Other addictive beverages, like coffee and sugar-laden drinks, also trigger histamine reactions. The net result is a 'histamine high.' This boosted energy and elation you experience is always short-lived and is always followed by an energy crash, plus other painful symptoms discussed above.

Before publishing her findings Virtue decided to test her theory and embark on a 30-day histamine-free diet.

"Within two days of going 'low-histamine,' I felt a youthful energy and exuberance that I had never experienced before. I felt well. I felt happy. And I knew it was due to the low-histamine diet… you cannot return to the old ways of bingeing upon histamine once you realize the process behind these binges."

SUGAR RUSH

Submerged in many alcoholic drinks are dangerous and highly addictive levels of sugar. Research collated in a *New York Times* article stated, "Cravings induced by sugar are comparable to those induced by addictive drugs like cocaine and nicotine."

Latest research revealed in *The New Zealand Listener* in 2018 reveals the physiological and neurological reasons your brain makes you crave sugar. I share some of these findings in the chapter Sweet Misery. It's only since researching and writing this book that I realized I was more addicted to sugar than alcohol.

Whew! That's a relief. But it's also not—because both are tough habits to crack. Tough, but not impossible. Knowledge is power, right?

In summary, not only is alcohol a highly addictive poison, but your cravings, your weight gain, low energy levels and less-than-optimal mental and emotional health may be fuelled as much by additives and sugar, as it is ethanol or alcohol itself.

You can heal your life and it begins with examining the facts. Consider becoming an amateur sleuth and adopting the role of an investigative journalist. Discover how alcohol is made, including all the artificial things that are added to many products to make it tastier and more alluring—and potentially more dangerous to your health.

Perhaps this may be all the motivation you need to develop a healthy intolerance for alcohol.

In the following pages we'll dive deeper into strategies to help ensure your successful sobriety, including: journaling

SWEET MISERY

Have you ever wondered if it's alcohol you're addicted to or whether you're craving sugar? You may also be surprised to learn how much sugar is hiding in your alcohol. You'd probably be blown away to learn that some studies suggest that sugar is 10 times more addictive than cocaine. Cocaine!

Personally, I have always favored the sweeter wines, Riesling, Pinot Gris and Gewurztraminer and others. What I didn't realize was it wasn't the variety of grapes I was attracted to but the higher sugar content.

Until I began researching my book *Mind Your Drink* I didn't even think about how much sugar I was ingesting, nor was I aware of how many alcohol manufacturers add extra sugar to the mix to keep you hooked.

Two or three glasses of wine can easily contain 3 teaspoons of sugar which is 75 percent of the recommended daily intake for women.

A vodka and cranberry easily hides a whopping seven-and-a-half teaspoons, while a G&T offers little to celebrate at four teaspoons of sugar.

Don't be fooled by companies like Coca-Cola who have developed new sub brands to sell 'healthy' alternatives like Cranberry Juice. I nearly got duped until I studied the labels and discovered the differences in sugar content.

Current laws don't compel alcohol companies to disclose what's hidden in booze, including added sugar. Although, higher than recommended levels of sulfites do have to be disclosed. A move in this direction, including sugar content and the addition of harmful artificial sweeteners, must surely be around the corner—especially as obesity levels continue to soar.

A recent report from the Australian Institute of Health and Welfare (AIHW) revealed that Australia has one of the highest rates of obesity in the world—a staggering 63% of adults are overweight and obese. Truly alarming.

Why is obesity an escalating issue? While food, nutrition, and exercise are all culpable nobody seems to be pointing the finger at epidemic levels of sugar-spiked alcohol consumption.

Instead, we're being fed the wrong messages and dispensed the wrong advice.

While beer is said to contain less sugar than other alcoholic alternatives, you only have to survey men's beer-guts to sense something is amiss.

No, drinking a lot doesn't make you look sexier, but it does taste nice.

No wonder my excess weight peeled off when I gave up booze. Plus, once I was free of the sugar cravings (and the withdrawals) it was easier to cut back.

"Sweets, like heroin, enter the body (and hence the brain) very rapidly," says neuroscientist Dr. Candace Pert.

"Sugar is a drug in a very real sense, and we're addicted to the 'up' feeling we get when our blood-sugar levels soar. This substance directly impacts your molecules of emotion—insulin being the main one. External drugs, internal chemicals, and the emotions— all of these use the exact same pathways and receptors," writes Candace Pert in *Everything You Need to Know to Feel Go(o)d.*

Sugar is a double-edged sword. Falling amounts of sugar can make you feel anxious, panicky, hyperactive, or depressed.

Too much sugar in your diet makes you irritable, keeps you hungry, speeds up the ageing process, and spikes irrational cravings.

"The demand for it can override your behavior just as a craving for heroin can, driving you not only to seek more and more sugary foods, but also to engage in behaviors that are associated with blood sugar on the rise. Unlike heroin, however, sugar is legal, plentiful, and cheap, so you're likely to satisfy that drive from the available supply and become hooked without even being aware of it," says Pert.

No wonder giving up alcohol is doubly hard. It's a quick highly addictive double-impact hit and an even quicker descent into sugar-fuelled, alcohol-saturated misery if you don't catch on quickly.

A word of caution. Don't even think about swapping your pre-mixes for drinks marketed as 'diet' alternatives. Increasing research warns of the extreme health hazards of Aspartame, an artificial sweetener marketed as Nutrasweet, Equal, and Spoonful (in the UK).

For a comprehensive summary of sugar in all its guises I highly Dr. Candace Pert' excellent book, *Everything You Need to Know to Feel Go(o)d.*

You'll also find a helpful summary of why sugar is bad for you and ways to reduce sugar cravings in the following article:

http://www.dailymail.co.uk/femail/food/article-3131012/We-reveal-sugar-alcoholic-drink-REALLY-contains.html

SAVVY SOBRIETY

Many people struggle to control alcohol because they're not motivated by sobriety. But, being sober isn't just about not drinking.

Sobriety is achieved by putting energy and effort toward something you really desire.

Knowing *why* you want something is just as important as knowing *what* you want.

Why do you want to control your drinking? To feel better about yourself? To achieve wellbeing goals? Because you're afraid that your drinking it taking over your body and your life? To inspire others? Because you're curious that what you've been hearing is true—life really is better sober? Or something else?

We'll explore more ways to help you discover your driving purpose later in this book, but first here are just a few benefits of achieving sobriety:

- Improved mental health and wellbeing

- Better physical health
- Improved emotional health
- Elevated spiritual health
- Saves money
- Enriches your relationships
- Is an indispensable part of fulfilment
- Energizes you
- Liberates you
- Will change your life and the lives of those who matter most to you

Being sober sounds great, and it is. But the challenge is that so many of us have been brainwashed into believing it's awesome to be drunk. As I share later in this book, many of the people we look up to, including our political leaders have a dysfunctional relationship with alcohol—no wonder it's hard to implement laws aimed at reducing alcohol harm.

But if it's cool to be high, why do so many of us want to quit? Why do thousands of people sign on for Dry July or make New Year's resolutions to lose the booze only to be coerced or bullied into drinking again?

Giving up drinking can feel like losing your best friend, even your lover—until you remind yourself how alcohol is a fickle companion who lets you down again and again.

Sobriety, now there's a forever friend.

She won't turn sour, she won't piss you off, or get mad at you, and she won't rob you blind. Sobriety won't hijack your brain and make you say and do things you'll wildly regret in the wake of hangover hell.

Sobriety is not seedy or unpleasant. Sobriety is a sophisticated, serene, stabilizer in a world gone mad.

. . .

Sober

Synonyms

1. Not drunk
2. Thoughtful, steady, down-to-earth and level-headed
3. Serene, earnest
4. Not addicted

Who doesn't want a friend like that?

Sadly, the opposite is also true. Some of my best, most trusted friends turn into tyrants, either at the time of drinking or in the days that follow. These are just a few of the changes I notice when they drink alcohol:

- Overly critical
- Short-tempered
- Tyrannical
- Moody
- Solemn
- Angry
- Silent
- Withdrawn

Here's a short excerpt from my Sobriety Journal:

29 Dec 2016.

> *"A terrible, terrible evening. Me hiding in fear. Brett on a rampage. Smashing my fridge (taking it physically out of the studio and hurling it to the ground). 'Stress' brought on by the windows he shattered when he mowed the lawn, his frustration at the fountain not going, mowing the front paddock and returning, his eyes flaming and puffy.*

> *And then drinking. Three bottles of beer, then driving to the store and returning with a giant bottle of Mount Gay rum which he knows I hate him drinking. It always makes him so aggressive. He drinks it straight from the bottle. I feel panic rising in my chest. I feel real fear. I fear for my life.*
>
> *Smashed pots, plants, my canvases strewn with horrid words I cannot decipher.*
>
> *I'm cowering because I could quickly become a victim of his frenzied attack. I fear he has lost his mind. He **has** lost his mind. He has lost control.*
>
> *I really hate alcohol. I hate what it steals from me. Our love. Our dreams.*

Although this frightening, truly terrorizing episode happened so long ago, I still feel the fear. That's what traumatic episodes do to us—their linger in our body waiting to be triggered—or, with help, resolved. It's a chilling reminder, but also a motivating one, which fuels my commitment for sobriety, and my devotion to helping others free themselves from harm, save their relationships, regain their sanity—and so many of the other benefits sobriety promises and *delivers*.

Unlike alcohol, sobriety can be trusted.

Throughout this book I'll discuss some of my strategies for living in a booze soaked world, including how I keep my energy and vibration levels high and don't allow drunks to dull my sparkle.

One simple strategy I do find helpful, however, is to pin inspiring quotes somewhere visible to remind me to censure the tendency to demand others change or to judge.

Letting go of judgment creates peace, strength, and ultimately increases joy. Becoming judgment-free and leading by example is also one of the key sobriety steps recommended by many successful addiction programs. This includes self-judgment and self-criticism.

My current go-to quote is by Abraham Hicks, "Let others vibrate how they vibrate and want the best for them. Never mind how they're flowing to you. You concentrate on how you're flowing because one who is connected to the energy stream is more powerful, more influential than a million who are not."

This quote, along with the image of a young woman in a glass jar, sending her loving light into the world, is pinned on my wall. The jar represents the shield she places around herself, to protect her from negative people and dark outside forces.

I also invite love, not fear or anger to guide my day. I'm not saying it's easy—if it were the world would be a happier place. I work to remember how my loved ones are when they're sober—how kind they are, how caring. This love extends to me too. I know I'm a nicer, kinder person sober than I am drunk.

Exercising self-love, however, means accepting that sometimes there comes a time when being around people who abuse alcohol becomes too toxic. Their drinking may undermine your health, threaten your resolve, or cause you to constantly fear for your life. There are times you may have to quit not only the booze but people, places, and relationships that hold you back.

Finding joy in sobriety is a lifestyle choice—a very personal, and very empowered and empowering choice. It's a choice you make with eyes wide open, determined to celebrate and make the most of your one precious life in every way.

Humor, as you'll also discover, goes a long way.

This man is giving birth to a six-pack…'Father and beers are doing swell.'

It's a picture I drew in my Sobriety Journal, in part to remind me how staying sober improves my waistline.

Call it like it is....would you like a shot of ethanol and a gallon of sugar with that?

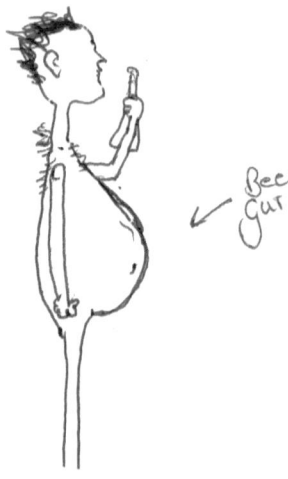

WOUNDED WARRIORS

If you're struggling with alcohol abuse or you're using booze to self-medicate, this doesn't necessarily make you an alcoholic—this doesn't mean you have a disorder or an incurable disease.

Self-medicating or anaesthetizing yourself with booze doesn't make you hopeless. But it does create an exponential increase that unless you become aware of how much you drink, why you drink and learn how to take back control, you'll continue to over-drink.

A great many people drink alcohol to mask or numb the symptoms of their wounds.

No one escapes walking in this world without some degree of hurt. For many people this hurt is profoundly deep.

The first cuts, experts (and songwriters) say are the deepest—very often these wounds are inflicted during childhood.

Tragically, what should be a happy time of innocence is one of incalculable pain. Incest, rape, physical abuse, emotional neglect—and many more horrid crimes, including murder, are often committed under the influence of alcohol.

Our local tavern, a sports and gambling bar, proudly tells patrons that they can bring their families, yet some 20 meters or so down the road a community noticeboard warns, "Kids are safer when you are sober. Ease up on the drink."

Tragically, it's a message that falls on far too many ears too deaf to hear, eyes too blind, and minds too inebriated to see the truth about alcohol.

Almost no-one escapes the toll of alcohol. Neither money, nor affluence, nor sobriety, nor age escapes its wrath. As I share in the opening of this book, my grandmother was four, and her brother aged six, and were outside the pub when their alcoholic father got into a drunken-brawl and murdered a man. Molly and her brother were forced apart—her brother was adopted and my grandmother spent her childhood being bounced out of foster homes. They never saw each other, or their parents, again.

Walking wounded? You bet. My grandmother spent her life seeking comfort from alcohol, even a stint in rehab couldn't dislodge the habit. Her brother, in adulthood, took his life.

Neither of them was ever offered help to heal the wounds of their past.

In *The Biology of Desire: why addiction is not a disease*, Marc Lewis shares the following testimony from an addiction counselor and former alcoholic,

"I have had a long hard look inside about how I feel personally about addiction. I do not feel that I have or had a disease. I see my past drinking as a behavioral problem, a learned response to dealing (or not dealing) with emotional pain and stress. Once I achieved the excavating of my wounds I no longer lived with the same anxiety or sense of dread/guilt and shame."

Personally, I have always been troubled by the preference of mainstream psychology to categorize and pathologize unwellness without delving deeper into its origins.

Instead, wounds are plastered over—seemly *cured* by a steady diet of pills and prescriptions. It was refreshing to read Lewis's book and this account. I encourage you to purchase a copy of his book. It's a brilliant exposé on the truth of addiction and the road to recovery.

Yes, I am overjoyed to say, times are slowly changing. *Slowly.* Unwellness is still a multi-billion dollar industry—there are powerful incentives to keep people dependent on the promise that the latest drug will cure.

Yet there is also an explosion of interest in alternative approaches to health and well-being and with it, the treatment of addiction. Three modern-day factors appear to herald the call for change:

- The escalating epidemic of depression, stress, anxiety and addiction
- The failure of the pharmaceutical industry to come up with sustainable solutions—let alone side-effect-free cures
- A flurry of reputable scientific studies validating the impact of therapies, once devalued and demoted as 'alternative'.

Transcendental meditation, prayer, massage, diet and a wide array of healing modalities, including energy healing, are on the ascent. Science it seems, has finally validated what many ancient cultures have always known—mind, body, spirit and environment are interconnected.

People are waking to the real reasons they drink.

As Legendary rock star Alice Cooper said in an interview, "I didn't realize that I was an alcoholic until I realized that alcohol was not for fun anymore. It was medicine."

You may, Cooper and others, may identify with the label 'alcoholic.'

You may find it empowers you, like finally being given a diagnosis that explains the symptoms of illness that has made you sick for so long.

"I feel better now that I know what it is," so many people say when told that what ails them has a name. But labels can be limiting. Labels can pathologize, categorize, and demoralize. What purpose does it serve to be labeled an alcoholic? What solution does it bring? Perhaps it helps fuel your will. Fantastic. But it just seems like a negative affirmation that feels bad.

Why not say, as I do when offered alcohol, "I don't drink." When people ask, "why not?" I smile and say, "I like it too much."

Rather than spend time on carefully manicured labels consider diving deeper and bringing to light the wounds or triggers that drive you to drink. Consider exorcizing the trauma that has severed your growth, stolen your childhood, blocked your joy and kept you stuck in a cycle of abuse.

Seek help.

- Seek help to heal the wounds of the past
- Seek help to free you from a toxic relationship
- Seek help to liberate you from untenable job stress
- Seek help from whatever or whoever causes you to over-drink.

Perhaps you don't drink to plaster over traumatic wounds. Perhaps your drinking habit is your quick-fix strategy to take the sharp edge off living in this world.

Whatever your reasons, whatever your motivations, whatever has attracted you to this book, it's my sincerest hope that you find encouragement, help, and healing in the pages that follow.

I'd like to encourage you to view this book as Home Rehab—your in-house holistic addiction recovery center.

Instead of forking out thousands of dollars to be treated by some of the world's most esteemed addiction specialists you'll find some of the best of the best in the pages that follow including:

- A diet of knowledge and education
- The latest developments in mind and body science, including neurotheology, neuroesthetics, psychotherapy and more
- Mind, body, and soul therapies—including energy psychology and holistic healing—including meditation

THE PATH TO SOBRIETY

I promise to break down the path to sobriety in ways you can easily understand and apply to your own life.

Knowledge is power. Ultimately long-term success in winning the war on alcohol can be explained through medical science and psychology — and marketing…how the booze barons encourage you to act against your best interests.

Understanding alcohol from all angles will offer substantive reasons for why it works.

Importantly, what I'd love you to take away from reading this book is that there is no one path to sobriety. You may or may not be able to go it alone, you may need help, you may need therapy, but regardless of the approach you take, controlling alcohol is a long-term lifestyle change.

Very often, as I've said, it may mean spotlighting and healing the wounds of your past.

Comedian and former addict Russel Brand shares his story of childhood sexual abuse in his book *Recovery: Freedom From Our Addic-*

tions. In his book he reinterprets The Twelve Step recovery process and champions the call for abstinence.

Similarly, Duff McKagan, the former bass guitarist of Guns N' Roses and one of the world's greatest rock musicians, shares how he used alcohol to self-medicate his agonizing anxiety. The origin of his pain he says, stemmed from being asked to lie to his mother about his father's affairs, their subsequent divorce and his father's own heavy drinking.

McKagan devised his own program of anxiety treatment and alcohol recovery. Read the inspiring story of a man who partied so hard he nearly died, in his book *It's so Easy and Other Lies*.

Anne Dowsett Johnson, a journalist and self-described recovering alcoholic, and the daughter of an alcoholic herself, urges us all to wake up to the wilful blindness to the damages of drinking in our culture, and explores disturbing trends and false promises peddled by alcohol barons in her book *Drink: The Intimate Relationship Between Women and Alcohol*. For Dowsett, medical intervention through prescribed anti-depressants played an instrumental role in her recovery.

AA's 12-step approach didn't work for stressed entrepreneur Russ Parry. But years of therapy, couple counseling, renewing his faith and a program of recovery offered by his church did—alongside changing his relationship to work. He shares his journey to abstinence in his book, *The Sober Entrepreneur*.

These are just some of the many people and books I have come to admire as I embarked on my own journey to understand why I drank so much and why I couldn't stop.

For these people, sharing their stories was part of their healing process —that and the desire to pay-it-forward. In my book, E*mploy Yourself* from my bestselling *Mid-Life Career Rescue* series, I share how health coach Sheree Clark numbed her job blues by over-drinking until she realized booze was never going to be a long-term sustainable solution.

She sold her business and created a new career as a healthy living coach. She still enjoys a drink—but says since her career change that she couldn't be happier or healthier.

As author and filmmaker Michael Moore said, "I want us all to face our fears and stop behaving like our goal in life is merely to survive. Surviving is for game show contestants stranded in the jungle or on a desert island. You are not stranded. Use your power. You deserve better."

I took these words to heart many years ago. Anxiety and depression run in my family—as does a tendency to place a stop-cap on dreams. As you've read, my grandmother grew up in foster care, plagued by the shame of her family secret—her father was murdered a man. It doesn't matter that he was drunk, that he only meant to land a punch. Murder is murder, right? At least it is to those quick to judge.

I'm sure that Molly's painful upbringing had an impact on how much she drank. She was such a beautiful women with so much truly tragic trauma, including the death of her first child—a much-longed for son who arrived into the world still-born.

My grandmother's upbringing also impacted my mother and her sister. My mom told me that she couldn't recall ever coming home from school without finding her mother in bed. My grandmother's emotional distance and attempts to numb her pain, in turn, impacted my mom's ability to give me the love I craved as a child.

My dad suffered the trauma of emotional neglect too. He was dumped in a boarding school when he was only four—supposedly for his highest good. He never knew his father, and only found out when he was in his 70s that he had a sister. Growing up, he never experienced a hug or knew true affection.

I understand now why, growing up, I, nor my siblings were ever hugged. We still don't. Hugging feels awkward, stiff, painful—foreign.

Like Amy Winehouse and so many others with wounded childhoods, early traumas can leave permanent scars that alcohol and other drugs appear to smooth.

Writing this book has awakened many painful memories, I found myself grieving for the feeling of belonging I never felt. But writing and time has healed these memories too—knowledge, truth, love and acceptance does that.

I've worked hard to overcome the wounds of my childhood—my adulthood too.

You should, too. Your past doesn't need to stop you.

"A lot of people feel like they're victims in life, and they'll often point to past events, perhaps growing up with an abusive parent or in a dysfunctional family," writes Rhonda Byrne in *The Secret*.

"Most psychologists believe that about 85 percent of families are dysfunctional, so all of a sudden you're not so unique. My parents were alcoholics. My dad abused me. My mother divorced him when I was six... I mean, that's almost everybody's story in some form or not," she says.

The author of the *Chicken Soup For The Soul* series, Jack Canfield, also speaks to this point: "The real question is, what are you going to do now? What do you choose now? Because you can either keep focusing on that, or you can focus on what you want. And when people start focusing on what they want, what they don't want falls away, and what they want expands, and the other part disappears."

In hindsight, you will see your life experiences as a gift. As Isabel Allende once said, "Without my unhappy childhood and dysfunctional family, what would I have to write about?"

I channel my life experiences into my books. I pay it forward and share how I learned to empower my mind, body, and soul. I studied Buddhist philosophy. I learned Transcendental and mindfulness meditation—and praise the life-altering magic of this beautiful tool as often as I can.

Something, fashion designer, Stellar McCartney has also done recently, when in a 2018 article she revealed how in her twenties she turned to meditation after her mother's death. "Transcendental Meditation keeps me sane," McCartney says.

At the time of writing she is 46, and wants everyone to have the chance to reap the same benefits, whether they have a raw emotional need for TM, like she did, or not. Which is why, despite her preference to keep her private life away from the spotlight, she gave her first interview on meditation.

Reading her account, and those of others, fortifies my own spiritual and wellbeing practices. As does reading self-empowerment and personal development books.

When I was struggling with my own anxiety and depression I devoured nearly every self-help book on the planet—and beyond. I went to healers and sought counseling.

I trained to be a hypnotherapist and counselor, studied psychology, and gained other therapeutic skills. I continue to pass on the knowledge I've learned to my clients and readers like you to help empower us all to live our best lives. It's a large part of the motivation behind sharing so much of my own personal story and vulnerabilities in *Mind Your Drink*. This is me 'unplugged.'

Every day I fight for my dreams.

We all enter this life, and leave it, with different challenges. Different parents, siblings, life experiences. The pain of your past doesn't need to define you. If you are prepared to be honest and vulnerable and to do the graft, you know what you need to do to empower your life and your work.

Throughout this book we'll explore a diverse range of strategies to help you either ease up on the drink or ditch it entirely. For some people, when they lose the triggers that drive their craving, control comes easily.

For others, alcohol is a serious and dangerously addictive substance—they come to accept that they just can't handle it.

Whatever camp you're in, you are the expert in your own life. You are not powerless to make a change for the better. Empowering yourself is the biggest, most vital, most life-affirming skill of all.

As former addict and leading neuroscientist Marc Lewis writes in this book, *The Biology of Desire: why addiction is not a disease,* alcoholism and addiction "can spring up in anyone's backyard. It attacks our politicians, our entertainers, our relatives, and often ourselves. It's become ubiquitous, expectable, like air pollution and cancer."

Shaming, blaming and naming is not the cure, compassion understanding, and living life on your terms is.

As Lewis also notes, "Many experts highlight the value of empowerment for overcoming addiction. In fact, most former addicts claim that empowerment, not powerlessness, was essential to them, especially in the latter stages of their recovery. Sensitivity to the meaning of empowerment in recovery may be greatest for those who've been disempowered in their social world, including women, minorities, the poor, and those with devastating family histories."

Abusing alcohol is not a disease. It's a coping strategy—one, before reading this book, you may not have been aware of.

As you read this book, you'll reclaim your power and decide whether alcohol has anything positive to contribute to your life at all, or whether you'd be better off putting your money, your energy, your time, your happiness and your health into something, or someone, who's a less abusive lover. Yes, you will decide—it's that simple, and at times, that difficult.

Throughout *Mind Your Drink,* we'll explore ways to heal the past and exorcize unhelpful emotions that keep you stuck in a cycle of destructive feelings.

As Candace Pert writes in, *Everything You Need to Know to Feel Go(o)d,* "Buried, painful emotions from the past make up what some psychologists and healers call a person's 'core emotional trauma'.

"The point of therapy—including bodywork, some kinds of chiropractic, and energy medicine—is to gently bring that wound to gradual awareness so it can be re-experienced and understood.

"Only then is choice possible, a faculty of your frontal cortex, allowing you to reintegrate any disowned parts of yourself; let go of old traumatic patterns, and become healed, or whole."

Lets take a deeper dive into how to control alcohol before it seizes the throttle and controls you.

CONTROL ALCOHOL BEFORE IT CONTROLS YOU

"Alcohol abuse can lead to major health problems—and can affect your ability to learn and function well. The best way to protect yourself from these problems is to never start drinking at all. It's a foolproof approach that works every time," says neuroscientist Dr. Susan Tapert.

Great advice for those who've never started, but what about those of us already fooled by alcohol?

If you're going to successfully kick or modify the drink habit you'll need some pretty compelling reasons to sustain your decision.

Many of us have bought into the cultural myth that drinking excessive amounts of alcohol makes us happy, cool, popular. But what if the opposite is also true? What if everything you have been told is a lie?

The truth about alcohol is that it is a highly addictive poison. Some people can handle it, but millions of people can't. There's no shame in admitting alcohol has you by its tail.

Booze impacts people differently. Your weight, height, the water composition in your body, your social group, unresolved traumas, and a whole host of other interesting factors all impact how quickly and how often you drink.

Do you truly know how it impacts you?

Do you become depressed or teary—sharing your tales of sadness, or wailing songs of melancholy, with anyone close enough to hear?

Perhaps alcohol gives you the confidence boost you lack or dulls the thunder of social anxiety.

Do you become gregarious, hyper-friendly—willing and ready to go to bed with anybody?

Perhaps you become impulsive—driving recklessly at great speed or daring yourself to achieve impossible physical feats, like diving through the air or surfing dangerously across a crowd of strangers.

Or does alcohol summon forth the warrior, the mutinous murderer or the vengeful vixen? Under the influence do you harm the ones you love? As you've read, even good people are capable of unfathomable brutality and even murder.

"There is no inexplicable defect in our personalities, no elusive flaw in our bodies. Alcohol is simply a highly addictive drug," writes Annie Gracie in her book *This Naked Mind.* "We find it hard to accept that we are all drinking the same addictive poison."

Alcohol weaves an often unpredictable, yet foreseeable path of harm in us all. Individual differences in brain chemistry, lifestyle choices, stress levels, upbringing, peer pressure, group-think and other factors trigger impulsivity, aggression, depression, and other emotional, cognitive and behavioral changes—all of which are seemingly beyond our control.

Alcohol changes who you are. These changes are hard, but not impossible, to predict.

"Anyone of us could be here," a prison-officer once told me while I was working in the bowels of a maximum-security prison. "Take

Hemi," he says, gesturing to a young, good-looking guy aged eighteen, now in jail for life. "He got pissed, got into a fight and the guy wound up dead."

Yep, I know that story well. I also know intimately the wide and bewildering range of effects triggered by alcohol abuse. Winding up in bed with strangers, euphoria which turns to dread, closeness that turns to rage, and feeling I no longer wanted to live—truly believing how peaceful it would be to throw myself from a cliff and fly through the sky. To die.

Take a moment and make a list of everything drinking steals or has stolen from you. Here are a few areas to consider:

- Harmonious relationships?
- Happiness?
- Career success?
- Custody of your children?
- Liberty and freedom?
- Security and safety?
- Sanity and peace of mind?
- Health and well-being?
- Your waistline?
- Money?
- Or something else?

For example, many people have either perpetuated or experienced domestic violence, been hospitalized, lost custody of their children, derailed a much-loved career, destroyed their most important relationships, suffered from an inoperable disease caused by alcohol abuse, nearly died—or did.

Controlling alcohol and the triggers that compel you to drink takes vigilance.

'There's so much marketing about alcohol, but I can't see any signs warning people of alcohol harm," I said to the woman at my local electorate office.

"They're silent," she said.

"They don't exist," I replied.

It makes you wonder. Out of sight, out of mind, right?

Why is that you can't escape the continual barrage of marketing messages inviting you to drink? Could it be there so much money spent on reactively fixing alcohol fall out and none left for proactive health initiatives—including education?

But you can right the imbalance and become more mindful of alcohol harm.

People who go to AA meetings, or other sobriety meet-ups, are continually reminded of how alcohol has no place in their life.

Many people who successfully control alcohol find other ways to remain vigilant. For example, I counteract all the positive messages the booze barons and happy drunks spin about the wonders of booze by constantly reminding myself of the negative aspects of drinking.

I also remind myself that alcohol is a poison dressed up as lolly water, that it's a neurotoxin, and that it makes me feel flat, discouraged and depressed. Affirming the negative is a simple way to counteract and rebalance the positive marketing spin.

As I shared in the opening of this book, keeping a Sobriety Journal is one of many strategies I share in this book, which works for me.

When I first created my Sobriety Journal I brainstormed and bullet-pointed some of the areas in which my excessive drinking was becoming problematic, personally and professionally.

As you read through this list give some thought to your own experiences.

Negative Physical Impact of Drinking Alcohol

Depression

Anxiety

Blackouts

Despondency

Cognitive impairments

Memory loss

Fearing for my safety

Negative Financial Impact of Drinking Alcohol

Reduced savings

Sucked away money that could be used to repay debt or diverted for a massage, flowers, beauty

Reduced productivity and work effectiveness

Diminished creativity that I can pour into money-making endeavors and things that spark joy

Negative Emotional Impact of Drinking Alcohol

Depression

Anxiety

Aggression—arguments with my partner

feeling blah

fear—especially when around other drunk people

Loss of confidence and self-esteem

<u>*Negative Spiritual Impact of Drinking Alcohol*</u>

Lower vibration

Dark Energies

Harmful spirits

Aggression

Shift from essence

'An ugly statue sits where your spirit should be." ~Rumi

Lack of mindfulness

Dis-ease

Disconnection from source energy

Reduced intuition

<u>*Negative Physical Impact of Drinking Alcohol*</u>

Aging

Weight-gain

Stress

Overload on liver

Increased likelihood of cancer—8 percent increase in risk for every standard drink you have

Ugliness—red eyes, pallid skin, bloating

Insomnia

Nutrient loss

Depletes almost every vitamin your body needs

Headaches

Eyestrain

<u>*Negative Relationship Impact of Drinking Alcohol*</u>

Increased arguments

Emotional distance and disconnection

Operating on different wavelengths

Breakdowns and meltdowns

Anger

Fear

Loss of love

Loss of respect

Neglect

I DIDN'T NEED a textbook or neuroscientist to warn me about alcohol harm, although further research illuminated the side-effects. But I did find it helpful to bring more mindfulness to the negative impact drinking was having in all aspects of my life.

As Rainer Maria Rilke once wrote (also in my Sobriety Journal): "Sickness is the means by which an organism frees itself from what is alien; so one must simply help it be sick, to have its whole sickness and to break out with it, since that is the way it gets better."

Dr. Candace Pert, formerly the chief of brain biochemistry at the National Institutes of Health in the US, revolutionized her field by discovering that emotions create biochemical compounds called peptides that serve as messengers in the brain; her team's work won the prestigious Albert Lasker Award, which is often a precursor to the Nobel Prize.

She urges us to honor all our feelings and look for the insight and hope of healing emotions provide. "When we don't admit to or accept responsibility for these less comfortable emotions, they can be more dangerous," she says

Take a moment and consider what alcohol steals or has stolen from you. Does this change how you perceive alcohol and addiction? Be grateful for the teaching.

THE SURPRISING JOY OF SOBRIETY

Is it more fun to have one? The 'one-and-done' club is growing in popularity, despite considerable pressure to have more. Would you be happier? I know I am—'one or none', that's my new mantra. Rule number one, I never, ever drink when stressed.

Sobriety is my sunshine, my light, the sparkling clarity of a life infused with beauty. I love being sober. I love feeling in control.

Controlling alcohol has freed me from the darkness and despair that once stalked me, and which still haunts so many.

Sure, I no longer have the quick fix-magic potions to addle my brain, mask my fears, vanquish my insecurities. Making friends with social anxiety didn't come in a seductively beveled crystal flute fizzing with bubbles. Nope, it took a lot of hard graft.

But I have something more as a result. Heart-wide open I have my spirit, my soul, my self. I am supported, nourished, and free to be me—authentically, warts, vulnerabilities, flaws and all. And it feels great. And I never want to go back to the blindfolded darkness of short-term highs and long-term lows.

Self-love, self-compassion, self-acceptance, and self-care—they're all part of my toolkit. They're part of your tool-kit too.

What do they all have in common?

Loving you.

Loving you more than trying to fit in with your drinking buddies. Respecting and loving your body and soul so much that you no longer crave toxins. Delighting in the fact you're riding a wave of new enlightened consciousness.

THE WORLD IS SOBERING UP

It's heartening to see the savvy sobers enjoying increasingly good company. Globally there's an awakening and with it a rebirth, a renaissance of sorts. Being boozed is a relic from the dark ages and this is the era of enlightenment. Sobriety is queen, abstinence her cohort.

Magazines are running pieces about the 'sober-curious' movement. *Elle* is printing headlines such as 'Why I Decided to Break Up With Alcohol'. Others are talking about how toxic and deadly alcohol is to your skin. *The Huffington Post* is running with 'What Alcohol Really Does to Your Sex Life', and *Men's Health* is asking 'Why Drinking a Little Booze Each Day May be Killing You'.

"I don't drink or smoke or have caffeine," music diva Jennifer Lopez was reported as saying, in a women's magazine. "That really wrecks your skin as you get older."

Yep, not only is sobriety for savvy connoisseurs of health and well-being, but being booze-free is becoming a status symbol.

Sober is the new drunk.

Think Colin Farrell, Russell Brand and Duff McKagan, bass guitarist of Guns N' Roses, and one of the world's greatest rock musicians.

Sober and boring? I don't think so! Instead, they're admired, celebrated, held up as the new cool.

When I tell people I don't drink they look at me wide-eyed and full of awe. "Wow! I don't think I could function without a drink," many of them say. "I wish I could quit."

They can, you can—where there's a will, there is a way. Quite simply drinking alcohol is a habit, something many of us do without stopping to question why.

As the health risks become more and more apparent, and more valued, coupled with the unearthing of the tactical untruths peddled by suppliers, alcohol is going the way of cigarettes—on a fast-track trajectory out the door.

"I want to live. I don't want to die," UK songstress Adele famously declared when she shared her decision to considerably scale back her booze binging.

"I didn't want to live, but I didn't want to die," Colin Farrell once said before finding the courage and the will to quit drinking and seek help.

Your health is your wealth and sobriety will make you rich, a hundred times over. You'll find plenty of people investing in the new currency of sobriety.

Where once you couldn't party without a cigarette in your hand, or socialize without ingesting a plume of toxic smoke at a pub, booze-free bars, nightclubs and communities are sprouting like poppy seeds all around the world.

HAVING A FREAKING GOOD TIME MINDFULLY

"*No Beers, Who Cares* (BWC) isn't about making anyone feel bad about drinking. It's a movement towards shifting attitudes around how and why we drink and helping people become more aware of their beliefs and habits and having a freaking good time doing so," says Claire Robbie, the founder *No Beers, Who Cares*.

Robbie describes her *No Beers, Who Cares* initiative as not anti-alcohol, but as a pro-mindfulness initiative.

"There's a shift around the world as people understand how incredible life can be without drinking and it's time to bring that high vibration to New Zealand," Robbie says, "and it's an amazing step towards living more mindfully."

Claire Robbie was a news reporter on TV3's Nightline before a tumultuous time led her to discover the life-changing benefits of yoga and meditation and life without alcohol.

At a low point in her life, what started as a hobby became an essential part of her healing process, and as her love for her new practices grew, so did the awareness that she had discovered a new vocation.

"The focus is less about giving something up, but boosting your awareness of how much you gain," Robbie says.

HACK YOUR HABITS JOYFULLY

"What we've seen is that giving up alcohol is a keystone habit. A keystone habit is one that unlocks your full well-being potential. Just a few of the benefits of going alcohol-free such as extra energy, motivation, vitality, productivity, money, and time, will begin to pave the way to the life you have always dreamed of," Robbie enthuses.

Whether you're tuning into *The Hello Sunday Morning* movement in Australia, *No Beers, Who Cares* in New Zealand, *Morning Gloryville* or *Off The Rocks* in the UK, or the ever-growing number of bars that have taken alcohol out of the mix, you'll find safety in numbers.

"When I first decided to undergo a long-term sober stint— total abstention from alcohol, for at least a few years and perhaps forever—I was full of dread, fear and feelings of deprivation, but after a while I realized how pivotal that decision was. It was only once I'd shelved alcohol that I was truly capable of sorting the rest of my life out. I then saw with absolute clarity how most people are addicted to something, and how the majority of those people are in denial about it," UK-based Jen Nelson, founder of Off The Rocks, says.

"I try not to waste time on regret, but if there's one thing I could go back and do differently, it would be to take a long and total break from alcohol a lot sooner than I did. Going sober for several years enabled me to identify the underlying causal reasons behind my once excessive drinking. Learning how to live sober also allowed me to cultivate proper coping techniques. I no longer celebrated every happiness with a drink and I stopped drowning my sorrows at the first sign of sadness. Recovery is so much more than giving something up, it's the way back to your authentic self."

How can you approach alcohol more mindfully? What might you be giving up by going alcohol free? How much might you gain? What are you prepared to change in your life? What would stop you?

Read on for further incentives on why sobriety is good for you, and why doing things to excess isn't just uncool but extremely dangerous —even fatal. Drink to excess, why would you? There comes a point in everyone's life when we decide, "I've had enough".

WEEK TWO: STRATEGIES FOR SOBRIETY

WEEK TWO: STRATEGIES FOR SOBRIETY

In the following section you'll find a tasting platter of strategies to support your successful sobriety. You may like to take a read through first and then pick 'n mix those that you think or feel are right for you.

1

HIGH ON BELIEVING: WRESTLING WITH THE GOD THING

As I wrote in the foreword to this book, while finishing my psychology degree at the young-old-age of 49 I decided to take a spiritual approach to the treatment of alcohol addiction. The topic proved challenging.

It was the final assignment needed to complete my third-year paper, Abnormal and Therapeutic Psychology. A lot was resting on it. I'd failed my first assignment where I had researched the causes and treatment of obesity. I was told this was because I hadn't consulted enough empirical data and scholarly articles—relying instead on people's personal accounts. I was keen to avoid the same mistake.

But I quickly discovered a lack of psychologically-validated research to cite.

Perplexed, I asked my lecturer why, when so many alcoholics swear that taking a spiritual approach was instrumental in their recovery, was there such a dearth of research?

"The theoretical etiologies of disorders do focus on cognitive, genetic, neurobiological, personality based theories —this reflects the bias of both the authors themselves and the current Western approaches," my lecturer, Dr. Gillian Craven, wrote back to me.

"This is for better or worse the zeitgeist of our time. Spiritual and environmental factors are starting to make a bit of an impact but are not fully accepted as a mainstream approach yet (particularly spiritual approaches). But every approach has its day... and as they do become more accepted maybe it is a matter of watch this space," she added.

This was back in 2014. In my view, spiritual approaches were, and continue to be, adopted by mainstream practitioners, including Deepak Chopra who offers addiction recovery programs at his Chopra Addiction and Wellness Center.

Alcoholics Anonymous also addresses spiritual issues, and many followers attribute placing their faith in God to their recovery.

The challenge for many psychologists, particularly those focused on academic research, is their inability to measure, quantify, and place spirituality in a test-tube.

"Science has sometimes been at odds with the notion that laypeople can cure themselves," writes Jarret Liotta in a *National Geographic article*, 'Does Science Show What 12 Steps Know?'

The purpose of *Mind Your Drink* is not to prove or disprove anyone's beliefs or to discredit any profession, but to present you with options, backed by my own experience, and the experience of others who have struggled to control alcohol—and succeeded.

An increasing number of people also adhere to the belief that God lies within us all—we are God—and it is time to connect to our inner guidance and the ultimate source of empowerment. Many great minds throughout time, including Leonardo da Vinci, subscribed to this view. Do you?

As we explore an eclectic and holistic range of strategies—spiritual, cognitive, feeling-based, and scientifically validated, to help you control alcohol, I encourage you to adopt an open mind and 'do a Leonardo da Vinci' and experiment with different approaches until you find what works for you.

Importantly, in the chapters which follow we'll strengthen your desire and fuel your motivation by creating a vision of victory, and imagining a better life alcohol-free.

2

BE FREE WHERE YOU ARE: HACK YOUR HABITS

"A habit is a redundant set of automatic unconscious thoughts, behaviors, and emotions that develop through repetition," writes Dr. Joe Dispenza in his book, *Becoming Supernatural: How Common People Are Doing the Uncommon.*

"It's when you've done something so many times that your body is programmed to become the mind. Over time, your body is dragging you to a predictable future based on what you've been doing in the past. Therefore, if you're not in the present moment, you're probably in a program," says Dispenza.

For many people, their new system of recovery is literally a carefully curated program of new habits involving healing, therapy and, very often, abstinence.

Truth dissolves lies and helps you hack your habits.

"At the exact moment when truth erupts the subconscious changes from wastebasket file to angel writing in a book of gold," writes Ray Bradbury in his book *Zen and the Art of Writing.*

When you name and repetitively hack the habits that trigger or support drinking you systematically reprogram old scripts with new ones that support and sustain sobriety.

If for example, you've maintained a habit, consciously or without truly thinking about it, such as having a drink when you knock of work, or when you cook a meal, create your own replacement therapy and switch the habit you want to quit with another habit that feels refreshing, rejuvenating and rewarding.

For example, instead of pouring a glass of wine, or downing a gin and tonic after work, I now find a beautiful place to go and meditate. Often, it's under my favorite tree.

When I lived in a bustling city I would seek peace and quiet in a church. Sometimes I go for a swim after work, or go for a walk. These and other habits nourish my mind, body and soul. They also offer the perfect distraction with the added and much valued additional benefits of elevating my energy and vibration.

I also love to read books instead of drinking. As you'll discover later, reading is the perfect escape and a tried and true strategy used by many people to aid their recovery. Oh, the places you can go, and the people you can become when you lose yourself in words.

Recently, I came across the beautiful writings of Zen Master Thich Nhat Hanh, a global spiritual leader, poet and peace activist, revered around the world for his powerful teachings and writings on mindfulness and peace. Hanh, a Vietnamese Buddhist monk who now lives in France, suffered tragic loss and significant trauma during the Vietnam War.

Hanh devoted his life to turning his anger into reducing hatred and crimes against humanity, and using his spiritual gifts to changing the world one word at a time.

In his book, *Be Free Where You Are,* he writes, "To live mindfully means to stop ingesting those kinds of poisons. Instead, choose to be in touch with what is wonderful, refreshing, and healing within yourself and around you."

Throughout *The Sobriety Experiment* you will discover how devoting your life to something other than drinking alcohol can transform your life. You may end up touching the lives of others who are suffering and who may crave the fix you and your story of reinvention can inspire. If you can kick the habit, they can too—right?

You'll also discover how devoting yourself to beauty—whether it's a beautiful book, a wonderful artwork, an uplifting piece of music, the lyrics of a song, indulging your hobby for exotic butterflies, or even creating beautiful food—can transform not only your soul but the souls of those who are touched and transformed by your beautiful new habits.

Ways to manifest and share beauty seem infinite. Piero Ferrucci, a transpersonal psychologist and the bestselling author of *The Power of Kindness*, has written a stunning book exploring the healing power of beauty and showing us how see the beauty of everyday in a new way.

Beauty and the Soul: The Extraordinary Power of Everyday Beauty to Heal Your Life weaves the threads of scientific research, spiritual practices and daily rituals, personal stories, and teachings from various wisdoms in a spell-binding tapestry that left me with a clear call to action—make beauty my guiding principal.

One of my favorite quotes comes from Picasso, "Art washes from the soul the dust of everyday life." For me, creativity is beauty. Art in its many forms, whether it is poetry, sculpture, a play, a painting, or a beautifully designed building. Even something as simple as a beautifully designed tap has such a powerful ability to spark joy and free me from groundhog day.

For me, this is spirituality: something that lifts me up at a much deeper level and allows me to transcend the mundane. Beauty offers this.

Some of the artists who were making abstract works in the past (when such art was not so common) were on a quest to see if art could inspire a transcendental state akin to the sublime feeling that nature could inspire. Artists such as Vasily Kandinsky, Kazimir Malevich, Mark Rothko—even Leonardo da Vinci hoped viewers would experience a spiritual revelation, or at least a deeply meditative feeling, while gazing at abstract surfaces, forms and symbols.

I love what the authors of a book about the artist Max Gimblett (*The Brush of All Things*) had to say about his art:

"For by accepting Gimblett's art, we come to understand the role painting can have in our lives; that it can be of use rather than decoration. Art shows us something about both nature and ourselves, it is where we go to gain sustenance."

I feel that way every time I look at the paintings I own which were created by him and which he entitled "Bite of The Golden Snake" and "Choice"—and other works I don't own but greatly admire.

A fellow New Zealander, Max Gimblett is a recovering alcoholic and an ordained Zen Buddhist Monk. He is the only New Zealand artist who has exhibited at the prestigious Guggenheim Gallery in New York. "Art is a not a hobby, he says, "It's a life and death thing."

Many people gain great joy, strength and comfort gazing or being surrounded by works of art—it doesn't have to be fancy or expensive, a child's drawing can elevate your soul and be especially freeing.

When I turned 50, using the natural knacks and talents that strengthen me, I devoted myself to creating my own publishing company, Blue Giraffe Publishing.

In doing so I honored my soul purpose—to be of service, empower and inspire others and create books of beauty. Having fun and being playful and child-like are also values and strengths of mine which sustain me.

This is why I commissioned my niece Freya, who was six-years old at the time, to draw a blue giraffe for my logo. I love that she gave the giraffe huge colorful spots and drew outside the lines.

Inspired by something one of my favorite muses, Gabrielle Bonheur "Coco" Chanel, once said, I asked Freya to add some wings.

"If you were born without wings, do nothing to prevent them from growing."

Coco had to overcome obstacles to success just like you and I. She suffered many hardships, including the death of her mother when she was young, being abandoned by a father who didn't love her, growing up in an orphanage, and the stigma of her early years which plagued her throughout her life.

She suffered extreme poverty, self-doubt, low self-esteem and craved love. People jealous of her talent, also spread malicious rumors and tried to undermine her success.

But she didn't let obstacles stop her from doing the work she loved. The pursuit of excellence born from her experience, fueled by her determination to be an independent woman, and the desire to liberate others, ultimately led to her success.

Her boundless imagination, strength of purpose and courageous spirit are an inspiration to young and old.

I reveal how the success secrets and strategies of extraordinary artists like Coco Chanel can help people like you and I succeed—personally and professionally—in my book *The Art of Success: Coco Chanel*.

In the next chapter, I also share how my experience of Interactive Drawing Therapy unearthed, and later healed my fear of standing out.

We'll dive deeper into the benefits of being less serious and adopting a child-like playfulness in the chapter Laugh and Play. How cool to learn that taking yourself less seriously triggers the dopaminergic reward system, a system known to play a pivotal role in drug reward and motivational behaviors.

Is it time to fire your harmful habits, make them redundant, give them their final marching orders, and employ new ones which help you to succeed? Let's take a look at some ways to hack your unhelpful habits and create a new program to aid your commitment to sobriety.

First up is the therapeutic tonic of creative expression. As you'll discover in the next chapter, creativity is like hanging out with your soul-mate—the one who brings life to life, heals your wounds, loves you unconditionally and lifts you higher.

3

POWERFUL CREATIVITY

Creative expression and communicating what you truly feel is one of our greatest joys and freedoms. It is a simple and effective way to inject more happiness into your life without needing alcohol. Creativity in its various guises is also a natural antidote to stress, anxiety and depression, which explains why art therapy is such a potent and popular tool.

Art therapy is a form of experiential therapy, an approach to recovery and healing that addresses emotional and spiritual needs through creative or physical activity. People don't need to have a background in the arts or any artistic talent to participate. They need only to be open to experiencing and engaging actively to benefit.

I have trained in a technique called Interactive Drawing Therapy and have found it to be an incredible tool in my own life and in my sessions with others. The simplest of drawings, a line, a color, a scrawled phrase or word can powerfully access parts of the psyche we often repress, bringing it to light. In an alchemical process, wounds are spun into gold.

When I first trained in Interactive Drawing Therapy the teacher asked for a volunteer. No hands were raised so he picked me. What harm could it do, I thought, being as skilled as I was at keeping a lid firmly on my feelings.

"Draw an animal," he said.

Sure, I thought. Great. Harmless. I drew a giraffe.

"Put some color on the page," the teacher gently guided.

My giraffe became pink with green, purple and yellow spots. What fun I thought.

"Where is she?" the teacher asked. "Draw this on the page."

I drew large grey and black rectangles, symbolizing office blocks, cars belching smoke, and a road, not unlike Lambton Quay, in Wellington, New Zealand where I went to work in a job I hated every weekday.

"Put some words on the page," the teacher whispered.

"She doesn't want to stand out."

And then it dawned on me, just as the words slipped onto the page. That giraffe was me. And the fact was I did stand out—naturally. I had always been different. And I had struggled unsuccessfully to belong.

"She can't help but stand out," my tutor affirmed. "It's who she is."

For me, this awareness was so new, so potent, so transformative, that I knew instantly there was work to do. I began to understand the deep social anxiety I had felt as a child and carried with me through adolescence—and with it the drinking to belong, to bolster the confidence I never felt, to hide the discomfort of living in my own skin.

I wonder, if you were an animal who would you be and why? Asking this question so directly, often yields substantially different, more rational, carefully considered choices, than those which arise through the techniques of tools like Interactive Drawing Therapy (IDT). The strength of IDT is its ability to access what is repressed, hidden and buried in the subconscious and bring it to light for healing.

Job stress, as we have discussed briefly, is a major reason many people over-drink. Again, drawing came to my rescue. I had become quite accomplished at pretending I loved my job—I couldn't afford to admit the truth.

As I share in my book, *Mid-Life Career Rescue The Call for Change*, "I was a single mum, the only one able to support my young daughter and myself. I used to go home with a brave face, but inside I was tired and depressed. My self-esteem was so low I thought no one would hire me. I tried to go to work, grit my teeth and bear it.

I wanted to make a difference in people's lives. But that wasn't what my boss wanted from me. "You could make a lot of money here," he said. "You just need to be more selfish." For a while, I tried to be someone else—motivated only by money, but every day my values were compromised, and the skills I loved weren't used.

My job started making me ill. It got so bad I got shingles—a painful virus affecting the central nervous system. I felt trapped and unable to leave. My colleagues at work had similar experiences. It really was such a toxic workplace. Several people had heart attacks, and the amount of alcohol people consumed after work to numb the pain was staggering.

I NEEDED A CAREER RESCUE. In desperation, I agreed to see a career counselor. During my first session, I was asked to draw a picture. I drew a grey bird in a black cage.

"The door is open, but she's forgotten how to fly," I told her.

This drawing brought tears to her eyes. Although I didn't understand why at the time, I can see now that she felt my pain at feeling so caught and trapped by my situation.

Through our sessions and the structured exercises we completed together, I rebuilt my confidence and strengthened my awareness of my skills, and most importantly, I learned how to dream.

The work the career counselor did with me was so important, so vital—saving me from despair. It led me to not just finding a job I loved, but later creating one that gave me a sense of purpose.

What she taught me literally gave me my life back. Happily, I can now serve others in this way too—as an author, qualified holistic therapist, counselor, life and career coach, and a trainer of other coaches who also aspire to make a difference in other people's lives.

If you're reading this book and recognize yourself in my story, if job stress or a toxic workplace is causing you to over drink, don't wait too long for help. I promise that your happy place is out there—it may even mean employing yourself. Now, that's ultimate freedom!

THERAPY CAN BE FUN—AND FREE!

Many addiction and rehab centers use art therapy as part of their therapeutic offering, and report that clients find engaging in creative arts highly satisfying and fun. It's a playful way of relaxing and an enjoyable way to address some of the more complex aspects of rehab.

Creative activity provides a way to process some of the stressful emotions and anxieties that can emerge during treatment. After rehab, activities like painting, sculpting or drawing can be used throughout the individual's life as a way to express feelings, explore creativity, and reduce stress.

Best of all, it's a tool anyone can access, anywhere, at any time , and the effects are long-lasting. You can engage in creativity whenever you feel the need to escape the madness of this world.

But you don't need to go to rehab or analyze how and why creativity works to understand it's magic.

Art in all its guises heals and empowers. Have you ever wondered why silencing or controlling peoples creative expression is the first things marauding tyrants and dictators silence or destroy?

Leonardo da Vinci, a great scientist once said, "Art is the queen of all sciences communicating to the world." Art permeates the inner and outer worlds and elevates our soul.

My grandmother Molly was a naturally gifted and self-taught artist. Her escape, when she needed one, was painting flowers and landscapes in oil colors.

Molly also loved to play the piano, the accordion, and even the banjo and sing for others. Perhaps it was her Irish ancestry which unleashed the happy, confident entertainer. I can still hear her beautifully manicured nails tapping along the ivory keys of the piano. Art banished her heavy episodes of drinking—when she sang, painted, created she never needed a drink.

I have a tiny painting of Molly's in my shed, a small bunch of violets framed in a custom-made frame my grandfather made for her. Reg Fairweather (beautiful name) was a talented wood turner and furniture maker. His was a hobby, a beautiful retreat he found great joy and personal expression in.

I wonder now, was that his way of escaping and coping when my grandmother's drinking got out of control? Or was it Reg's way of coping or distancing himself from his own pain? At the time of writing, I've only just learned that Reg's mother, my great-grandmother, died not long after giving birth. It's a trauma that had, until now, remained a secret.

"I write songs to deal with things I otherwise might not be able to," a young woman once said about her budding music career, hobbies and dreams.

"For me to be happy is about pleasing only my heart and not worrying about what others think," says Interior designer Olimpia Orsini about her magically surreal lair in her home away from home in Rome's bohemian Campo Marzio.

"I love what a camera does," says landscape photographer Alicia Taylor. "It opens up people to connect with you, it can take you on an amazing journey, and probably is the only time I feel I've got the guts to do something is when I've got the camera in my hands. I feel like it's a key to the world."

"Knitting saved my life," the waitress at my local cafe told me recently. She told me how her hobby has provided the ultimate cure for her anxiety, and of the joy she finds in knitting for friends.

Without the anxiety of feeling different, author Isabel Allende, says she wouldn't have been driven to create. "Writing, when all is said and done, is an attempt to understand one's own circumstance and to clarify the confusion of existence, including insecurities that do not torment normal people, only chronic non-conformists."

What do these people all have in common? They harness the power of creative expression to rise above the challenges of life.

Personally, I love to write paint, take photographs and have dabbled in a great deal many other things during my life—including making stained glass Tiffany-style lampshades, pottery, knitting, crochet, cross-stitch. You name it, I've tried it. They take me out of this world, out of my mind, into the realms of the divine. I find great comfort there.

Get drunk on creating—yes, please! It's a positive addiction I'm happy to feed.

"I love the chaos. I do everything I'm not meant to do. I used to drink like an animal, but now I use my art to express the chaos in my mind," says Sir Antony Hopkins about the joy he finds in painting. "I used to take myself so seriously. I have an obsessive personality. I do everything fast. I want to do everything I can because time is running out", he says. "I want to express color. Maybe it's reaching for some sort of divine."

Don't get caught up in the classical definitions of an artist when you think about creativity, you don't have to be an artist, painter or sculptor to be creative. Expressing your thoughts or imagining what doesn't yet exist and then bringing it into being lies at the heart of creative expression. You could harness the transformational power of creativity by:

- Imagining or dreaming what could be, for example, your life of sobriety
- Challenging the status quo, as I am in the writing of this book, or generating solutions and new ideas
- Designing new products or services, perhaps instead of drinking you will pour your heart and soul into creating something you are proud of
- Expressing thoughts and feelings, visually, that are too big or too difficult to put into words
- Or doing something else that helps you deal with life and creates joy in your heart.

One of the most liberating features of the creative process is that it triggers moments of vitality and connection.

"The arts address the idea of an aesthetic experience," says Ken Robinson, an internationally recognized leader in the development of creativity.

"An aesthetic experience is one in which the senses are operating at their peak, when you are present in the current moment, when you are resonating with the excitement of this thing that you are experiencing, when you are fully alive."

Being fully alive is part of the enchantment that creative expression holds. This transformational process connects you to your authentic self. But to free yourself you must act. As Shakespeare once said, "Joy's soul lies in the doing."

How can you harness the power of creativity in your own life?

In the next chapter, we'll explore more deeply the transformational power of pepping up your peptides and changing the way you feel naturally.

4

PEP UP YOUR PEPTIDES

"As our feelings change, this mixture of peptides travels throughout your body and your brain. And they're literally changing the chemistry of every cell in your body," says neuroscientist Dr. Candace Pert.

What you feel has a powerful effect on your mind and your behavior, attracting, or repealing from you what you desire—including health and vitality. Call it the law of attraction, the law of manifestation, or whatever you like, but know that the mind-body connection is backed by strong empirical science.

Dr. Candace Pert, formerly the chief of brain biochemistry at the National Institutes of Health in the US, revolutionized her field by discovering that emotions create biochemical compounds called peptides that serve as messengers in the brain; her team's work won the prestigious Albert Lasker Award, which is often a precursor to the Nobel Prize.

Pert's breakthrough discovery changed the way scientists understood the mind-body connection.

Her discovery of the opiate receptor, the mechanism by which a class of chemicals (peptides) alters the mind and body, and subsequent research, led her to an understanding of the way emotions function as a regulatory system in the body.

Because of her revolutionary work on emotions and the mind-body connection, Dr. Pert appeared in the film, *What the Bleep Do We Know,* and her work helped shift the paradigm from "emotions as neuroscience" to "emotions as biology, " *and* "emotions as physics."

So, what does all this mean for you and your quest for sobriety?

Many people use alcohol to numb their emotions and mask their pain. But as Dr. Pert's research highlights repression creates imbalance and leads to ill-health.

"My research has shown me that when emotions are expressed—which is to say that the biochemicals that are the substrate of emotion are flowing freely, all systems are united and made whole. When emotions are repressed, denied, not allowed to whatever they may be, our network pathways get blocked, stopping the flow of the vital feel-good, unifying chemicals that run both our biology and behavior," says Pert.

As you've already discovered alcohol is a depressant and aggravates anxiety and other mental imbalances. Too often, when people start to experience low mood or suffer mental illness they head to the doctor or schedule an appointment with a therapist.

However many psychologists and western doctors treat the mind as "disembodied, a phenomenon with little or no connection to the physical body," says Pert. "Conversely, physicians treat the body with no regard for the mind or the emotions. But the body and mind are not separate, and we cannot treat one without the other."

I endorse this professionally and personally and have seen many people return to good health when they stop ingesting toxins, particularly alcohol. My daughter was too-quickly diagnosed as having bipolar and prescribed medication. She was never asked about external events that may have been triggering acute stress, nor asked about her health behaviors (or rather, non-health behaviors) that may have exacerbated her condition. Nor was she counseled in any way so that she could process and transcend feelings that kept her blocked.

After a period of counseling, particularly trauma therapy following a violent assault and attempted strangulation by her then partner, Hannah is now alcohol-free and healthy.

Extensive counseling, having a constructive outlet for her feelings, changing her environment and removing herself from negative influences, and working on her self-esteem has transformed her life. Dr. Pert would no doubt say that she has 'pepped up her peptides."

"I've always kind of known that the energy you emanate from within attracts the situations and people that you need," Pert explains.

"We're not just little hunks of meat. We're vibrating like a tuning fork

—we send out a vibration to other people. We broadcast and receive. Thus the emotions orchestrate the interactions among all our organs and systems to control that."

Emotions are meant to be felt temporarily, flowing through and out of you so they don't become stuck in your cells and tissues. This is why having an outlet to express your emotions healthily is so vital—especially when painful emotions keep replaying through your conscious and subconscious mind.

Memories are emotions tangled with thoughts, and these can become implanted not just in your brain but in your body too. There are different theories about how exactly this works, but Dr. Pert explains that memories can be found stored biochemically in the synapses where neurons (brain cells) connect to each other.

"The sensitivity of the receptors are part of memory and pattern storage," she once said. "The peptide network extends beyond the hippocampus, to organs, tissue, skin, muscle and endocrine glands.

They all have peptides receptors on them and can access and store emotional information. This means the emotional memory is stored in many places in the body, not just the brain. The autonomic nervous system is pivotal to this entire understanding."

WE ARE ALL a bundle of nerves

The autonomic nervous system is where you experience the flood of physical reactions to your emotions—it's the system that switches hormones on and off, changes your breathing and heart-rate patterns, and more in response to fear and stress.

As Colette Baron-Reid, a survivor of rape and a recovering alcohol and drug addict, shared in her book, *Uncharted: The Journey Through Uncertainty to Infinite Possibility*, "Even if you haven't studied the science of how energy affects and forms patterns in the physical world, you have experienced it, as I have. Once, I ran into an old friend with whom I had severed ties years before. My relationship with this person had been constantly in chaos, unhealthy, and not serving either of us, so we had grown apart.

"I had tremendous anxiety whenever I was around this friend, triggered by the friend's history of anger and my history around abuse. Over and over, I found myself back experiencing the energy of my 19-year-old self and the rape, when I couldn't defend myself and capitulated out of fear.

"After the friendship ended, I rarely thought about this person, and I assumed I had simply moved on, but when I saw this person approaching on the sidewalk, I felt a sense of panic and quickly crossed the street. I asked myself, "When am I?" (not where but when) and realized I wasn't present in the now; I was experiencing the energy of the past.

"Deep breathing and tuning into the Observer reconnected me to my soul and small self. I imagined myself in the hand of God, surrounded by love and light, and I sent my former friend the intention of compassion. The nightmare ended as the energy in my body shifted. I was no longer disempowered by the stored energy that had infused the memory."

Pep up your peptides—find a healthy outlet for your emotions. Make finding a way to release all those stuck energies your mission.

Journaling and writing morning pages are some of my favorite ways to express any stinky feelings that bog me down in a rut. Meditation is another—it's an amazingly alchemical tool that helps me stress less, and eliminate so much unnecessary negativity from my life. They are all some of the daily rituals I share in the next chapter, Magic Mornings.

5

MAGIC MORNINGS

"If you win the morning, you win the day," says millionaire author, podcaster and polymath Tim Ferriss. Despite his phenomenal success, Tim suffers from anxiety and credits a robust morning routine and other health behaviors with giving him more bounce throughout the day.

Ferriss kick-starts his day with 10-20 minutes of transcendental meditation, five to 10 minutes of journaling or Morning Pages, making his bed, and a healthy dose of positive vibes. He also does at least 30 seconds of light exercise. 30 seconds!

"Getting into my body, even for 30 seconds, has a dramatic effect on my mood and quiets mental chatter," Ferriss wrote in his book *Tools of Titans*.

I've followed a similar ritual for years—long before I discovered Tim Ferris. But whenever I am tempted to flag my meditation or my ritual of writing in my journal, I find it helpful to remind myself these are the tools Titans like Tim use to achieve phenomenal results.

Below are just a few of the many *Magic Morning* routines and rituals you can use to prime your day for miracles:

• **M**editation and mindfulness—enjoy some sacred silence

• **A**ffirmations—empower your beliefs with feeling-based reminders of your intentions

• **G**oals to go for—set your priorities, including health and well-being activities (exercise etc.)

• **I**nspiration—journaling, visualization, reading

• **C**o-create—partner with spirit, tap into your Higher Self, evoke the muse…and get ready to create

Importantly, complete these crucial focusing activities *before* you get to work.

I experience many of these activities simultaneously when I meditate, write my Morning Pages, and consult the oracles; and also when I go for a walk in nature, listen to an uplifting audiobook or podcast, or sip my morning coffee.

Ferriss, in a podcast episode, sums up the potency of similar mindful practices: "It's easy to become obsessed with pushing the ball forward as a Type-A personality and end up a perfectionist who is always future-focused.

"The Five-Minute Journal is a therapeutic intervention, for me at least, because I am that person. That allows me to not only get more done during the day but to also feel better throughout the entire day, to be a happier person, to be a more content person—which is not something that comes naturally to me."

I'm not alone in knowing the positive difference daily habits like journaling or taking the time to reconnect with my higher self, makes to my resilience and happiness levels.

Get your day off to a high-vibration start. Choose, develop, and apply your own Magic Morning routines. In the next chapter you'll discover why meditation is my favorite way to start the day.

6

MINDFUL MEDITATION—CULTIVATING INNER POWER

"Meditation is not just blissing out under a mango tree," says French Buddhist monk and molecular geneticist Matthieu Ricard. "It completely changes your brain and therefore changes what you are."

Quietening your overactive mind through mindfulness training techniques like meditation is a wonderful way to boost your *joie de vivre*. Meditation helps you to take control of your mental chatterbox and create some quiet space, so you can hear the voice within. This changes how you respond to what's happening in your life and increases your ability to tap into a higher level of wisdom when making decisions.

Science has proven that when people meditate they alter their brains in a good way—lowering stress levels amongst many other important things. Ridding yourself of self-limiting thoughts, controlling your reactions, discovering an inner contact with a creative source, and having more creative insights are just a few of the other benefits that can flow. The whole experience is primarily one of wholeness, rightness, and power.

Steve Jobs, a lifelong practitioner of meditation, confirmed the connection between meditation, creativity and life success: "If you just sit and observe, you will see how restless your mind is. If you try to calm it, it only makes it worse, but over time it does calm, and when it does, there's room to hear more subtle things—that's when your intuition starts to blossom and you start to see things more clearly and be in the present more.

"Your mind just slows down, and you see a tremendous expanse in the moment. You see so much more than you could see before. It's a discipline. You have to practice it."

There are many forms of meditation, including breathing meditations, walking meditations, Buddhist meditations, Transcendental Meditation and more. Whichever form you choose, the main thing to remember is that its benefits are only a few breaths away and the only thing you need is your attention.

Meditation can be done in short bursts of time, even while on the bus or train. To really be of benefit many people recommend meditating first thing in the morning, and towards the end of the day, for 20 minutes each time. You may already feel pressed for time but the benefits of creating some space in your diary will pay dividends.

Our brains never get a break and the results can be increased stress, anxiety, insomnia and if left unchecked, even depression. But, remember—there is something you can do—meditate.

Meditation changes brain patterns, soothes and connects you to your Higher Self. It's one of the most powerful bounce strategies you'll ever discover.

"It's the Swiss army knife of medical tools, for conditions both small and large," writes Arianna Huffington, the founder of *The Huffington Post* and author of *Thrive*.

So, what's the buzz? Recent research published in *New Scientist* has revealed that meditation can help to calm people and reduce anxiety and depression. The research found that regular meditation can tame the amygdala, an area of the brain which is the hub of fear memory.

People who meditate regularly are less likely to be shocked, flustered, surprised, or as angry as other people, and have a greater stress tolerance threshold as a result.

By meditating regularly, the brain is reoriented from a stressful fight-or-flight response to one of acceptance, a shift that increases contentment, enthusiasm, and feelings of happiness.

Meditation can shape our brains for the better. Watch this video on YouTube—you'll see the incredible results verified by science. http://youtu.be/m8rRzTtP7Tc

I've been meditating for over 25 years now and love it. And while it can be challenging to find time during busy or stressful periods, it really is the key to boosting creativity, harnessing intuition, building resilience, and creating a calmer and happier outlook in general. These are all important factors in maintaining the energy and focus to create and sustain sobriety success.

Here are a few of the many ways a regular meditative practice will help you claim and keep your energy and success levels high:

- Decreased stress and anxiety
- Improved focus, memory, and learning ability
- Heightened recharging capacity
- Higher IQ and more efficient brain functioning
- Increased blood circulation and reduced hyperactivity in the brain, slower wavelengths and decreased beta waves (Beta State:13—30Hz) means more time between thoughts which leads to more skillful decision making
- Increased Theta State (4—8Hz) and Delta States (1—3 Hz)

which deepens awareness and strengthens intuition and visualization skills
- Increased creativity and connection with your higher intelligence
- More energy

When Tim Ferriss, who suffers from anxiety and practices transcendental meditation, sat down with more than 200 people at the height of their field for his book, *Tools of Titans*, he found that 80% followed some form of guided mindfulness practice.

It took Ferriss a while to get into meditation, he says in a podcast episode about his own morning routine. But since he discovered that the majority of world-class performers meditated, he also decided to follow the habit.

His practice takes up 21 minutes a day: one minute to get settled and 20 minutes to meditate.

Ferriss recommends two apps for those wanting some help getting started—*Headspace* or *Calm*.

"Start small, rig the game so you can win it, get in five sessions before you get too ambitious with length," says Ferriss.

"You have to win those early sessions so you establish it as a habit, so you don't have the cognitive fatigue of that practice."

Make meditating for at least 20 minutes a day part of your daily routine for optimum success and well-being.

In the next chapter, we'll look at how regularly taking time to focus on the present moment yields remarkable benefits.

7

THE POWER OF NOW

Yoga, meditation, and the journaling practice that follows in the next chapter are all ways of finding stillness and peace by living in the now.

"The moment that judgment stops through acceptance of what it is, you are free of the mind. You have made room for love, for joy, for peace," writes Eckhart Tolle in *The Power of Now*.

So often we are disconnected from the present, either leapfrogging into the future or living in the ghostlands of past hurts, wounds, traumas or disappointments. You may have tricked yourself to fall in love with alcohol again, remembering the 'happy' days and conveniently forgetting the toll drinking took.

The power of now is remaining in the present moment and taking one day at a time.

Living one day at a time is also a fundamental tenet of AA's 12-Step Program. "Just for today I will not drink," says 12-step devotee Russel Brand. By not getting too far ahead and focusing on the power of right now, that day, it avoids overwhelm and feeling like the climb toward eternal sobriety is too high.

The Just for Today card that AA and Al-anon members carry in their pocket or purse is a popular aid. Those carrying it refer to the affirming reminders when they feel tempted to drink, or something, someone, or just life in general, rattles them.

Here are a few affirmations I sourced from the Internet:

- Just for today, I will try to live through this day only, and not tackle all my problems at once. I can do something for twelve hours that would appall me if I felt that I had to keep it up for a lifetime.
- Just for today, I will be happy. This assumes to be true what Abraham Lincoln said, that most folks are as happy as they make up their minds to be.
- Just for today, I will adjust myself to what is, and not try to adjust everything to my own desires. I will take my luck as it comes, and fit myself to it.
- Just for today, I will try to strengthen my mind. I will study. I will learn something useful. I will not be a mental loafer. I will read something that requires effort, thought and concentration.
- Just for today, I will exercise my soul in three ways: I will do somebody a good turn, and not get found out; if anybody knows of it, it will not count. I will do at least two things I don't want to do just for exercise. I will not show anyone that my feelings are hurt; they may be hurt, but today I will not show it.
- Just for today, I will be agreeable. I will look as well as I can, dress becomingly, keep my voice low, be courteous, criticize not one bit. I won't find fault with anything, nor try to improve or regulate anybody but myself.
- Just for today, I will have a program. I may not follow it exactly, but I will have it. I will save myself from two pests: hurry and indecision.
- Just for today, I will have a quiet half hour all by myself and

relax. During this half hour, sometime, I will try to get a better perspective of my life.
- Just for today, I will be unafraid. Especially I will not be afraid to enjoy what is beautiful and to believe that as I give to the world, so the world will give to me.

A pocket-sized version of this is available at most 12-Step meetings such as Alcoholics Anonymous or Al-Anon

Source: alcoholselfhelpnews.wordpress.com

Look closely at your current circumstances to see if you are fully present and grounded in your commitment to remain sober. Be mindful of times when you are reacting out of past conditioning and unconscious expectations.

Consider creating your own pocket-sized Just For Today affirmations. If you find yourself triggered, or tempted to drink, return to the now and your intentions for today.

In the next chapter we'll look at how journaling can empower your sobriety.

8

JOURNAL YOUR WAY TO JOYFUL SOBRIETY

For many people journalling their way to sobriety has been an important part of their recovery.

Journaling is a simple yet supportive means of helping you express your feelings and track your thoughts and progress. It's a friend when you are in need, a co-creative partner in your success, a cheerleader and a gentle nag-buddy on your life journey.

To minimize stress and boost your bounce mindset, one form of journaling is writing Morning Pages, a strategy developed by Julia Cameron, a recovering alcoholic and the author of *The Artist's Way*.

The writing is just a stream of consciousness, writing out whatever you are feeling—good (or what one of my clients calls the "sunnies") or not so good ("the uglies").

"It's a way of clearing the mind—a farewell to what has been and a hello to what will be," Cameron says.

"Write down just what is crossing your consciousness. Cloud thoughts that move across consciousness. Meeting your shadow and taking it out for a cup of coffee so it doesn't eddy your consciousness during the day."

The point of this writing is to work with your subconscious and let it work its magic in the creative, healing process.

Start where you are—commit to a daily practice of writing Morning Pages and journal for self-exploration.

You can find out more about Morning Pages here http://juliacameronlive.com/basic-tools/morning-pages/

THE SOBRIETY JOURNAL

Another form of journaling to support your recovery or to help you cut back on booze is creating a Sobriety Journal—a repository for all things inspirational, supportive and motivating.

I've already shared a few excerpts from my Sobriety Journal with you.

Your Sobriety Journal doesn't need to be fancy, just your go-to place to jot down your thoughts and to place inspirational images.

I prefer mine with no lines. This allows me total freedom. You'll find some nice blank ones from artist supply stores. I love the Fabriano Black Book 190G A4 Landscape available online from www.gordonharris.co.nz.

My current sobriety journal begins with a couple of opening quotes, one of which I included in this book:

> *"I gave up alcohol in 1980. I enjoyed it far too much, to the point where I frequently got intoxicated. Everything in my life changed for the better when I stopped. It was the right decision."* ~ Deepak Chopra

Deepak's words spoke to me—reminding me that it's not that alcohol is intrinsically evil, but rather it's just too darned tempting. The fact that a professional man as astute and competent as Deepak Chopra is could only control alcohol by completely stopping sustains my own quest for success. Deepak is a medical doctor, spiritual guru to movie stars and also the founder of the Chopra Addiction & Wellness Center.

I also jotted down something Adele, the UK singing, songwriting legend, once said during an interview:

> *"I used to be a massive drinker, now I might only have two glasses a week—having a hangover with a child is torture. I used to love being drunk, but as I got more famous I would wake up the next morning and think, "What the fuck did I say and who the fuck did I say it to?"*
>
> *"I'm not as indulgent as I was then (21)—I don't have time to fall apart...I'm very cautious, whereas I was never cautious before...I go out of my way to avoid anything remotely dangerous...I don't want to die."*

The next pages of my Sobriety Journal include reminders of the negative results of drinking too much alcohol. My focus then turns to the positive results of sobriety in the pages that follow—weightless, looking younger, saving money, improved brain functioning, increased spiritual connection, transcendence and more! Life really is more beautiful sober.

There is no order to my journal. I write what I feel, what I need to express. For example, my entry on the 2nd of April 2016 read:

> *"This was to be my beginning of alcohol-free—although I had none yesterday, nor the other day. My lover has disappeared into a bottle of rum, Mount Gay...and already begun to get aggressive. I decided to*

have a few drinks. How can we be together if we are not on the same wave-length?

But I see the error in my logic now...and it has only cost me disappointment re my willpower. But in all else I am fine. I've come to the shed to begin this journal. He is hugging the wall outside. "I'm relaxing," he drawls when I ask him what he is doing. I'm going to get cream for our dessert and a ginger beer (before he takes the car)."

Later I added, *"I left him to do his thing...when I returned he was talking, I think to Chris about trips...I was glad to see him immersed in his passion and not drinking. I made him a meal, brought him mosquito spray, candles and went to bed. He slept it off in the spare room."*

Over a year later I can look back on this time and feel empowered by how much has changed for the better.

Whenever you need to work things through or you talk yourself into a bit of a funk turn to your journal.

You can process things and express your feelings safely and tap into the wisdom of your higher consciousness. This will aid healing and transform negative energies into agents of positive change.

You'll also find positive reminders of your intentions. Instead of saying "I want a drink" and "I am so over this," and retelling the story that allowed for drunkenness and failure, turn to your beautiful book. It's the place in which you're creating and telling a new life story.

I often notice that my anxiety increases when I don't have a special book in which to purge and reshape my thoughts.

Whenever this happens, I go to my journal and write my way back to sanity. I also reread some of the most empowering and encouraging quotes from other people who have also struggled to maintain a healthy mindset.

Top of my list was Jessie Burton's empowering words, "Always picture succeeding, never let it fade. Always picture success, no matter how badly things seem to be going in the moment."

When I read these words they remind me that I have been picturing failure. I was telling myself messages of failure. I was feeling failure. These reminders kick-start a more positive focus.

Jesse Burton, the author of *The Muse and The Miniaturist*, is very inspiring to me because she is so honest about her own battles with mental health—including anxiety.

Blogging and sharing your thoughts with others is another form of cathartic journaling—as is writing a book like this.

"You could have talked more about your personal experience so that other writers can more easily relate to you," wrote an advance reader of one of my earlier books.

You'll notice in this chapter and throughout this book that I've woven in more of my experiences, the highs and the lows, the successes and the failures, as a result.

The point of this writing is to work with your subconscious and let it work its magic in the creative, healing process.

Keep a Sobriety Journal. It may not work for you, but you will never know until you try.

DIVE DEEPER...

. . .

The Sobriety Journal: The Easy Way to Stop Drinking: The Effortless Path to Being Happy, Healthy and Motivated Without Alcohol is available in eBook and Print.

This guided book leaves you free to create your own bespoke journal tailored to support your needs. It includes, Journal Writing Prompts, Empowering and Inspirational Quotes and Recovery Exercises that can be of use in your daily journal writing, working with your sponsor or used in a recovery group.

9

ELEVATE YOUR MINDSET

If worry or anxiety causes you to reach for the bottle, consider elevating your mindset. When you create an intention to empower your mindset you set your vibrations into alignment, making it easier to follow through with actions that support you.

His Holiness the 14th Dalai Lama once said, "Negative thoughts are like weeds, but positive thoughts are like flowers—they need nurturing every day."

Leonardo da Vinci proactively fertilized his mind and empowered his resolve by focusing on his dreams, goals, and aspirations.

"You cannot help being good, because your hand and your mind, being accustomed to gather flowers would ill know how to pluck thorns," he once wrote.

To steady himself against self-doubt or the attacks of others, he actively cultivated an elevated mindset by using affirmations, journaling, meditating, channeling and accessing the spiritual realms, and surrounded himself with like-minded, aspirational and inspirational people. By doing so, he developed grit and the ability to bounce back from extreme adversity.

Granted, he wasn't known to be a huge drinker, but his daily habits, reverence for nature, and scientific knowledge may explain why. As I shared in the beginning of *The Sobriety Experiment*, da Vinci once wisely said, "Extremes are to be avoided."

If you actively cultivate a success mindset you automatically increase your resilience and ability to bounce back from setbacks because your mind and elevated energy will create a barrier to discouragement. This helps cut back the thorns of self-doubt, procrastination, fear, and any of the other things toxic to your happiness and success.

I also believe vibrating on a higher level expels toxins from your body. I know this from my own experience when one Valentine's day I decided to enjoy some champagne. My drinking was controlled, measured. I drank water, enjoyed a good meal. I didn't drink because I was stressed.

And yet that night I was so very sick. I threw up. I felt like crap. But when the wine was purged I had no hangover, just diamond-like clarity that I was blessed. Blessed that my body no longer needed, craved or would tolerate alcohol.

Oprah once said that one of the best ways to cultivate a success mindset is to think like a queen: "A queen is not afraid to fail. Failure is another stepping stone to greatness."

So yes, in a sense, I had failed. Failed not to drink. But greatness came in a stronger, clearer way, knowing how much better life is sober.

As I shared earlier, Rainer Maria Rilke once wrote: "Sickness is the means by which an organism frees itself from what is alien; so one must simply help it be sick, to have its whole sickness and to break out with it, since that is the way it gets better."

Similarly, J.K. Rowling encourages making failure part of your bounce-back strategy. "Failure is inevitable—make it a strength," she says.

So, be gentle with yourself on your sobriety journey. Falling off the wagon is not the failure. Failure is not getting back on.

IMPRESS THIS UPON YOUR MIND—ATTITUDE is everything. As Buddhists say, life is suffering—it's how you react to life that counts.

"With our thoughts, we make the world," Buddha once said. Set your vibrations high with your loving, thoughtful reminders of the benefits of controlling alcohol.

And remember to nurture the flowering of your sobriety every day.

10

FACE YOUR DEMONS

In 2017 movie superstar Brad Pitt revealed he had a shocking drinking problem that wrecked his marriage and tore his young family apart.

"I feel retarded when it comes to expressing my emotions," he said as he opened up about his battle with alcohol and how he struggled to express his feelings to his family.

To help him kick the alcohol habit he opted to face his demons and learn how to express and handle emotions by seeking the services of a qualified and skilled counselor.

Asking for help, whether this is addiction counseling, relationship therapy, stress at work, or something else, isn't easy for many successful people. However, it's often what you need to gain a fresh perspective, overcome obstacles, heal wounds and expand your life.

If your drinking is troubling you, seek help with whatever issues are causing havoc in your life. You need only ask. In the resources section of this book is a list of some of many organizations with with expertise in helping.

As a qualified counselor and holistic therapist, I know that very often talk-therapy empowered by techniques such as Cognitive Behavioral Therapy (CBT), Rational Emotive Behavioral Therapy (REBT—you'll find an example later in this book) and other modalities can be extremely effective. As a holistic practitioner and life coach I also know there is a wide range of alternative help and healing approaches that yield remarkable, extremely quick results.

Many people chose to connect or reconnect with lapsed spiritual or religious rituals. Whether you elect to seek the services of a therapist, put your faith in God, divine wisdom, spirituality or something else, the truth is very often that safety, guidance and strength comes from a place within.

However, it's also important to recognize that many people abuse alcohol as a way to self-medicate or block out extreme trauma, including incest, sexual abuse, and rape. If the wounds of the past and unhealed traumas are driving you to drink, consider seeking the help of a skilled therapist, counselor or coach.

Be sure that whoever you turn to for help has a proven track-record of success in helping clients with similar issues.

Do some research to find the person with the expertise and style that resonates best with you. Some people prefer a soft, gentle approach—others need someone more challenging. One size definitely doesn't fit all.

We'll explore some therapeutic and spiritual approaches to healing common issues, including stress, anxiety, and depression, in the following chapters.

11

GET ANGRY

American author Bede Jarrett once said, "The world often continues to allow evil because it isn't angry enough."

Passionate anger, used constructively, can be a powerful motivator for sustained sobriety. It was for me. As I shared in the beginning of this book, it wasn't until I became frightened, fearful and then bloody angry that I decided something had to change. And fast.

Anger and the desire to right injustice can also lead you to your life purpose. This same anger fuels my writing now, shaping many of the chapters and sections (especially those dealing with how we are fed lies, kept in the dark regarding the truth about alcohol and manipulated by marketing).

Other people have been fuelled by anger too. Grant Cardone shares in his book, *Be Obsessed or Be Average*, how his anger was piqued by the parting words of an insensitive drug and alcohol counselor when he left rehab.

"He told me I would amount to nothing. That I had a disease. That I couldn't be cured. I resolved that day that I would never go back."

On a mission to prove he wasn't worthless and to make his family proud again his obsessive quest for success (and to remain drug and alcohol free) has transformed his life.

As comedian, actor and recovering addict Russell Brand writes in his book, *Recovery: Freedom from our Addictions*, "Here's some good news for the fallen, for those of you that are reading this in despair, the junkies, the allies, the crack-heads, anorexics, bulimics, dyspeptics, perverts, codependent, love-addicted, hopeless cases, I now believe addiction to be a calling. A blessing."

What presses your buttons? It may be specific things going on in your life now or wider issues about alcohol in general, such as injustice, slack alcohol control, lack of funded help for those suffering addiction or the escalating profits of booze barons.

Gain greater awareness of the source of your anger by exploring why your buttons are being pushed.

For example, many communities are angry at the ease with which alcohol resellers can ply their trade in their neighborhoods, setting up near schools and other prominent spots. And they're fighting back, lobbying to Councils to limit the number of licenses.

A recent addition to my own injustice-fuelled anger followed a suicide awareness program by our major newspaper, *The New Zealand Herald*. New Zealand has a horrendous and shameful number of suicides. Every 67 hours a young person in New Zealand kills themselves. That's more than one person every three days, or 130 a year.

Our youth suicide rate (25 and under) is the second worst in the developed world. The teen rate (15-19) is the worst, so high it raises the global average. Why?

Could it be that when in 1999 the legal purchasing age was lowered from 20 to 18 alcohol-related suicide idealization, depression, and low self-worth raised their ugly heads? Despite several calls for legislation to raise the drinking age again, and the overwhelming evidence presented by *The New Zealand Herald* that alcohol is a causal factor in the majority of teen suicides, lawmakers overwhelmingly favor the status quo. The legal drinking age remains locked at 18 and suicide rates continue to soar.

So, who is influencing the lawmakers? Alcohol lobbyists? You decide! At the time of writing I have just submitted my first request to Parliament requesting this information under The Official Information Act.

I'm still puzzled by the knighthood awarded to the late beer baron Douglas Myers. The then 71-year-old former Lion Nathan head was made a Knight Companion of the NZ Order of Merit for services to business and the community. Myers was one of New Zealand's most prominent businessmen, having worked his way up through Lion Nathan to build a personal fortune estimated to be worth $900 million.

Former Minister of Parliament Paul Goldsmith, who co-authored a biography titled, *The Myers*, said Myers was passionately committed to improving the country's economic performance for the good of all Kiwis. I'm still trying to figure out what specific steps he took to reduce the harm his alcoholic beverages aided and abetted.

This is only one of many examples I can personally cite. Another, I have already shared was the Wellington City Council taking The New Zealand police to court when the Police were trying to reduce harm, including violence, by opposing an application to increase licensing opening hours. The Council was seeking an extension to 5am, backed by bar owners, including the proprietors of a local strip club.

Former Wellington area commander Inspector Chris Bensemann was reported in the newspaper as saying there was little point in the council "sitting on its hands", as it was plain to see there was a problem with drunk and disorderly people in Courtenay Place in the early hours.

"There needs to be an acceptance that there is alcohol harm in our community," he said. "We have to move forward with this, and we have to be courageous. If we just throw our hands up in the air and say it's too hard, that would be sad."

The Council's response?

Former Wellington Mayor Celia Wade-Brown asked Bensemann to back up his claim with statistics, saying the council preferred to base its decisions on good data, and proceeded with taking the Police to Court.

Below is a copy of some email correspondence I had with the Council. Amongst the many things that riled me was the excessive use of ratepayer money to fight the case—money that I felt could have been better directed at helping those in need (I have removed the name of person for Privacy Act reasons):

> Re: Information Request - Cost of legal fees to Wellington City Council to defend LAP in High Court.
>
> On 23/01/2015, at 3:02 PM, DH
>
> <DH@wcc.govt.nz> wrote:
>
> Dear Cassandra
>
> Further to my email dated 7 November 2014, I can now provide you with the outstanding information from your request- the total cost for legal spend defending the Council's Local Alcohol Policy.
>
> The legal cost to date was $104,442.00 (excluding GST).
>
> Kind regards
>
> D.
>
> Manager, IRO | Governance Directorate | Wellington City Council

From: Worklifesolutions [mailto:cassandra@worklifesolutions.co.nz]

Sent: Friday, 23 January 2015 3:40 p.m.

To: DH

Subject: Re: Information Request - Cost of legal fees to Wellington City Council to defend LAP in High Court.

Thanks for following through D. Can you confirm the outcome

Many thanks

Cassandra

On 23/01/2015, at 3:49 PM, DH

<DH@wcc.govt.nz> wrote:

Hi Cassandra

Here is a link to the outcome of the court case- in case you have not already seen this.

http://www.stuff.co.nz/business/industries/65254965/authority-rejects-capitals-5am-liquorsale-hours.html

Kind regards

D

THE DECISION, said the Wellington City Council's proposed liquor plan had overstepped its authority, giving itself enforcement powers that contradicted the law.

What presses your buttons? Are there any ways you could you use your anger to benefit others and bring about positive change? Or are you going to throw your hands in the air and say it's way too hard?

Perhaps expressing gratitude instead is the ultimate sobriety cure. In the next chapter we'll discover why…

12

GLORIOUS GRATITUDES

You may have heard about the benefits of expressing gratitude, but are you truly grateful? Do you spend time every day acknowledging what's right in your life or do you focus on what sucks? Often when we're stressed negative emotions, including criticism, become the flavor of the day—and it's a sour, putrid flavor at that.

If you want to instantly feel better start acknowledging your blessings, write them down, and even better, tell people you care about why you're grateful that they're in your life.

I've been keeping a gratitude diary for years. In fact, the positive feelings I gain from spending a few moments counting my blessings is literally addictive. Happily, positively so.

Recovering alcoholic, Anne Dowsett Johnston, also credits her gratitude list with helping her love herself and her life again after experiencing much pain. "For several years now, I have begun each morning with a gratitude list, one that lists my challenges as well as my blessings—especially when I feel broken, which reminds me how much I loved and was loved. There is some strange alchemy associated with gratitude. Somewhere along the way of doing these lists, I fell in love with my life again."

So what's going on? Why does expressing gratitude feel so good? In part, because feeling grateful activates the region in the brain that produces dopamine. Add a sprinkling of gratitude toward others and you intensify the effect by increasing activity in social dopamine circuits, says neuroscientist Dr. Alex Korb, author of *The Upward Spiral: Using Neuroscience to Reverse the Course of Depression*. All of this improves your relationships, makes social interactions more enjoyable, and fills your day with love.

"Trying to think of things you are grateful for forces you to focus on the positive aspects of your life. This simple act increases serotonin production," Korb says. And what does serotonin do? It makes your life look more glorious and helps you feel great.

Korb says, "It's not finding gratitude that matters most; it's remembering to look in the first place. Remembering to be grateful is a form of emotional intelligence."

As the brain learns to go in search of positive things in your life, it becomes more skilled at finding them, he explains. 'Then, it simply takes less effort to be grateful. Everything is interconnected. Gratitude improves sleep. Sleep reduces pain. Reduced pain improves your mood. Improved mood reduces anxiety."

Sometimes it's hard to feel optimistic and grateful when you're feeling run down, harassed or depleted. However, if Viktor Frankl, the Austrian psychiatrist who survived the horrors of the Nazi death camps, can, you can too. Frankl developed a therapy he named logo therapy, and wrote about it in his excellent book, *Man's Search for Meaning*. He believes that it is not the situation which defines and controls us but our attitudes and reactions. Somehow, he urges, we must endeavor to look for meaning and express gratefulness during even the most challenging and horrific of times.

Living in constant gratitude for what we do have versus over-focusing on what we don't have, increases confidence, hope, feelings of satisfaction and happiness—and resilience. These positive, feel-good emotions are all necessary utensils in your toolkit.

Our attitude liberates us. Who would have thought that such a simple strategy could provide such a kaleidoscope of benefits?

13

CONSULT THE ORACLES

A sobriety ritual I love is beginning my day being intuitively guided by oracle cards. Not everyone believes in mysticism—but I do. And so do a great many others.

"If you want to be a serious writer or intellectual you can't say you're a mystic because no one will talk to you again," says American author (and professional tarot card reader) Jessa Crispin, slightly tongue-in-cheek.

But, it may surprise you to know that many Titans consult oracles to improve their mindset, boost their productivity and performance, and sustain their commitment to sobriety.

Subjects such as astrology, psychic phenomena, spirituality, and a fascination with tarot and oracle cards have helped many creative people and successful entrepreneurs overcome doubt, strengthen their beliefs, clarify their direction and find meaning in challenging situations.

As I share in my book *The Art of Success: How Extraordinary Artists Can Help You Succeed in Business and Life,* Coco Chanel found great wisdom, peace, comfort, and healing, from oracle cards and an eclectic array of spiritual rituals.

Oracle reader and spiritual adviser Colette Barron-Reid credits this spiritual practice, and others, with saving her life and helping her recover from chronic alcoholism and drug abuse.

"Faith in the guidance of Spirit gives you the courage to take risks because you're assured that whatever happens, a Higher Power is on your side and you will survive," says Barron-Reid.

"Increasing numbers of people are looking to ancient oracles to receive personal guidance because they are not getting the answers and insights they need when they consult the usual sources of psychology and science," she says.

However, there are some highly influential psychologists who do value the wisdom and intuitive guidance that oracles herald.

Of all the psychological theories in the West, that of revered Swiss psychologist Carl Jung stands out as most applicable.

Jung wrote about Tarot on several occasions, seeing it as depicting archetypes of transformation like those he found in myths, dreams, and alchemy.

He described its divinatory abilities as similar to the ancient divination text I Ching, and to astrology. Later in life Jung established a group which attempted to integrate insights about a person based on multiple divination systems including Tarot.

Jung, Crispin, Colette Barron-Reid, and other healers, myself included, are proud to join many others who invite people to experience a new, or rather an old way, of finding hope, courage and comfort to live an inspired, joyful life.

The following excerpt from one of Collette Baron-Reid's excellent suite of oracle cards may sustain your quest to continue being alcohol-free:

> The Horse King always comes to lend you the power to go the distance, forging ahead whatever the weather. You will most certainly reach your perfect destination with this noble Ally. He lets you know that some person or circumstance brought through synchronicity will certainly appear to help you with your endeavors.
>
> You aren't meant to go this part of the journey alone.
>
> This is also an important time to delegate authority to others so that they may assist you. Currently, you're magnetic to powerful people who are in a position to help make your dreams come true. The Horse King asks that you remain open to those who are sent to aid you. You can be assured that you will be lifted up and will ride high in victory.

Consider experimenting with oracles and making these, and other spiritual practices, part of your daily sobriety ritual. It may feel like something out of left-field, but you never know until you try.

14

PURPOSEFUL SOBRIETY

Create an extraordinary life and create a life of meaning by prioritizing your purpose. By living your soul purpose, and sharing your gifts with the world, you consciously or unconsciously tap into universal needs and higher levels of consciousness. This boosts your energy, elevates your success, and yields mind-bending productivity. Not only will this blazing energy create the ultimate distraction but it will also lift your spirit with the ultimate of natural highs—all of which enables phenomenal results.

Paulo Coelho, for example, wrote *The Alchemist* in less than two weeks following his own search for meaning and purpose. The book's main theme is about finding one's destiny. And it's a theme that tapped a universal chord.

Your purpose communicates who you are, clarifies your priorities, and determines the creations your actions produce.

BENEFITS OF CREATING with purpose include:

- Tapping into your life's purpose gives you an edge; it stokes the flames of passion, enthusiasm, drive, and tenacity needed to succeed
- A sense of purpose can give you the courage, and clarity of vision needed to thrive
- Purpose fuels the embers of flagging motivation and latent dreams
- A sense of purpose can lead you to the work you were born to do and allows you the freedom to be authentically and purposefully you
- Discovering your true calling opens you up to the dreams the Universe has for you—bigger than you may dream for yourself
- Creating with purpose connects you with divine intelligence, universal energy, and the laws of attraction—magnetizing fans to you

A LIFE LIVED on purpose is the most meaningful, powerful and happiest life there is.

LOOK FOR THE GIFT

Sometimes in life, as with photography, you need a negative to develop the positive. What at the time seemed like a low point can, with hindsight, prove to be the most life-changing and meaningful experience.

A classic and powerful bounce strategy is to reframe setbacks and look for the treasures they may yield.

In *The Book of Joy*, two great spiritual teachers, the Dalai Lama and Archbishop Desmond Tutu, men who have both known tremendous suffering, encourage us all to look for the gifts contained within adversity. One of these gifts is the opportunity to be reborn.

"When I spoke about mothers and childbirth, it seems to be a wonderful metaphor, actually, that nothing beautiful in the end comes without a measure of some pain, some frustration, some suffering," writes the Dalai Lama. "This is the nature of things. This is how our universe has been made up."

In the same book, the Dalai Lama shares how the gift of being exiled from his beloved Tibet provided the opportunity to give birth to a new way of being and to share his teachings and Buddhist philosophy throughout the world. "Life is suffering," he says. "It's how you react to life that changes your karma", he teaches. "I'm just one human being, but I believe each one of us has a responsibility to contribute to a happier humanity."

It is no coincidence that successful and revered people see the cup half full, look for ways to add more to peoples' lives rather than play the victim, and demand that life treats them more favorably.

"If I had been brought up protected and happy, what the devil would I write about?" says Isabel Allende of her troubled childhood. The gift of her previous unhappiness creates bounce in the lives of millions of readers who are enchanted by her words and are inspired by Allende's tales of passion, courage, endurance, and hope.

IF YOU NEED MORE HELP to find and live your life purpose you can read my book, *Find Your Passion and Purpose: Four Easy Steps to Discover a Job You Want and Live the Life You Love*, available as a paperback and eBook.

Or you may prefer to take my online course and watch inspirational and practical videos and other strategies to help you to fulfill your potential—https://the-coaching-lab.teachable.com/p/follow-your-passion-and-purpose-to-prosperity.

15

BOOZE BUSTERS: LOOK FOR YOUR HEROES

Gather examples of people living a sober life who inspire you. Allow them to be your virtual mentors. This will offset the mistaken belief that you, or others, may have that people who don't drink are losers. Consider how you can use their success to guide and encourage you.

Some of my own personal role models include:

- Julia Cameron, author of *The Artists Way*
- Duff McKagan, music legend
- Collette Baron-Reid, intuitive counselor & author
- Deepak Chopra, guru
- Denzel Washington, actor
- Colin Farrell, actor

. . . and many, many more courageous and enlightened men and women who find joy in sobriety.

With neither drugs and alcohol in his life, how does Colin Farrell let off steam?

"Run around. Whatever. Go up on hikes. I go into nature a lot, man. I go into nature a lot. I find nature pulls the steam out of you and f***s it over its own shoulder. I go on road trips and go to the cinema and hang out with my kids," he said in a 2017 interview in The Independent.

"I put on a bit of music. I just live. I just live it without being poisoned the way I was poisoned for years."

Farrell says it's not difficult to have that kind of self-evolution in Los Angeles where he lives.

"No, I think Los Angeles is a good place for it, actually. I am not talking Hollywood. Hollywood is a state of being and also a zip code. But Los Angeles is a very forgiving city. You can be whatever you want. It is actually a good place to reinvent yourself. Los Angeles is an incredible place and there are incredible support groups. There are alternative ways of looking at things. There are people from all over the world. So, there is not one particular behavior that's followed."

Following your own path, as Farrell and others say, rather than the booze pack, is a great sobriety strategy, and one that works for me. Looking at things differently, challenging norms, accepted practices and beliefs (like getting wasted means you're hip and cool) is relatively easy—where you suspend the fears and mistaken beliefs that kept you stuck.

Adopting a range of holistic strategies, including exercise, music, and meditation, empowering my self-esteem, and clearing out old scripts, along with other techniques I share is this book has enabled me to become a heroine for myself, my loved ones and other's who want to live their best life.

Find your heroes and discover and follow their success strategies. Become someone else's hero or heroine and pay it forward by sharing your journey to sobriety.

16

JUMPING WITH JOY

Authentic joy, rather than drunk delirium, has phenomenal energy and incredible versatility. In *The Book of Joy* the Dalai Lama shares that Paul Ekman, a longtime friend, and famed emotions researcher, has written that joy is associated with feelings as varied as:

- Pleasure (of the five senses)
- Amusement (from a chuckle to a belly laugh)
- Contentment (a calmer kind of satisfaction)
- Excitement (in response to novelty or challenge)
- Relief (following upon another emotion, such as fear, anxiety, and even pleasure)
- Wonder (before something astonishing and admirable)
- Ecstasy or bliss (transporting us outside ourselves)
- Exultation (at having accomplished a difficult or daring task)
- Radiant pride (when our children earn a special honor)
- Elevation (from having witnessed an act of kindness, generosity, or compassion)
- Gratitude (the appreciation of a selfless act of which one is the beneficiary)

Buddhist scholar and former scientist Matthieu Ricard has added three other more exalted states of joy: rejoicing (in someone else's happiness, what Buddhists call *mudita*), delight or enchantment (a shining kind of contentment) and spiritual radiance (a serene joy born from deep well-being and benevolence).

When you tap into your joy, you tap into an unlimited reservoir of energy and enthusiasm.

The French take it further—of course! *Jouissance*, literally means orgasmic joy. It's derived from the word from *jouir* ("to enjoy"). *Jouissance* is to enjoy something a lot!

One of my favorite creativity experts, Mihaly Czikszentmihaly refers to this as a state of "flow."

In a popular YouTube talk he asks, "What makes a life worth living? Money cannot make us happy," he says. Instead, he urges us to learn from people who find pleasure and lasting satisfaction in activities that bring about this state of transcendent flow.

This is where your soul meets the road—accelerating you toward your preferred future and fueling your success.

Find something that sparks joy and keep hugely interested in it by feeding and nurturing your *jouissance* every day.

Find joy in whatever is present in your life today.

Encourage yourself, challenge any mistaken assumptions that finding joy is not possible for you, and boost your belief by collecting examples of people who followed their joy and made a rewarding career, enriched their lives and stayed sober. Collette Baron-Reid is just one of many inspiring examples…oh, and when I follow my joy I inspire myself!

17

MIND POWER

Your mind is so incredibly vital to the success or failure of virtually everything you do, from relationships, health, work, and finances to overall happiness.

Thoughts do become things, and your body experiences what the mind believes. This is why challenging and conquering your fears and mistaken beliefs is so important.

Happily, you can trick you mind into gravitating towards what you want and away from what you don't.

"I have learned how to deceive people into health for their benefit," writes Bernie Siegel, M.D., author of *A Book of Miracles* and *The Art of Healing*.

"Doctors can kill or cure with 'wordswordswords' when they become 'swordswordswords.' We all have the potential for self-induced healing built into us. The key is to know how to achieve your potential," Siegel says.

Many of the things that influence your thoughts, feelings, and behaviors are invisible; a great many lurk in the realm of the subconscious mind.

The function of your subconscious mind is to store and retrieve data. Its job is to ensure that you respond exactly the way you are programmed.

"By the time you reach the age of 21, you've already permanently stored more than one hundred times the contents of the entire Encyclopedia Britannica," says motivational writer Brian Tracey.

And much of this information is rubbish, false, incomplete, or obsolete.

Your subconscious mind is like a huge memory bank. Its capacity is virtually unlimited. It permanently stores everything that ever happens to you. What is limited is your ability to consciously recall many of the scripts programmed into your mind.

You may not even be aware of limiting beliefs that are holding you back. Boosting your self-awareness will change that, coupled with a willingness to grow.

One of the most important things you can commit to realizing is that you exist in more than the physical world. The mental world, the emotional world, and the spiritual world all exert a powerful influence over you—whether you are consciously tapping into them or not.

"What most people never realize is that the physical realm is merely a 'printout' of the other three," writes T. Harv Eker.

Any limiting and unhelpful beliefs or repressed experiences preventing you from changing your relationship to alcohol cannot be changed in the physical world. They can only be changed in the "program"—the mental, emotional, and spiritual worlds.

Which is why *The Sobriety Experiment* takes a holistic approach to health and happiness. Alongside the latest developments and most successful addiction cures, passion, joy, faith, prayer, meditation, courage, dreams, purpose, and mindfulness practices are some of the strategies we'll discuss in this book.

Creating a beautiful mind is one of the most important and effective places you can empower.

BY THE WAY, did you know that you have more than one mind?

18

YOUR BEAUTIFUL MINDS

Conventionally we're told we only have one mind—our brain. However scientific advancements are increasingly confirming what ancient cultures and mystics have known for centuries. We have access to three minds—potentially more—and they're all critical tools in your self-empowerment and recovery process.

- The conscious mind
- The rational mind
- The subconscious mind
- The superconscious mind

The conscious and rational minds are thought to be responsible for only 5% of our behaviors. A whopping 95% of habits and behavioral triggers and programs are activated by the subconscious mind. Uniting these minds into one coherent and coordinated vision, and drawing upon your spiritual or superconscious mind will help you yield supernatural resolve, resilience, and results.

THE CONSCIOUS MIND

What is consciousness? Does anyone really know what it is? As with so many labels created by humans, even the experts can't seem to agree on one universal definition.

"How do physical processes in the brain give rise to the self-aware **mind** and to feelings as profoundly varied as love or hate, aesthetic pleasure or spiritual yearning? These questions today are among the most hotly debated issues among scientists and philosophers," David J. Chalmers writes in an article in Oxford University Press.

Arguably the simplest definition of the conscious mind is what we are aware of when we fully present. When we lose consciousness the lights of awareness go out. We don't even need to be physically asleep. Alcohol, for example, dulls the lights of our conscious mind, we lose control and often aren't aware of who we were before we went into an altered state.

Alcohol hijacks our consciousness. Once they're on a roll with alcohol very often they can't even remember what they said or did. One of the major reasons people drink in the first place is often to forget.

"When my son committed suicide I drank and drank and drank. I drank so I could sleep. I drank to ease my pain. I drank to forget. And then I stopped," my hairdresser told me.

Alcohol as medicine has been a tried and true remedy for thousands of years—as a short-term cure, it can be powerfully effective. But as a long-term cure? Well, I'll let the statistics presented throughout this book speak for themselves.

Raising your consciousness, including the reasons why you drink, the harm alcohol does, and how life can be more beautiful without alcohol is only one part of the sobriety solution.

To really succeed you need to unite and draw upon all your minds. Empowering your conscious mind, while ignoring the subconscious and superconscious minds is like trying to balance on a one-legged stool—easy if you're a circus clown but pretty futile unless you want to end up the fool.

THE RATIONAL MIND

Your rational mind is your analytical, thinking brain. It's the mind that much of society values most. Many people believe this is a major mistake. Think about it. You can rationalize anything if you want to—and many people who drink, do. Very convincingly.

Politicians and lobbyists, in particular, are very skilled at using rational arguments to great advantage. Take lowering the drinking age in New Zealand, for example. The rational argument presented was, they can vote when they are eighteen, so they're old enough to drink responsibly.

That's like saying, they're old enough to choose whether to wear a crash helmet. Wearing helmets, along with not texting when you are driving was made law because it was the only way to reduce harm—giving people the choice to opt in or out didn't cut it.

Significant research proves that not only is alcohol harmful, but teenagers' brain development does not fully mature until they are twenty-five. Hmmm, why not raise the voting age, instead of lowering the drinking age? There's a thought!

Your rational mind, in some respects, is inferior. It's often a trickster—telling you that you want to drink, even when you've told yourself that you don't. Your rational mind is easily hijacked by savvy marketers who remind you that you like drinking, that it's okay to drink, you'll be more popular, happier—drinking is fun…you can stop anytime.

Yeah, right.

As Dr. Joe Dispenza, shares in his book *Becoming Supernatural,* many commercials, advertising, and marketing messages seek to hijack or disorientate the inhibitory processes of the conscious mind, bypassing the analytical mind so that one becomes highly responsive to suggestions and information in the subconscious mind.

"As the conscious mind is busy and preoccupied trying to figure things out, the subconscious mind takes it all in without discretion. If you can disorient people with information (or in today's world, disinformation), shock, or confusion, you just opened the door to programming their subconscious mind."

As you'll discover below, if you're harboring wounds, repressing emotions or lack conscious awareness you'll find yourself more easily manipulated by those with questionable motives.

The analytical mind separates the conscious mind from the subconscious mind. One of the major purposes of many therapies and healing modalities, including meditation, is to help people transcend their analytical minds. Slowing your brain waves down, tuning into your body, and being more present, for example, helps to move you out of your thinking brain, past your analytical mind, into the operating system of the subconscious mind, where many automatic programs and unconscious habits hangout.

THE SUBCONSCIOUS MIND

Again, what constitutes the subconscious mind is hotly contested. However, I agree with the compelling scientific research confirming your body is your subconscious mind.

Ancient mystics and 'alternative' healers have always known and accepted this universal truth.

"A huge amount of emotionally mediated information is being exchanged throughout the body and brain, much of which never rises up into our consciousness. This is why I say: Your body is your subconscious mind," says Dr. Pert, the neuroscientist, and pharmacologist who discovered the opiate receptor, the cellular binding site for endorphins in the brain.

Her research confirms what I and others have known and told their clients for years—listen to your body barometer…your body never lies. Does your body really crave alcohol, or is it your mind? I go into more detail in the chapter, *Your Body Barometer.*

Your body is a storehouse of memories—positive and negative. Releasing negative, often extremely traumatic, memories locked in your body is an essential part of healing and recovery for many people who struggle with booze.

The escalating awareness of the mind-body relationship by mainstream scientists, in part, explains why 'alternative' therapies are gaining increasing traction and relevance, including acupuncture, therapeutic massage, cranial massage, and energy healing techniques to name but a few. For so long, too long, these powerful healing modalities were dismissed as witchcraft, fluff, and other demeaning claims.

"Trauma is absorbed and stored in the body and can be unblocked by correcting the energy flow. My theory of the psychosomatic network includes subconscious memories stored in the body, specifically in the receptors on every cell surface. You can see how closely all three—information, emotions, and electrical energy—are related and comprise what we experience as energy moving, a phenomenon often accompanied by a release of past trauma that is felt in the body—your subconscious mind," says Dr. Pert.

THE SUPERCONSCIOUS MIND

A third, less well-known state of awareness, certainly one that few main-stream medical professionals believe in, is called the superconscious— the source of who and what we are in our highest spiritual reality. Also commonly referred to as the 'soul' or 'higher Self, your superconscious mind is known by many names.

The physical center of superconsciousness is believed by many people to be in the frontal lobe of the brain, at a point midway between the eyebrows, also known as the Christ center, God center or spiritual eye. The more we are able to draw our energy and awareness upward to the Christ or God center, the higher our level of awareness.

Leonardo da Vinci, who was always a pioneering, curious and open-minded scientist, spent much of his career searching for the soul.

"Do you know that our **soul** is composed of harmony?" Leonardo once said.

"Beauty is the bridge to the divine," others have concurred. Crossing into the realms of the divine takes an integrated approach of body, mind, and spirit. This is why embracing your soul power and adopting spiritual approaches to healing alcohol dependence and addiction are so vital.

Thinking and feeling, heart versus head, mind versus body, have played a dual battle for supremacy throughout history as the center for knowledge. Yet in truth neither is supreme. The power you give to one over the other is only in your perceptions.

However, many people, myself included, believe for balance, all must work as one. One of the experts I have always revered is my muse and mentor Leonardo da Vinci—a man who has always challenged conventional thought and let his own experience be his strongest guide.

Leonardo was fascinated with how the heart functioned, but also the pineal gland, a small structure about the size of a pea, located in the middle of the brain. He believed, as did René Descartes, a French philosopher, mathematician, and scientist, that the pineal gland was where the soul attached to the body, passions resided and provided a direct channel to a higher divine, intelligence.

Perhaps this was how Leonardo was able to accurately predict the future. However, at the time, his soulful thoughts were considered heretical—The Church, not man or women, was the guardian of the soul, and priests (said to be God's only legitimate representatives on Earth) were the only people capable of offering healing.

Some 500 years later leading-edge neuroscientists, including Dr. Candace Pert and Dr. Joe Dispenza and a great deal many other leading-edge scientists, have moved to the 'other side' calling us all to access the god within, commune directly with the divine, and embrace the supremacy of our higher conscious minds.

Catching up with Leonardo's views, in his book, *Becoming Supernatural: How Common People Are Doing the Uncommon,* Dr. Dispenza devotes a fascinating chapter to the wonders and miraculous healing powers of your pineal gland. It's a fascinating chapter I highly recommend reading.

"As you now know, when we as a consciousness move beyond the world of the senses in this three-dimensional reality, we can tap into frequencies that carry specific information beyond the vibration of matter and the speed of light," he enthuses.

What does this mean for you? As I wrote at the beginning of this book, for too long science has been at odds with the notion that laypeople can cure themselves. The truth, now made manifest in brain scans, and extraordinary stories of self-sustained recovery of addiction, and other severe illnesses is that you no longer have to buy into the story of possessing a hopeless, incurable disease.

You can, and will, heal yourself.

As Dr. Candace Pert shares in her book, *Everything You Need to Know to Feel Go(o)d*, The Dalai Lama, who called science "the slayer of religion," had lent his expertise in meditation to several studies of consciousness.

In his talk to neuroscientists, billed as "The Science and Clinical Applications of Meditation," the news that advancements in brain-imaging technology had led to an interest in finding consciousness in the brain, was seen as a significant advancement, given that most neuroscientists still didn't use the word consciousness, let alone super-consciousness their work.

Dr. Pert shares the following humorous example, "The Dalai Lama had something to say about emotions: 'If you want a happy life, you must . . .' and he swiped his arm in a broad gesture to indicate the words get rid of, 'negative emotions, like hatred, anger, and jealousy.' And then he joked, 'If neuroscientists can find the locations in the brain of these things... and can take them out, I will be the first to have the operation!' bringing down the house in laughter."

Do you believe in the existence and healing power of super consciousness?

Superconsciousness is also that level of awareness that we experience when we are in a state of flow, and our mind is in a calm and blissful state. Alongside spiritual and physical healing, it is the underlying mechanism behind intuition and also attributed to enhanced creativity and successful problem-solving.

Personally, I have found tapping into my superconscious and increasing my daily spiritual practices, do more to sustain my commitment to sobriety than any other intervention I have tried so far.

Meditation, as I expand upon later in this book is one of the most important things I have ever learned. Following the end of my alcohol-fuelled engagement my despair was unbearable. I didn't want to live, and I didn't want to die. I had to survive. If not for me, for my daughter, then aged five.

I read about the benefits of meditation and made learning how to do it my new obsession.

"You'll never be able to meditate," I was told by an accomplished meditator, in large part because of my profound despair and also my very busy, hyperactive mind and acute social anxiety.

Well, no greater challenge has ever been laid. 'Why can't I?' I thought, indignation rising. 'What's so special about you that means you can and I can't.' I felt anger and injustice bite—why was I being excluded from 'the club' of happy meditators. And envy rose too—she was happy. I wasn't. She had a loving relationship. I didn't. I felt like she was saying that I wanted what she had.

Just as we are all told repeatedly we can never be happy in a world without booze, how exciting, liberating and empowering it was to prove doomsayers wrong.

So, I made it my mission to learn Transcendental Meditation for no other reason than this was the technique 'the gatekeeping' happy-camper practiced. To say it was life-changing doesn't come close to capturing how profoundly grateful I am.

LEARNING TO MEDITATE WAS LIFE-SAVING.

If you're sitting on the fence, or believe you'll never be able to master it, believe me when I say, give it a go. Find a technique that works for you—and meditate throughout the day. Every day.

"There's a future you—a you who already exists in the eternal present moment—who is actually calling himself or herself to the more familiar you who is reading this book," says Dr. Dispenza. "And that future you is more loving, more evolved, more conscious, more present, more kind, more exuberant, more mindful, more willful, more connected, more supernatural, and more whole. That is who's waiting for you to change your energy to match his or her energy on a daily basis so you can find that future you—who actually exists in the eternal now."

Everyone has the potential to experience superconsciousness, but in most people, it lies dormant. Numerous studies have shown that meditation is the most direct way to awaken the superconscious. It's also one of the most powerful, cost-effective and portable tools in your sobriety tool-kit. We'll explore the significant benefits of meditation later in this book.

Some of the many other simple and powerful ways to access the wisdom and support of higher knowledge include:

- Journaling
- Prayer
- Following your passions
- Surrounding yourself with like-minded people
- Immersing yourself in nature
- Retreating into solitude
- Reading sacred books and accessing ancient knowledge of the spiritual realms
- Consulting the Akashic Records, or "Hall of Knowledge

Honor the mind-body and spiritual dimension. When your spirit and soul-self is off-center, the odds are your work and relationships will be too.

For a fascinating discussion of the 7 spiritual minds contained within the energy centers of the body, I encourage you to purchase a copy of Dr. Joe. Dispenza's, *Becoming Supernatural: How Common People Are Doing the Uncommon.* Each center, referred to as chakras (meaning wheels in ancient East Indian Vedic texts), produces its own chemical hormonal expression, which then activates the organs, tissues, and cells in each area.

Learning how to bring these centers into alignment is a powerful tool.

While we're talking about your minds, remember you also have three brains—your rational brain, your emotional brain and your intuitive brain or gut. Marvelous—assuming you're not pickling them both by overdrinking.

19

WHAT'S YOUR TRUTH? DO YOU REALLY BELIEVE THE LIES?

"Strength of mind rests in sobriety," clever-thinking Pythagoras once said. Do you believe this is true? Or do you think only alcohol can deliver strength, courage, happiness?

Researchers say we start with the conclusions *we want to be true* and then work backward to justify our behavior—paving the journey with rational beliefs. There are those scoundrels again, the conscious and analytical minds.

This is 'self-preserving' logic—logic that serves the story we want to tell.

Changing your beliefs, everything you think you know and hold to be true is necessary for sustainable change.

Examine your beliefs about alcohol, how many of the below are relevant to you?

• Alcohol relaxes me.

• Alcohol helps me switch off my mind.

- I can't have fun if I don't drink.

- Alcohol relieves my stress.

- One drink won't harm me. I can stop easily.

CHANGING or challenging your beliefs is a central theme of therapies such as Cognitive Behavior Therapy (CBT). A major component of CBT is that thoughts, feelings, and behaviors are intertwined—influence one aspect and the others cannot escape being influenced also.

For example, feelings are impacted by your thoughts and behaviors, and your feelings impact your thoughts and behaviors. Knowing this and then leveraging off their dependencies gives you a level of power. You can improve any unwanted facet by addressing the other two.

This explains in part why, when I a person tries a new behavior, like running (instead of drinking) they experience a dopamine spike and feel happier.

In short, if you have feelings that bring you down or you want to avoid, you can modify them by changing your thoughts and behaviors.

Clearly, CBT doesn't have a monopoly on helping people. There are plenty of therapeutic approaches available today, and not all of them involve talking. It's important that you find one that resonates with you.

However, I do find CBT a useful and easy to apply tool—one which you can easily master and apply yourself to challenge mistaken beliefs and distorted thinking.

COGNITIVE DISTORTIONS

When we over-rely on cognitive distortions, we usually interpret events in such a way that fuels emotions such as anxiety, depression, or anger. All-or-nothing thinking, overgeneralization, mental filters, disqualifying positives, and jumping to conclusions, are some examples of distortions.

CBT helps to spotlight any mistaken beliefs, negative views of yourself, the world around you and your future, by studying your thought patterns.

Many people suffer flawed perceptions called cognitive distortions. These distortions are like a solar eclipse that blackens the light and darkens the way you view the world. Some of these cognitive distortions are listed below.

ABSOLUTE ALL-OR-NOTHING THINKING: All-or-nothing thinking refers to thinking in extremes. You are either a success or a failure; a winner or a loser, perceiving situations in absolute, black-and-white categories. Another example might be a belief that people who don't drink are missing out on the fun.

This cognitive distortion can disrupt attempts to change behavior, such as sticking to a period of sobriety or not drinking at all. If you think about your decision in all-or-nothing terms, it is likely that one slip-up will derail all of your efforts.

Relapse is very common—but it doesn't have to be a permanent fixture. The danger of absolute thinking is that you'll be too hard and say and think anything short of 100% might as well be 0%, so if you stick to your diet 90% of the time, all-or-nothing thinking will have you believe that you've totally failed and that you might as well drink whatever you want.

OVERGENERALIZATION: When you draw a conclusion about something based on just one example, you are overgeneralizing. The problem with this flawed thinking is that you will tend to view negative events or people as a never-ending pattern of defeat.

For example, after saying to your fiancé that you wanted to have a break from drinking, and he distanced himself emotionally from you, you might overgeneralize by thinking you'll never be loved unless you drink.

As a result, you may feel quite hopeless or fear abandonment. If your partner does leave you for any reason unless this flawed thinking has been challenged, you'll apply the same belief to your new relationship —and even attract another boozer.

This happened to me. Again and again. Over fifteen years ago, things really got bad. In my case, my fiancé distanced himself emotionally from me, increased his drinking—including snorting vodka up his nose (perhaps to get me to reject him first) and eventually did abandon me. In fact, he simply disappeared and stopped returning my calls.

To gain closure, I left my engagement ring on his doorstep!

My CBT therapist asked, where is your evidence that *everyone* will abandon you if you don't drink? And, where are examples of people who are happily married and sober? Both questions stimulated my thinking, helped me reframe my overgeneralized and unhealthy beliefs, and see my relationship, and my fiancé for what it was—broken.

I talk more about how I survived alcohol-fuelled suicidal depression in a chapter dedicated to the darkest period of my life. You'll find it toward the end of this book.

Mental filter: Dwelling only on the negatives. Focusing only on what you'll be giving up, rather than what you'll be gaining (health, happiness, slimness, clarity, and energy—to name just a few) is your negative mental filter at work.

In my example, it took the passage of time, a great deal of therapy, cultivating optimism and opening myself to spirituality to shift my negative filters.

DISQUALIFYING THE POSITIVE: Filtering out all the **positive** evidence about ourselves and our behavior and amplifying the negative is an extreme form of all-or-nothing thinking. I entered an art competition many years ago, when they rang me to tell me I'd won, not only could I not believe it, but I told them they'd made a mistake. "That other guy's painting was better than mine," I told them. "Mine isn't that good."

What does this have to do with alcohol control? It's a prime example of how little or how much valuing ourselves, our talents, and rating our self- esteem can infect so many areas of our lives. In my situation, disqualifying the positive also meant dating and drinking with the wrong men.

Similarly, if you habitually disqualify the negative, the chances are you'll turn a blind eye to sobriety initiatives such as mindful drinking which celebrate the positive aspect of remaining sober. Perhaps testing 'positive' for excess blood-alcohol and losing your license might change your mind!

JUMPING TO CONCLUSIONS: Assuming your thoughts, feelings or beliefs are true without any supporting evidence is the hallmark of someone who leaps to conclusions.

Some easy and powerful ways to change your thought are to expose your thoughts to rational analysis. This is why forming CBT questions, also known as Socratic questions, such as those below can herald profound and simple change:

"Where is your evidence for this (belief). How might the opposite also be true?"

"Where is your evidence that people who don't drink are losers? Who do you know who is sober, fun and successful? (Check out the chapter Booze Busters for some suggestions).

OTHER INTERVENTIONS IN CBT INCLUDE:

- Relaxation training for anxiety
- Assertiveness training to improve relationships
- Self-monitoring education to improve insight
- Cognitive restructuring to modify thinking patterns

By changing your thoughts to become more informed and challenging cognitive distortions you can improve your feelings and behaviors.

Many of the strategies and insights provided in this book use information to help provide insight and reshape your thoughts and feelings about alcohol—including exposing some of the tactics used by booze barons and big business in their attempts to increase profits.

Others provide relaxation tips, including meditation, journaling, yoga, and exercise. Others provide more spiritual and faith-based tools.

Of course, there are many feeling-based tools to help you express and transform your feelings positively.

But all of them will empower you with information that will aid your recovery.

Let's kick off by exploring your beliefs about sobriety. First up, mind over mojitos. . .

20

MIND OVER MOJITOS: MINDFUL DRINKING

Mindful drinking is one of the planet's fastest-growing movements. Increasing numbers of people are evaluating their relationship to booze, either adopting lengthy periods of being completely booze-free, cutting-back and taking control of how regularly they drink or quitting altogether to boost their health, happiness, and success.

Mindful drinking is boosting your awareness of why you drink, how much you drink and the consequences of your drinking. It's not about cutting alcohol from your life entirely, although many people do.

Mindful drinking involves taking a holistic approach and being fully aware of how each drink you consume affects your mood, behavior, thoughts, health, decision-making and your relationships.

Rather than drinking purely out of habit and mindlessly opening a bottle of wine and swishing it down every night with dinner, or cracking open a few beers after work, adopting a more mindful approach will bring added awareness to your drinking behavior in order to transform things for the better.

Making a conscious and rational decision to control alcohol is only part of the battle. Not only is alcohol highly addictive, but it's an intrinsic part of Western Culture. Your unconscious mind has been conditioned over a lifetime to associate alcohol with relaxing, managing stress, partying, socializing and being cool.

Throughout this book you'll find a range of holistic and easy to implement strategies to help you approach alcohol more healthily, reduce your reliance and dependence on booze, and curb your drinking.

You'll also find plenty of healthy, alcohol-free drinks you'll enjoy in my book, *Mind Over Mojitos: How Moderating Your Drinking Can Change Your Life:Easy Alcohol-Free Recipes for Happier Hours & a Joy Filled Life. Read to the end for a preview.*

21

A VISION OF VICTORY

"Begin with the end in mind," encourages Steven Covey in his runaway bestselling book *The Seven Habits of Highly Successful People*.

Your vision is your "why;" it's the furnace that stokes your desire and fuels your dreams. It's the big picture view of your long-term future and aspirations.

If you lack a 'big picture' view, you can easily fall into bad habits, lose focus, or prematurely give up on your commitment to sobriety.

What is your vision? What does your life look like when you control alcohol? Is it a growing income that funds your lifestyle now that you've cut back on booze? Is it better mental, emotional and physical health? Or is improved relationships, and making right the wrongs of the past. Perhaps it's getting your kids back? Is it being one year alcohol free and taking it from there?

"There are women succeeding beyond their wildest dreams because of their sobriety," the poet Mary Karr once wrote.

Strengthen your vision by clarifying your reasons for wanting to succeed.

I committed to a period of sobriety because I wanted to deepen my spirituality. I also wanted to inspire and help others, including my daughter and those I love deeply.

I also wanted to walk-my-walk—helping others control their relationship to alcohol and discovering how an alcohol-free life could be more beautiful, created a powerful sense of purpose which fulfilled and empowered me.

As I wrote in the introduction of this book, the harm alcohol created evoked an anger which I wanted to channel for the wider social good. I wanted to right what I saw as a deep injustice.

"You go where your vision is. Think big, feel big, and know in your heart that you are one with God," says Joseph Murphy, Ph.D., author, and New Thought minister.

"And you will project a radiance, a glow, a confidence, a joy, and a healing vibration which blesses all who come within your orbit now and forevermore."

That's the Law of Attraction, the Law of Manifestation, The Law of Intention all wrapped into one.

Define your vision. See it clearly in your mind and heart. Engage all the senses until it becomes your living reality.

IMAGINE BETTER

Abraham Lincoln once imagined a world where sobriety was mainstream. "I desire to see the time when education-and by its means, morality, sobriety, enterprise and industry—shall become much more general than at present, and should be gratified to have it in my power to contribute something to the advancement of any measure which might have a tendency to accelerate the happy period."

Imagining better, coupled with visualization techniques are the most powerful mind exercises you can do. No doubt you've heard the saying, 'Out of sight, out of mind.'

"What practical strategies are you going to implement as a result of reading this book?" I wrote to an advance reader.

Her reply was, "Drawing/painting and writing all the things I have in my mind. Getting my specific sobriety journal that is solely for my new intention out and having it constantly with me, feeding it every day."

Empower your intentions by writing them down. Create a vision board, or create a movie, and review your intentions daily. Consider creating a Sobriety Journal to boost your desire and determination and to manifest your intentions.

Another variation of this is to create a sobriety dream board. This is where manifesting your preferred future really happens.

I have covered the wall of my writing room with images of the self-empowerment books I have written and plan to write, feedback from people who have told me how much they have loved my posts with alcohol-free alternatives, and how my words have helped them control alcohol and changed their lives. I also have feeling-based images of what sobriety means to me—including a photo of me and my partner on vacation (feeling awesome, happy, and completely booze-free).

I have also created motivational images with photos and quotes by people I admire who live life sober.

Every time I sit in my writing chair looking at my sobriety board, it is a motivational kick-start; a feeling-based affirmation of not only who I admire and what I yearn for, but the successes I have already manifested.

So many things I've visualized and affirmed on my sobriety board are now my living realities. And the others? I have no doubt that they soon will be!

Creating a sacred space that displays what you want brings it to life. What you focus on expands. Place love, success, health and happiness center stage. Create visual affirmations and place them in a space where you see them often.

"The law of attraction is forming your entire life experience and it is doing that through your thoughts. When you are visualizing, you are emitting a powerful frequency out into the Universe," writes Rhonda Byrne in her popular book *The Secret*.

Whether you believe in magic or not, we know that visualization works. Olympic athletes have been using it for decades to improve performance. *Psychology Today* reported that the brain patterns activated when a weightlifter lifts heavy weights are also similarly activated when the lifter just imagined (visualized) lifting weights."

BRAIN GYM

In the traditions of Napoleon Hill, Earl Nightingale, and Maxwell Maltz, author Jack Canfield also emphasizes the importance of focusing on a vision and creating compelling and vivid pictures in your mind in order to achieve your goals. Canfield cites neuropsychologists who study expectancy theory to support his view on the significance of visualization.

Scientists once believed that people responded to information flowing into the brain from the outside world. But today, they've figured out that we respond to what the brain, based on prior experiences, expects to happen next.

Scientists have discovered that the mind is such a powerful instrument, it can deliver literally everything you want. **But you must believe that what you want is possible.**

This is where visualization works its magic. Seeing is believing!

By programming your brain to expect that something will happen a certain way, you achieve exactly what you anticipate.

How do you create a vision or sobriety board that works? It's simple: Your vision board should focus on how you want, or expect, to *feel*. Because you're aiming for health, happiness, joy, and prosperity, you'll *expect* to feel great! So, be sure to evoke these feelings on your sobriety wall.

To create the life of your dreams, focus on your joy. Allow the Universe to give you every good thing you deserve, by being a magnet to them. To magnetize every single thing you desire, you must be a magnet of love and manifest your preferred future by imagining better.

What, if anything, are you doing to keep your dream of happy sobriety visible?

Bring your vision of sobriety into being. It doesn't have to be a wall—it could be a poster board you can move around. Or, as my partner and I once did when visualizing the million-dollar property we dreamed of buying (and later purchased), you can create a manifestation fridge!

22

LOVE IS THE DRUG: FOLLOW YOUR PASSION

Lose the booze and replace the desire for alcohol with a healthy, positive addiction.

Passion is a source of unlimited energy from your soul that enables you to achieve extraordinary results. It's the fire that ignites your potential and inspires you to be who you really are. When you do what you love it's like hanging out with your best friend—with less Pinot and fewer craft beers.

Following your passion and claiming your authentic self is a great way to boost your vitality. Whether you call it joy, love or obsession or desire, these powerful heart-felt emotions are natural opiates for your mind, body, and soul.

When you're feeling anxious, depressed, stressed, hung-over or drunk, doing things which feed your soul are often the first things to be traded. Nothing seems to spark joy. But, when you do something that enlivens your spirit you may be amazed at how quickly fire ignites.

Passion brings the energy or chi of love, giving you energy, vitality and a heightened sense of well-being. It's one of the greatest stress-busters and most powerful drugs of all— promoting the generation of endorphins, the feel-good chemicals that will give you a natural high.

THE POWER OF PASSION

"Nothing great in the world has been accomplished without passion," the philosopher G.W.F. Hegel once said. Denzel Washington and many other successfully sober people agree. "You only live once, so do what you feel passionate about, take chances professionally, don't be afraid to fail," Washington says.

Washington also said, "I made a commitment to completely cut drinking and anything that might hamper me from getting my mind and body together. And the floodgates of goodness have opened upon me— spiritually and financially.

- Passion is energy. Without energy, you have nothing
- To be passionate is to be fully alive
- Passion is about emotion, feeling, zest, and enthusiasm
- Passion is about intensity, fervor, ardor, and zeal
- Passion is about fire
- Passion is about eagerness and preoccupation
- Passion is about excitement and animation
- Passion is about determination and self-belief
- Passion, like love and joy, is contagious
- Passion can't be faked. It's the mark of authenticity

PASSION FUELS inner purpose and fires the flames of your imagination. It gives you a reason for living and the confidence and drive to pursue your dreams. Passion enables you to unleash latent forces and God-given talents.

When you find and follow your passion, you'll find your sweet spot.

You'll be emboldened by love—thus powering your creativity, courage, resolve, and tenacity. You'll also bounce back from setbacks, and refuse to allow failure to stop you—increasing your likelihood of achieving extraordinary success.

Before Grant Cardone built five successful companies (and counting), became a multimillionaire, and wrote bestselling books he was broke, jobless, and addicted to drugs and alcohol.

Cardone had grown up with big dreams, but friends and family told him to be more reasonable and less demanding. If he played by the rules, they said, he could enjoy everyone else's version of middle-class success. But when he tried it their way, he says that was when he hit rock bottom.

Then he tried the opposite approach. He said NO to the haters and naysayers and said YES to his burning, obsession. He reclaimed his passion to be a business rock star, a super salesman, a huge philanthropist. He wanted to live in a mansion and even own an airplane. Obsession, he says, made all of his wildest dreams come true. And it can help you achieve massive success too.

INSTEAD OF DRINKING **focus on what excites you**

"I find things I like and I do them," says James Patterson, arguably one of the most financially successful authors today. Patterson is also the son of an alcoholic.

Feel the power that comes from focusing on your passionate obsession. What do you love doing? What inspires you? What makes you feel joyful?

Channel your passions into your career or pour it into a hobby. Even five minutes a day doing something you love can give you back your mojo and take your mind off the need to drink.

Laurie, a hobbyist lepidopterist escapes the need to drink by studying and enjoying his collection of exotic butterflies.

"Knitting saved my life," Lauren, the waitress at my local cafe told me recently. She told me how her hobby has provided the ultimate cure for her anxiety, and of the joy she finds in knitting for friends.

I love to write—it's one of several favorite obsessions, and the perfect activity to do instead of drink, especially when I write books like this to help and empower others. It's a similar ploy that's worked well for Russell Brand (*Recovery: Freedom From Our Addictions*), and Julia Cameron (*The Artist's Way*), and other 'creatives' who've channeled their creative energy into helping others.

Your passion may start as a hobby or as a way to cure your blues, but could very well turn out to be your ticket to a more fulfilling career. That's how things rolled for Claire Robbie. At a low point in her life, and drinking way too much, what started as a way of healing became an essential part of her sobriety process. And as her love for her new practices grew, so did the sense that she had discovered a new vocation. Robbie founded No Beers? Who Cares! to encourage and support people to jump on the alcohol-free bandwagon.

Another go-to-booze-replacement strategy that I love is to head off for a swim in the sea or go for a brisk walk. In the next chapter, we'll take a look at the life-changing magic of exercise, including how Duff McKagan, bass guitarist of Guns N' Roses, cycled his way back from a vodka-induced near-death situation.

"I could feel this healthy new kind of pain searing ever muscle fiber and neutron in my body. I was on fucking fire—and I liked it," McKagan said.

He was hooked!

Set your soul on fire with exercise in the next chapter.

23

MOVE! SET YOUR SOUL ON FIRE.

Many people lead sedentary lives, but the most successful alcohol-free people praise the benefits of exercise. Many use their exercise as a mind-spa and say it provides the ultimate feel-good distraction.

Duff McKagan, wrote in his biography, *It's So Easy and Other Lies,* "Initially I rode my heavy old mountain bike just to stave off the shakes, but I quickly realized riding made me feel better. And it filled the time."

The first few days after quitting alcohol McKagan says he just rode around aimlessly and, without realizing how long he'd been gone, discovered he'd been riding eight hours. He credits the resulting soreness with giving him back his life.

"My muscles ached each morning. I hadn't exercised in years. But the soreness lifted my spirit. Not spirit, as in mood, but my actual spirit. My body was so wrecked with abuse that my spirit was the only thing keeping me afloat."

Later McKagan decided to challenge himself with harder rides. "These increasing hard rides came to represent a form of self-flagellation, a way to punish myself for all the damage I had done to myself and others."

Numerous studies have shown that exercise promotes the production of positive endorphins, which play a key role in making you feel better about yourself and your capacity to cope.

Vitamin D sufficiency, along with diet and exercise, has emerged as one of the most important success factors in human health.

During times of low mood or stress or when you're trying to give up the booze, you can become lethargic. Convincing yourself that you don't even have the energy or time to exercise can increase feelings of depression and irritability.

In the one-sided state of depression, there is very little electrical activity in the brain. A person on a stationary bike has more electrical activity in their brain than a person watching an educational video. The truly depressed person will have such low electrical activity that making basic decisions, including the mood-enhancing decision to exercise (even just a little), becomes very difficult.

Researchers also confirm there is a strong link between breathing, outside energy and beneficial brainwave patterns. This may explain why so many people say that walking is their meditation—clearing their minds, and allowing space for good ideas to flourish.

Getting up and moving, embracing the flow of 'chi' in your entire system will enable you to activate both hemispheres of your brain– bringing a new perspective as well as greater tolerance to life's stressors.

Exercise needn't require self-flagellation. Listen to your body barometer when it tells you to exercise more and sloth less.

Discipline yourself to go out and get some fresh air—ideally somewhere not too frenzied, like a park, not a busy street.

Combine brisk walking with deep breathing to boost your energy levels, short-term memory, and state of mind.

When your breathing is calm and steady, your body is in a nurtured state which helps strengthen your immune system. This will help you ward off colds and snuffles and the desire to self-medicate with booze.

Commit to a regular exercise regime and a healthier diet. Be consistent so that changes easily fall into place and become life-affirming habits.

Yoga, as you'll discover in the next chapter is a wonderfully restorative, gentle form of exercise—one which many people credit with restoring their spirit.

24

YOGA

As you read in the chapter Mindful Drinking, Claire Robbie, founder of No Beers? Who Cares!, credits discovering how the life-changing benefits of yoga and meditation helped her love her new life without alcohol. Robbie says yoga and meditation became an essential part of her healing process.

Russell Brand is also a devoted yogi, as are many recovering addicts. Brand's story of how he went from being a drug and alcohol addict to being a yoga teacher and meditator is inspiring. Sober for over a decade now, Russell has his own yoga studio with a mission to help people who may be going through the same struggles he went through.

"*Samskara saksat karanat purvajati jnanam.* Through sustained focus and meditation on our patterns, habits, and conditioning, we gain knowledge and understanding of our past and how we can change the patterns that aren't serving us to live more freely and fully," says Yoga Sutra III.

Here are a few of the many reported benefits of yoga:

- Improvements in perceived stress, depression, anxiety, energy, fatigue, and well-being
- Reduced tension, anger, and hostility
- Reduced headaches and back pain
- Improved sleep quality
- Improved breathing and deeper relaxation
- Greater spiritual connection

Yoga, relaxation, and mindfulness practices work behind-the-scenes to help lower the stress hormone cortisol.

Just two 90-minute classes a week is enough to notice an improved stress response, even in those who report being highly distressed, according to research on yoga and meditation coming out of Germany. Study participants noted a decrease in stress, anxiety, and depression.

"Available reviews of a wide range of yoga practices suggest they can reduce the impact of exaggerated stress responses and may be helpful for both anxiety and depression. In this respect, yoga functions like other self-soothing techniques, such as meditation, relaxation, exercise, or even socializing with friends," says an article posted by Harvard Medical School.

"By reducing perceived stress and anxiety, yoga appears to modulate stress response systems. This, in turn, decreases physiological arousal —for example, reducing the heart rate, lowering blood pressure, and easing respiration. There is also evidence that yoga practices help increase heart rate variability, an indicator of the body's ability to respond to stress more flexibly."

Researchers at the Walter Reed Army Medical Center in Washington, D.C., are offering a yogic method of deep relaxation to veterans returning from combat in Iraq and Afghanistan. Dr. Kristie Gore, a psychologist at Walter Reed, says the military hopes that yoga-based treatments will be more acceptable to the soldiers and less stigmatizing than traditional psychotherapy. The center now uses yoga and yogic relaxation in post-deployment PTSD awareness courses and plans to conduct a controlled trial of their effectiveness in the future.

Yoga classes don't have to be difficult. They can vary from gentle and soothing to strenuous and challenging; the choice of style tends to be based on personal preference and physical ability.

Hatha yoga is the most common type of yoga practiced in the United States and combines three elements: physical poses, called *asanas*; controlled breathing practiced in conjunction with asanas; and a short period of deep relaxation or meditation.

Nurture your body and soul with regular yoga sessions. Consider adopting a meditation practice, if you haven't already.

25

TRUST YOUR GUT

What do Albert Einstein, Bill Gates, Oprah Winfrey and Richard Branson have in common? The answer is, they trust their intuition. Each one of them credit this wise "inner guide", in part, to their personal and professional success, as is the case with so many other successful people.

Just like love, intuition is challenging to define, despite the huge part it plays in our everyday lives. Steve Jobs called it, "More powerful than intellect."

While Webster's defines intuition as "quick and ready insight," you may know it as: a gut feeling, a natural mental skill, a sixth sense, an inner knowing, a feeling, an instinct, a hunch, a premonition, wisdom from a Higher power, a still, quiet inner voice, an inner compass that points you to success and abundance; a gift from Spirit. But however people define intuition, we all *intuitively* know just what it is.

"There is a voice within if only we would listen to it, that tells us so certainly when to go forth into the unknown," writes Elisabeth Kubler-

Ross, a Swiss-American psychiatrist, pioneer in near-death studies and the author of the groundbreaking book *On Death and Dying.*

Kubler-Ross also said, "Learn to get in touch with the silence within yourself and know that everything in this life has a purpose."

You are born with this inner knowing and when you listen to it and act on its wisdom you are guided unfailingly towards your hopes and dreams—and your life purpose. Whether you act on your intuition is another thing.

WHY DON'T SOME PEOPLE LISTEN TO THEIR INTUITION?

In a world that seems to value logic and facts over emotions and feelings, to follow one's heart, or listen to your intuition, can seem foolhardy to many people. Perhaps this is because intuition, like spirituality, can't be seen or scientifically measured.

Many people may tell you that you need to think rationally and use your head, not your heart, in order to gather the "facts" and "evidence" you need to make "sound" decisions.

But the truth is that your mind can't always be relied on, especially when you are about to make big changes in your life. Your rational mind can "fool" you into doubting your abilities or make you catastrophize about how things will turn out. Things can get out of control and the smallest concern becomes a mountain of anxiety.

"If I stop drinking I won't cope, I'll lose my friends, I'll be an outcast, people will think I'm a failure," and other similar negative thoughts. Thus the unhelpful, self-sabotaging script may come into play.

This is where intuition can help. Your 'in-tuition', is your inner teacher, your wisest counsel, your most supportive ally.

Some of us have the ability to tap into intuitive guidance more easily than others. But, like any skill, the more you practice using it, the better you will get.

YOUR INTUITIVE INTELLIGENCE

Listed below are just a few reasons why intuitive intelligence is a skill you should master.

TRUSTING your gut in life will help give you:

- Confidence when you have nothing to go on, and no concrete experience or information on which to base your decision
- Clarity in the face of a tsunami of choices and possibilities
- A faster ability to make the right choice, rather than becoming bogged down in months or years of analysis
- Awareness of opportunities you may not have considered
- Inspiration and a friendly pep-talk when you need one
- Trusting your gut can save your life

THE INFINITE INTELLIGENCE OF YOUR SUBCONSCIOUS MIND

"The infinite intelligence within your subconscious mind can reveal to you everything you need to know at every moment in time and point in space, provided you are open-minded and receptive", writes Joseph Murphy in *The Power of Your Subconscious Mind*.

"Within the subconscious mind, you will find the solution to every problem, and the cause for every effect. Because you can draw out the hidden powers, you come into actual possession of the power and wisdom necessary to move forward in abundance, security and joy."

Sounds great! How do you gain this knowledge? By tapping into the power of emotions and listening to your own infinite intelligence.

This is where the subconscious mind rules—it's the storehouse of emotions, unlike the ego and conscious mind that rationalizes everything it can.

The rational mind has its place, of course. The trouble is, all too often it dominates, very often talking us out of or into things that rob of us of joy and fulfillment.

Is intuition better than concrete, measurable facts?

That depends! Some decisions require logic and analysis. The rational information necessary to easily make the right decision may be readily available or easy to source.

But there are times, especially when you are changing your life when you have nothing, or very little, verifiable information. That's when knowing how to access, listen and act on your intuition can be most helpful.

When I began writing this book I acted on an inspired idea without any market research. I honestly didn't 'know', for sure if my book would sell, but in my heart, I felt that sharing my story and the techniques that had helped me, and also my clients, would inspire others too. I gave myself a pep-talk throughout the writing process and applied myself with more confidence than I truly felt.

And, as you read from the reviews, my intuitive hunch proved right. First, I began by researching sophisticated and easy drinks which would be great alternatives to drinking alcohol. Again, my intuition guided me. I kept being directed to make the book fun, and light-hearted and to 'beat' the booze barons at their own game by using similar ploys they do to make their beverages sound desirable.

Here's a fun recipe from one of my other sobriety books, *Mind Over Mojitos*:

H_2O Clean & Collected

When you think premixed drinks, do you think "loaded with alcohol, neurotoxins, carcinogens, sugar, additives and a whole lot of unnecessary calories?" Well so did we.

This thought-enhancing drink is guaranteed to satisfy the thirst of those who want a lot of indulgence, while still embracing a healthy lifestyle—H_2O Clean & Collected is created for people like you and me, who care about what we put in our bodies and are sick of artificial highs, and alcoholic sugar-loaded drinks bloating our shelves and stomachs.

Full of personality, it is light bodied, with incisive lemon/lime flavors, a seductive balance of acidity, guilt-free sweetness (zero sugar, zero carbs, zero preservatives) with a lasting finish.

Ingredients

- Water (fresh rain or spring water if available)
- Ice
- Slice of organic lemon or lime

Method

Pour water into your favorite stunning glass, I prefer crystal and sometimes a lovely champagne flute is elegant.

Garnish with fruit or add a wee drop of freshly squeezed juice or your fav healthy syrup.

If bubbles make your soul sing, whip out your SodaStream, or (RTD) bottled soda, pump up the volume and enjoy a natural high.

100% clean and natural!

Thank you to Russ Perry, author of *The Sober Entrepreneur* for sharing his go-to-drink of choice—sparkling water, with a dash of lime. Sometimes the simpler things in life are the best.

In fact, this drink is so good perhaps we should bottle it!

BEST OF ALL, after following my intuition, I received great feedback:

"*Cassandra is such a wonderful guide throughout the book to show how Sobriety doesn't have to be a prison sentence and it can be fun. I love the sassy and sexy recipes. I also really appreciated her take on the importance of a good glass and that aesthetics are everything when it comes to sobriety and a sexy non-alcoholic beverage that still makes you feel like an adult.*"

Russ Perry, author of *The Sober Entrepreneur* also left a review, "Fun, simple and just what's needed for a creative break to drinking (that can seriously change your life!)."

If you'd love some ideas or are curious, *Mind Over Mojitos: How Moderating Your Drinking Can Change Your Life: Easy Alcohol-Free Recipes for Happier Hours & a Joy-Filled Life* is available in print and paperback.

STEERING YOU THE RIGHT WAY

President and Editor-in-Chief of *The Huffington Post,* Arianna Huffington, writes in her bestselling book, *Thrive*, "Even when we're not at a fork in the road, wondering what to do and trying to hear that inner voice, our intuition is always there, always reading the situation, always trying to steer us the right way.

"But can we hear it? Are we paying attention? Are we living a life that keeps the pathway to our intuition unblocked? Feeding and nurturing our intuition, and living a life in which we can make use of its wisdom, is one key way to thrive, at work and in life."

TUNING IN TO YOUR INTUITION

Listed below are some tips and strategies that will help you feed, nurture, and tap into your inner success coach:

THE BODY BAROMETER. The body never lies. Your body language is one of the primary ways your heart and intuition guide you. When you are in tune with your intuition you are more likely to experience:

- A feeling of limitless energy
- A feeling of weightlessness and lightness
- A feeling of being happy and motivated
- Excitement, zest, and animation.

These signs are all clues to your passion and purpose. Passionate feelings are the ways your intuition guides your decisions about what is right, given who you are and who you want to be.

What signs does your body give you when you are being true to yourself and living soberly?

What warning signs does your body give you when you are off track?

ASK OPEN, generative questions. Intuitive information reveals itself more easily when you ask yourself open questions such as, "How can I begin to bring more money into my life?" or "What business or self-employment opportunity could I choose that will be both fun and financially rewarding?"

These are just a few sample questions—so many people drink because of financial pressure and stress. Create your own generative questions that are most relevant for you, but don't try and force a reply. Your intuition will reveal the answer in a variety of ways. There's no one right way to receive intuitive wisdom. It may come in the form of a hunch, a gut feeling, an inner voice, an image, or in a dream.

What questions do you want answers to? Prompt your intuition by writing down some good open questions. For instance, if your biggest concern about how to go alcohol-free, "Where can I find someone to help me have fun without drinking?"

Pay extra attention over the next three weeks to special "go-incidences" or insights.

For example, as I was writing one of the chapters in this book called, *Hooked on a Feeling*, I walked into a local cafe and the song, Hooked on a Feeling by the band Blue Swede was playing on the sound system. What are the odds!

The lyrics of the song also inspired me to write a chapter titled, High on Believing—spirituality, and faith is such an important part of peoples' recovery. Maintaining a believing mindset is another critical factor in achieving goals of any kind—something I cover in my book, *Developing a Millionaire Mindset*.

Create some space. If you're constantly stressed and always wishing for more time, money, freedom, or energy, you need to create some time for "sacred idleness." All those signs of stress are signals from your intuition that it's time to slow down. Take a comfort break. Give yourself the rejuvenating gift of some time off to reflect on your life.

What do you truly want? What fills your soul? What can you let go of? What are the blessings in your life? These are all questions to ask your intuitive guidance system. Listen to the answers, reflect, and act.

Listen to inner wisdom now, pay attention to intuitions, feelings, and hunches. They're not random responses generated by the brain and nervous system to keep them busy, but data from the unified field that surrounds you.

"Everything we ever need to know is in this field, to be revealed at exactly the right time. The more deeply we pay attention the quicker the messages are received and the more effectively we can act upon them," says intuitive astrologer, Sarah Varcas. "There is a lot of information available to those willing to listen, watch and learn."

Hot Tip! Taking the time to meditate, write, and dream new dreams will pay off in a big way and is an important step in creating the abundant, peaceful and prosperous life you deserve.

What steps can you take to learn more about meditation?

How can you create some space for "sacred idleness" in your life? What can you let go of?

CALL UPON YOUR Archetypal Symbol

Another way to embrace your intuition is to call upon archetypal symbols. According to renowned psychologist Carl Jung, archetypes are inherited memories represented in the mind as universal symbols and can be observed in your dreams.

Jean Wiley, a self-employed Professional Intuitive Astrologer agrees. "10 years ago when I was really struggling with how to find my voice, swimming in that river of conformity, and hiding so much of myself for so long, what I would do was dream of David Bowie.

"He didn't come to me in my dreams, but he was my symbol. He was everything that was authentic and envelope-pushing, and innovative and interesting, and thumbed his nose at everything that was conventional and conforming. And I would dream about David Bowie and I would wake up in the morning and I would feel better."

Who could you call upon to give you courage, direction, and strength?

If you're looking for additional instructions on how to connect with your archetypal symbol I recommend Deepak Chopra's incredible book *The Spontaneous Fulfillment of Desire: Harnessing the Infinite Power of Coincidence*.

For more help with valuing and trusting your intuition and higher wisdom I also recommend Lynn Robinson's books, including *Trust Your Gut*.

WHAT YOU TRULY WANT TO BECOME

"Your time is limited, so don't waste it living someone else's life. Don't be trapped by dogma—which is living with the results of other people's thinking," said Steve Jobs, co-founder of Apple Inc. "Don't let the noise of other's opinions drown out your own inner voice. And most importantly, have the courage to follow your heart and intuition. It already knows what you truly want to become. Everything else is secondary."

The reality is that many people spend their lives ignoring their real calling, their passion, and their true path with heart—especially when they're drunk!

And remember, decisions based purely on the analysis of the cold, hard, objective facts ignore what it is to be human, to be fully alive. If you want to wake every morning looking forward to your life, then getting in touch with your emotions is a vital part of any decision-making and planning process.

INTUITION IS **the Gateway to Your Authentic Self**

"Your sixth sense is your authentic self," says intuitive author and business psychic Sonia Choquette. And this authenticity is the thing you want in life. It's what attracts others to you, and it's what sets you apart in the crowd. There's no one else like you in the world. When you trust your intuition, you trust your SELF.

Intuition is the language of the soul speaking through the heart. Your intuition may not make logical sense, but it makes heartfelt sense and speaks to your need to be whole and have integrity. Intuition rather than logic offers a way to break out of old struggles, self-limiting mindsets and limitations, and to reach the clouds.

Look For and Heed the Signs

There's a lovely scene in a movie called *Man On A Wire* about a high-wire walker Philippe Petit, who, while reading the newspaper in France, experienced a lightning flash of insight.

Staring down at an article about the proposed building of the World Trade Centre he knew what he wanted to do and become—the first, and only man to walk across New York's World Trade Centre, supported by nothing but a wire stretching across the twin towers. 1,368 feet above Manhattan!

At the time, the buildings, later destroyed in the 2011 attacks, were still only in the concept and design phase. But Philippe ripped out the newspaper cuttings and set about planning how he would make his dream come true.

Inspirational people are like vitamins for our souls. Philippe's pursuit of passion is inspiring on so many levels. Not only did he succeed, but he also excited so many others.

Barry Greenhouse, for example, an insurance executive at the time, served as the 'inside man' and help with logistics, spicing up his life in the process. His intuitive daring and courage also captured moviemakers, who later brought this amazing feat to international screens.

The film of Philippe's quest was awarded the Grand Jury Prize at the

2008 Sundance Festival. In February 2009, the film won the BAFTA for Outstanding British Film, the Independent Spirit Awards, and the Academy Award for Best Documentary Feature. Philippe Petit's, and the movie's success is further testament to the power of passion and listening to your intuition.

You may not have such 'lofty' or death-defying aspirations, but if you listen to your intuition you will summon the courage, drive, passion, and fortitude to pursue your own path with heart. Perhaps you too will inspire people and meet with the success others only dream of.

What can Philippe teach you?

- Listen to and follow your intuitive spark of excitement
- Surround yourself with people who believe in your dreams
- Minimize distractions—maintain absolute, unswerving focus
- Be playful, whilst being safe
- Let go of your safety net. Trust your skill and preparation
- Commit your all—put everything on the line if necessary
- Do what you love
- Practice. Practice. Practice
- Design a fail-proof strategy
- Leave nothing to chance—this is your life we're talking about
- Just do it!

LISTENING to your inner self is a very important part of re-creating and strengthening your authentic or true self.

Knowing how to slow down and tap into your intuition or "inner knowing" will help you not only gain greater self-mastery and control, but also give you some essential tools to have on hand to help you ride the winds of change and to strengthen your sense of self.

Personally, I find that when I trust my gut I am more empowered to do what is right for me and that other people's criticisms and toxic taunts bounce off me more easily. In a world where sometimes a kind word seems as scarce as red diamonds this is a priceless gift.

While we're talking about toxic people check out the next chapter, relationship rehab!

26

RELATIONSHIP REHAB

In a universe where "like goes to like" and "birds of a feather flock together," we attract to us that which we emanate.

Everything connects to everything else, especially when it comes to the health of your relationships.

Leonardo da Vinci once said, "Marriage is like putting your hand into a bag of snakes in the hope of pulling out an eel."

Read into this what you will, but the theme is clear. Make good choices and marry well, keep your relationship in good health, or don't marry at all.

Be on guard for relationships that are dragging you down. Sometimes this means investing more time and energy into making things work, or having a bit more patience when people important to you aren't at their sober best. Take the good with the bad, don't give up too easily, work at it and recognize that nothing is absolutely perfect.

If people try to pull you down, take a step back and explore their motives. Fear is often the culprit. The fear that you may surpass them.

The fear that your successful sobriety will highlight their own failings. Or the fear that you will leave them.

If you can't make things work, professionally or personally, be prepared to quit. Divorce your job, your boss, your partner—anyone who is toxic to your health and happiness.

"I knew I had a lot to deal with. For one thing, I had to cut it off with my wife Linda. She was not understanding about the situation. How could I have expected her to be? Our relationship was based on getting fucked up together," writes Duff McKagan in his autobiography.

Getting your head bitten off or feeling like you're surrounded by a vat of snakes, or being held back, will only deflate your ability to become alcohol-free. Or, as I share later in this book, being in a toxic relationship could end your life.

Let's look at the importance of surrounding yourself with a supportive community of like-minded people.

SOBRIETY BUDDIES

A central tenet of Alcoholic Anonymous's successful program is regular meet-ups and seasoned group members *"sponsoring"* newer members, guiding them through the process of *"working the steps."*

But you don't need to join AA to benefit from collegial support and the therapeutic benefits of talking about your recovery as well as any problems you experience along the way. If you want to join, that's great. Many recovering alcoholics, like Russel Brand say that without AA's 12-Step Program he would still be an addict—or dead.

Duff McKagan, says, other than having a Librium drip in his arms while he was in hospital to help him through the shakes and alcohol withdrawal, he had no program, no AA, no community—just a few friends, and his bike.

The simplest definition of sobriety buddies is supportive people that share the same values, beliefs, and aspirations.

Your sobriety buddies are the ones who always have your back no matter how flat or down you feel. They're the ones that you can show your vulnerable, wounded, self-doubting self and they'll still love and support you unconditionally—worry warts and all.

Your sobriety buddies can also help motivate and reenergize you and cheerlead your successes.

As you've already discovered, sometimes to flourish you need to break free of your current tribe and find one that breathes fresh air into your life, lifts you higher and brings out the best in you. Your best-fit sobriety buddies are committed co-creators and enthusiastic supporters in one another's mutual success.

Your sobriety buddies are a great team of supportive others—whether they be significant friends, partners, or family members, or those found online through wonderful Facebook groups and webinars. They may even be your clients.

I found many of my buddies online when I devoted myself to living and working with purpose and passion—including freeing myself from being controlled by alcohol. We've never met in person, but we stay connected and share success strategies via Facebook, emails and occasionally we link-up on video conferencing calls.

One of my key cheerleaders is my partner, Lorenzo. We got together over lunch one day and bounced some ideas around for this book. He also helps me keep my alcohol consumption in check.

When you choose to step out of limiting thoughts and open your heart to others, you'll find the people who want to share and celebrate the journey with you. You'll find your sobriety buddies.

My readers have become sobriety buddies by reaching out to me and interviewing me on their podcasts and success summits. Recently,

Sheree Clark, a fabulous and influential healthy-living coach based in the US, discovered my book *Mid-life Career Rescue: The Call for Change* and showcased it on American television.

She also included an interview with me in her fabulous "What the Fork" summit. You'll find a link to this interview and the TV clip on my media page at www.cassandragaisford.com/media. You'll also find an interview where she shares how job stress caused her to drink way too much. Changing careers was her ultimate sobriety cure. Listen to our chat, From Despairing Business Owner to Joyful Solopreneur—http://www.cassandragaisford.com/podcast.

Many successful authors and podcasters found their sobriety buddies by following their enthusiasms and passionate purposes to share what they learn with others.

Here are a few ways to find your buddies:

• Scan Facebook for like-minded people and groups—you'll find a few suggestions at the back of this book.

• Create a Facebook community of your own—show up and encourage others

• Listen to podcasts which inspire you to become the best sober version of you.

• Check out Meetup.com and find a group of like-minded souls to meet up with in person

• Speak from your heart, and reach out to those you love, or feel could help

If you're having trouble finding your team, there are many networks within the community that can assist you. This could be your local Church, the LifeLine Service, AA, or the services offered to the community by your Local Council, e.g., Citizens Advice Bureau.

Your own friends and family could also be a great help if you are willing to listen to their suggestions.

Remember, "A problem shared is a problem halved." Gather a team of supportive or like-minded people who will nourish, cheerlead, challenge, and support you when you are tempted to abuse alcohol, feel flat or overwhelmed and who get a buzz from helping you succeed.

Next up is a favorite recovery strategy, and it's one you can do from the privacy of your own home—prayer therapy.

27

PRAYER THERAPY

Harness the energies of love and boost your ability to bounce and tenacity to succeed with the sacred daily ritual of prayer.

If prayer is something you are unfamiliar with or hold negative associations about, don't be deterred. Whatever your experience or belief system, prayer is simply a form of spiritual communion. It's a very simple and potent tool used successfully by many resilient people.

Many people have lost their union with God because of the hypocritical dogma which has polluted many faith systems. However, prayer comes in many shapes, colors, and textures.

Many recovering alcoholics, prosperous creatives and successful business people, including Deepak Chopra, Julia Cameron, Wayne Dyer and Louise Hay, refer to prayer in several forms, including describing it as the voice of God, intuition, higher self, inner goddess, or their Sacred Divine.

In her book *Illuminata: A Return to Prayer*, Marianne Williamson speaks of prayer as a way of "focusing our eyes," dramatically transforming our orientation, releasing us "from the snares of lower energies," and aligning "our internal energies with truth".

Prayer, or invoking a higher power, is revered by many for its power to help them reclaim their strength, find their inner power and overcome tragedy.

Scientific (4-step) prayer therapy is another form of invoking the guidance and help of a higher power. "It is the only real answer to the great deception," writes Joseph Murphy (PhD.) in his excellent book, *The Miracle of Mind Dynamics*. "Let the light of God shine in your mind, and you will neutralize the harmful effects of the negatives implanted in your subconscious mind."

The four steps Murphy suggests are:

- Recognition of the healing presence of Infinite Intelligence
- Complete acceptance of the One Power
- Affirmation of the Truth
- Rejoice and give thanks for the answer

"Faith is action in love," Mother Theresa once said. Whatever mode of prayer or invocation you use, read them slowly and deliberately and notice how the energies in your mind, body and soul shift.

The indicator of God's presence in you is the presence of peace, harmony, abundance, and joy.

Take the time to stop and pray from your heart. The words that you use aren't as important compared to the strength of your desire to connect with The Divine.

Ask and pray for a solution. Without asking there can be no answering.

Be open to a response appearing which is different from your expectations—and know that your prayers are heard and answered.

I have many ways of praying, including:

- Asking for guidance directly
- Journaling my *prayers*—writing out questions, heartaches, and struggles
- Going for a prayer walk
- Connecting with source energy and enjoying a silent retreat
- Reading prayers I have written or that others have created which speak to and guide me.
- And, importantly by reciting my access prayer which enables me to connect to the wisdom of the Akashic records, God energy, and my guides and loved ones in spirit. I use a similar prayer to help others who contact me for help and guidance and who wish to have a soul reading to reveal their soul self and soul history and soul purpose in its true beauty and magnificence.

You can learn more about this service on my website.

The beauty of prayer is that it's all about listening to the quite, but unmistakable guidance and strength of Spirit, and it's available to anyone, regardless of faith, gender, race, or any other discriminatory bias. As you listen, don't expect to hear a voice. But do expect God to tug at your heart, move your conscience, or help you realize something you need to do or change. Very often I experience profound joy and peace and a deep sense of coming home to Self. Sometimes this feeling is often accompanied by tears.

28

HEALING HYPNOSIS

UK based hypnotherapist Marissa Peer says that there are only three things you need to know about your mind: it likes what is familiar, it responds to the pictures in your head, and it gravitates to what you desire.

To get the tremendous power of your unconscious mind behind your goals, you will need to program it for success. A simple and exceedingly effective way to do this is through hypnosis.

"Emotional problems work much more on the 'feeling level' than the 'thinking level' which is why just trying to think differently is so hard," say the UK-based hypnotherapists at Uncommon Knowledge.

"We use hypnosis to help you feel different quickly which then makes you think differently about a situation."

You can access hypnosis sessions from the comfort of your home via instant download. There's an endless array of scripts on offer to help you overcome addictions, stop alcohol relapse, eliminate self-doubt, reduce anxiety, boost confidence, and much more.

But a word of caution first—the Internet is awash with websites which offer hypnosis products and services that have not been created by experienced and qualified professionals. Some of these programs are of limited or no use, while others may do more harm than good.

"Hypnosis is the epitome of mind-body medicine. It can enable the mind to tell the body how to react and modify the messages that the body sends to the mind," reported the *New York Times* in a recent article.

I purchased the "Stay off Alcohol" program from Hypnosis Downloads.com based in the UK. In the early days of my unsuccessful attempts to scale back my drinking I listened to it every night before going to sleep. I found myself smiling in agreement to the soothing and totally sobering acknowledgement about what alcohol was stealing from me and the positive reinforcing reminders of all the reasons remaining alcohol free was what I really needed.

I'm in the process of completing my Better Living with Hypnosis Hypnotist certification training with Dr. Steve G. Jones, a registered Clinical Hypnotherapist, and Founder of the American Alliance of Hypnotists. It's from Dr. Jones that I first learned of the Akashic records, which is also offered as part of his consciousness-raising training.

Harness the power of your mind to put weight into your dreams, and to help you remove obstacles to your success. Let hypnosis take the pressure off. Experiment with this powerful technique and reprogram your subconscious mind for success.

I invite you to sign up for my newsletter to be the first to know when I release the following hypnosis downloads:

- The Flowering of Your True Potential
- Party Without Alcohol
- Stay Off Alcohol Forever

- Mindfully Moderate Drinking

Don't forget about the transformational power of self-hypnosis techniques including affirmations and the self-soothing strategies I shared previously. Kind, encouraging, and sometimes stroppy, self-talk can really help. Talk yourself up and enjoy a natural high.

29

AFFIRM YOUR DESIRE FOR SOBRIETY: SELF-SOOTHE

When you feel flat, worried or crave a drink, your default thoughts can veer towards the negative. You may find yourself saying, *'I'm broke. I won't succeed. I don't know how I'll cope without drinking.'* Or something else equally discouraging.

The trouble is these negative affirmations will become your reality. And you don't want that to happen, do you?

To affirm something, is declaring it to be true. An affirmation is also a statement you intend to be true. Listen to your words—are your intentions setting you up for failure or success?

Claim back your power and self-soothe. Harness the power of positive affirmations to convince yourself you'll succeed or get through whatever is troubling you. Create and hold a vision for what you know, or wish can be true.

"I am the greatest," Muhammad Ali used to say repeatedly. "I said that even before I knew I was. I figured that if I said it enough, I would convince the world that I really was the greatest."

A superhero in and out of the boxing ring Mohammed Ali was a fast-talking world-conquering superhero (1942 - 2016).

Similarly, many people experiencing profound grief or trauma often turn to affirmations for comfort. "All is well. Everything is working out for my highest good," Louise Hay, the author of *You Can Heal Your Life*, used to say. "Out of this situation, only good will come."

As you'll discover later, the power of hope is a magical thing.

Affirmations repeated regularly work because they program your mind and activate the part of the brain that acts as a filter—registering what's important to you and screening out what you no longer value.

Another reason affirmations work is that they create a dynamic tension. If what you are affirming has more bounce than what you currently believe, the tension between the two different realities becomes uncomfortable.

To rid yourself of the tension you can either accept the status quo and stop saying the affirmation, or raise your reality and energetic vibrations higher by making your affirmation and reality match.

Plant your affirmations deeper by framing them emotionally. Instead of, "Obstacles do not bend me", experiment with "I feel strong in the face of obstacles they do not bend me", for example.

Or, "I am joyfully building greater resilience—every day I grow stronger."

These emotion-laden statements engage your heart-center so that deeper, more resilient changes can take root.

Deeper changes create greater, habitual, instinctive resilience and conviction and resilience to remain sober.

Here are a few of my favorite sobriety affirmations:

- I love the energy and vitality I feel being free of alcohol

- I love waking up feeling clear-headed. clear-hearted, my energy bright and looking forward to my day
- I trust that all is well in my life
- I look at life from a higher perspective
- Happiness and joy flow easily—the longer I embrace sobriety the more joy I feel
- I'm a manifestation magnet, my commitment to sobriety has opened the floodgates of goodness upon me—spiritually and financially

CREATING EMPOWERING, heart-centered affirmations is fun! I adapted the last one from a Denzel Washington quote I have on my wall. Have a go at creating your own, keep them somewhere you can see regularly and repeat them often—especially if you find your resolve wavering.

30

RATIONAL EMOTIVE BEHAVIORAL THERAPY

When I completed my counseling training many years ago I was introduced to Albert Ellis's Rational Emotive Behaviour Therapy (REBT). REBT originated in the mid 1950's as Ellis became increasingly aware and frustrated by the ineffectiveness of traditional psychoanalysis to produce change in his patients.

The REBT worldview is that people often make themselves emotional victims by their own distorted, unrealistic, and irrational thinking patterns. Ellis takes an essentially optimistic view of people, but criticizes some humanistic approaches as being too soft at times and failing to address the fact that people can virtually "self-destruct" through irrational and muddled thinking.

According to Ellis and the REBT worldview, all people are born with self-defeating tendencies. When something goes against your goals, your values or desires, feelings of failure, rejection, etc., can set in; but you have a choice.

You have a choice of feeling terrified, panicky, depressed, self-pitying, self-doubting, etc.—and succumbing to these emotions.

But these feelings can prevent you from making positive changes—and may drive you to drink.

Which emotion you choose, according to REBT practitioners, is thought to mainly depend on your belief system—not your goals and values, but what you tell yourself when your goals and values are thwarted or blocked.

We all have a rational set of beliefs called "preferences." In this context, "rational" means self-helping beliefs, such as, "I don't like what is going on." "I wish it weren't so." "How annoying?" "Let's see what I can do about it."

Many people very frequently pick irrational beliefs, referred to as "demands," such as, "Because I don't like what is going on, it absolutely should not be allowed." "It can't happen." "I can't stand it." "Everyone should love me–if they don't, I am worthless." "It's horrible, I think I'll give up" (or, when taken to the extreme, "I'll kill myself").

Ellis' therapeutic approach is not to challenge the clients' goals and values, but instead *attack* their absolute demands about achieving these values. The emphasis of the therapy is on changing the way the client thinks about the behavior or the upsetting event, rather than on changing the behavior itself.

This is a critical point—it is not the actual event but our view of the event that is critical.

The task of the REBT therapist is to correct clients' thought patterns and minimize irrational ideas, while simultaneously helping them to change their dysfunctional feelings and behaviors. Challenging the irrational statement is key to changing an entire philosophy of life.

THE ABCDEF METHOD

Perhaps Ellis's most important concrete methodological contribution is his A-B-C–D-E-F theory, which can be summarized as follows:

A - the "objective" facts, events, behaviors that an individual encounters. (I call this, 'the activating event').

B - the person's beliefs about 'A'

C - the emotional consequences, or how a person feels and acts about 'A'

D - disputing 'B' irrational beliefs

E - the effect that disputation has on the client

F - new feelings and behaviors

EXAMPLE:

I helped a friend apply the ABCDE method following a Boxing Day alcohol-fuelled drama which impacted his son. The following is an edited extract (I have changed names to protect people's privacy):

A - THE ACTIVATING EVENT AND "OBJECTIVE" facts, events, behaviors encountered.

Following Boxing Day, Tim, who is nineteen, rang and told his father, Simon about an alleged assault between him and his mother's new boyfriend. Tim says both his mom and her boyfriend were drunk.

B - THE BELIEFS ABOUT 'A'

Simon is waiting to speak to the 'old-one' (his ex) to determine the facts but believes his son's account of what happens. The 'old one' is not returning his call.

He believes the reason she is not returning his call is because she is at fault, and that an assault did occur.

C - THE EMOTIONAL CONSEQUENCES, or how Simon feels and acts about 'A'

Simon's emotions are heightened. He's feeling frustrated, powerless, angry, resentful and fearful for his son's safety. Yet, aspects of his son's version of what happened concern him. He feels confused as to what really occurred.

Simon drinks 3 bottles of beer and goes to the bottle store to buy more.

Simon believes alcohol relaxes him, minimizes stress, and helps him stay calmer and in control while he waits.

Over the course of the evening (3 hours) he drinks five 500ml bottles of beer (11 standard drinks.) Feeling stressed, I join him—minimizing my drinking by consuming small quantities in six crystal glasses (in total 500 ml, or 2.2 standard drinks.)

After speaking to 'the old one' and his son on a three-way call, and resolving all misunderstandings, I asked how he feels now that he knows his son is not at risk. He shuts me down and says, "I don't want to talk about it."

He doesn't speak to me again that evening.

D - DISPUTING 'B' irrational beliefs

Rather than work myself into a state, I challenged my belief that by drinking with Simon we would both be relaxed. Alcohol is a depressant, it depletes your energy, and increases symptoms of stress already triggered by external events, I reminded myself.

It increases anxiety, melancholy, gloom, and aggression, which is why Tim's mom and her partner argued, and why Tim 'lunged' at this stepfather when he told him to mind his business.

I counsel myself, "Alcohol is ethanol, a flammable, colorless chemical compound—it's poison, also used to fuel cars, masquerading as a happy drink."

E - EFFECT that disputation has

The episode strengthened my resolve never to drink during times of stress, and my conviction that I don't want to ingest poisons.

Simon's knowledge that his ex is an alcoholic causes him to question his own dependency on alcohol during times of stress.

This change in thinking affects Simon by making him more committed to controlling his drinking and being a role model to his son.

F - NEW FEELINGS and behaviors

Simon and I felt calmer and more optimistic about the benefits of not drinking.

Simon felt more empowered and in control now that he has discovered the truth about his ex's drinking and how her relationship with a man who drinks excessively affects his son.

He decides to take control by helping Tim find a way to gain his independence and leave home, knowing that despite urging his ex to seek help for her drinking that, as with other times, this may have fallen on deaf ears.

Tim successfully finds work that he loves which means he is seldom at home, and tells his father that alcohol has no place in his own life. Tim is happier sober!

Your A-B-C–D-E-F Strategy

The A-B-C–D-E-F Strategy provides a process to approach drinking behavior more mindfully and to be your own therapist or counsel. It's simple, easy to use and incredibly quick and powerful.

Consider applying this technique to a current or past stressful situation, and wheeling it out again when you are faced with trauma, stress or events that may trigger a desire to drink in the mistaken belief that it will help you cope.

31

BOOK THERAPY

Art in all its many forms, whether it is poetry, sculpture, a play, a painting, a beautifully designed building, or the beautifully written, passion-inspired words in a book have such a powerful ability to uplift even the most despondent spirits.

For me, this is what spirituality is: something that lifts me up at a much deeper level and allows me to transcend the mundane.

Words are my go-to place for comfort, encouragement strength, advice, inspiration and empowerment. As a writer, books are my thing, and it's my heartfelt desire that this book provides all these qualities, feeling and support as you continue your journey to sobriety.

You will also find comfort in the words of other authors, both writers of fiction and non-fiction. I loved reading Duff McKagan's memoir, for example, and highlighted the page where he wrote, "I was sober, but thirsty. My mind had almost atrophied from lack of stimulation."

It was a powerful reminder of the healing power of gaining new knowledge.

McKagan felt the need to read. He wanted to experience things he missed out on in high school, he was curious about all the things he hadn't read and the knowledge he hadn't discovered.

When someone gave him a Ken Burns Civil War documentary he became enthralled and voraciously read non-fiction books on the topic. He moved onto fiction when he discovered Ernest Hemingway's book set on the Spanish Civil War.

"*For Whom The Bell Tolls* unlocked the world of literature. Hemingway's descriptions blew me away. When one of the characters talked about alcohol addiction, I cringed.

"'Of all men the drunkard is the foulest. The thief when he is not stealing is like another. The extortioner does not practice in the home. The murderer when he is at home can wash his hands. But the drunkard stinks and vomits in his own bed and dissolves his organs in alcohol,'" were the words of Hemmingway that had struck him so powerfully—strengthening his commitment to his own sobriety.

"In my new and lonely world of desert-island sobriety, I was at last connecting with something. If I was not yet finding my place in the world, I was at least finding places and ideas and people I could relate to, despise, or aspire to in these great books.

"As I moved on to other writers, working my way through literary classics alongside my steady stream of nonfiction, the authors also gave me confidence to use my own voice speaking and to use intelligent words, as opposed to a raised voice that had really only masked fear—fear of how to deal with uncomfortable or incomprehensible situations."

The space between the covers of his books became McKagan's place of solitude. "Reading continues to represent a meditative haven for me to this day," he says.

I couldn't agree more. It's hard to enjoy a book when you've drunk too much, but you can get 'drunk' on reading. I'm a bookaholic—whether it's writing them or reading them I also gain so much comfort.

I enjoy reading romance novels, and writing them under my pen name Mollie Mathews, for this very reason—pure fantasy and escapism.

Incidentally, while I was writing *The Sobriety Experiment*, a reader of my short-story romance shared the following with me:

> "I just read *Twist of Fate*, so sorry it was so short, but I lived myself in Jonathan's life. How it nearly matched my first marriage, then for a mere 23 years I found love and living with my childhood sweet heart until 2007 when fate struck he was injured in a car accident and has loss of memory of it.
>
> Same year his only son was sent to prison with 2 others on account of murder which he never did do for 10 years. On their 5th year he and his friend were released on parole, he was out 1 year and 2 months when he died of heart attack.
>
> Since then I lost my loving, funny full of life sweetheart. He now lives a life within himself, doesn't want to go on holidays or visit family or friends. He blames God for taking his son and has started to drink heavy from 2 in afternoon until 5.30 then locks all doors and just sits and watches TV. It feels like prison or boarding school where you are coupled up not allowed out.
>
> As I read it seems that Johnathan's marriage was a secluded one sided marriage. Thanks for the short story I truly loved it. I think I must ask my daughter in New Zealand to collect your books and send them to me.
>
> Please keep writing these kind of love stories they are really lovely and heartwarming to read.

Letters like these are why I love writing love stories. You can learn more about why I write romance here—https://molliemathews.wordpress.com/2017/01/28/why-i-write-romance/.

In short, as with my self-empowerment books, I passionately believe in the power of love to transform peoples lives.

32

MUSICOLOGY

Singer and songwriter Alanis Morissette once wrote, "The two most inspiring life forces are anger and joy—I could write 6 zillion songs about these two feelings alone."

Rehab, was one of Amy Winehouse most famous and tragically prophetic songs. Written and performed by her the lyrics are autobiographical and summarize Winehouse's refusal to enter a rehabilitation clinic.

"I asked my dad if he thought I needed to go. He said no, but I should give it a try. So I did, for just 15 minutes. I went in said 'hello' and explained that I drink because I am in love and have screwed up the relationship. Then I walked out."

Affirming this song, by singing the lyrics "They tried to make me go to rehab, I said, no, no, no", over and over and over again, and wearing it as a badge of defiant celebration can have done little to help her commit to becoming addiction-free.

As you well know, drinking alcohol won't repair a demanding relationship or fix a broken heart.

After her death, forensic investigators recovered one small and two large bottles of vodka from the bedroom where she was found dead. The coroner's report explained that Winehouse's blood alcohol content was 416 mg per 100 ml (0.416%) at the time of her death, more than five times the legal drink-drive limit. Somewhat euphemistically the coroner cited her death as 'misadventure,' adding to their verdict, "The unintended consequences of such potentially fatal levels was her sudden death."

So what's this got to do with musicology? As you read in the last chapter, words can empower and heal. The opposite is also true, as Amy's story powerfully illustrates.

Musicology is the study of music in a historical and cultural context, and music therapy is a specialized form of applied musicology for the purposes of healing.

THE RIGHT SONG can save your life.

"I didn't realize that I was an alcoholic until I realized that the alcohol was not for fun anymore. It was medicine," legendary rock star Alice Cooper said in an interview.

He turned things around by going into treatment and renewing his childhood roots in Christianity. He's now on a campaign to build awareness of mental illness and to save lives.

"I really believe everybody has a certain amount of mental disability. I think we are born with certain phobias, certain things we are afraid to talk about," Cooper said.

Part of his awareness strategies includes using his music as a tool for healing. Cooper wrote "Hey Stoopid," a song about teen suicide, which includes the lyrics: "No doubt you're stressin' out/That ain't what rock n' roll's about/Get off that one-way trip down lonely street."

"That song, in particular, I've gotten so many emails: 'That song saved my life,'" Cooper said.

What's your go-to sobriety soundtrack? What lyrics, sounds or tempos support, heal and empower you? Perhaps your music therapy involves playing a musical instrument. Or, have you considered writing your own sobriety songs and penning some lyrics to help improve your physical, emotional, mental and spiritual health. Who knows, you may just strike a chord with others and create a hit.

And if you don't? You will have provided a therapeutic outlet to express your feelings.

Good vibrations will help you relax. Sound therapy meditation is another practice that encourages deep relaxation and mindfulness. All you need to do is lie back and let the good vibes wash over you. Specific vibrations and frequencies enable you to regenerate and rebalance on mental, emotion, physical and spiritual levels.

I've experienced Tibetan crystal bowl healing and found the experience profound. Consider giving this, or rhythmic drumming, or another form of sound healing a bash. Sound healing journeys are especially helpful for people who find it difficult to relax, suffer from insomnia, anxiety or other disturbances affecting the nervous system. By being exposed to specific rhythms, our brain waves slow down to a Theta state, which we usually only achieve in a deep state of hypnosis, meditation and relaxation.

GOOD VIBRATIONS

My daughter Hannah Joy, contributed a chapter about the power of music to help, in my book Bounce: Overcoming Adversity, Building Resilience and Finding Joy.

Hannah is a gifted writer with an AMAZING voice, and an instinctive feel for music. Before she could walk or talk she would jive along to her favorite songs—one of which was Mustang Sally from the movie *The Commitments*. Below is an edited extract from her chapter:

> Pythagoras was the first known person to use Music Therapy to help people with mental afflictions. This practice has been used to overcome adversity for thousands of years.
>
> We first begin to respond to music in the womb. In the last trimester as babies we are able to hear musical sound.
>
> We develop our innate capacity to move to a beat and to feel a beat. The rhythm of our mother's heartbeat is the first beat we respond to as fetuses.
>
> Tones and sounds affect our psychology. Listening to peaceful music can help you to sleep, just as upbeat music can lift your mood. If I ever feeling sad I put on a happy song.
>
> Music can be used for comfort. Music can be used to empower the passage of sadness. Music can induce a relaxation response—especially some classical music.
>
> It's not just the melodies though, it's also the lyrics and the stories people tell with their words. For me, the lyrics in Taylor Swift's 1989 album helped me to overcome a terrible breakup.
>
> Her vulnerability and the rawness of her lyrics were so uplifting for me. It helped me feel less alone in my experience to know that she had felt the same confusions and frustrations too. This was the album where she released the song "Shake it Off."
>
> Shaking it off is a brilliant way to bounce back. Sometimes we get far too bogged down in reality and we simply need to return to our inner child and have some fun. Plug in those headphones, put a happy playlist on Spotify and dance around the house.
>
> Sound healing, whether it's from your favorite song, the rhythmic wash of waves on the seashore, or an ancient musical instrument is

one of the cheapest and easiest ways to access healing and to recover when life's hurdles knock us down.

If you need some help bouncing go search for your favorite sounds. Incidentally, my commitment to sobriety has inspired my daughter and her friends. Yay!

33

MASSAGE

Many people drink to reduce stress without tackling the real culprits. While this may provide a short-term fix, in the medium and longer term it only increases the issues.

One of my favorite ways to de-stress is to go for a massage; so many people mistakenly think massage is an indulgence rather than a health behavior.

But, as a recovering alcoholic once told me, "I'd rather get a massage and get the problem rubbed out than taking a pill and just feel drugged out."

Many rehabilitation programs have added massage to their regimen of treatments. Some centers also use acupuncture and Reiki in rehabilitation programs.

"Massage has had a positive effect on every medical condition we've looked at," says Dr. Tiffany Field.

Studies show that people in the early stages of withdrawal from alcohol have considerably reduced levels of the feel-good hormone dopamine in their bloodstream. Until your body readjusts and you begin to enjoy other activities and stimuli in place of alcohol, you are susceptible to relapse.

Some studies also suggest that a one-hour massage results in benefits equivalent to a 6-hour sleep.

Sounds good to me, especially when I'm feeling fatigued. Lack of sleep increases anxiety and depression and can tempt you to restore the balance or self-soothe by reaching for alcohol.

One of the many reasons massage can be super helpful in the treatment of alcohol addiction is that your body reacts to massage in a similar way to alcohol and drugs. Massage is pleasurable for most people, and triggers the release of happiness hormones like dopamine and feel-good endorphins.

Therapeutic massage can play a unique and important part in reawakening the reward and pleasure pathways in your nervous system. Regular massage will help sway you away from alcohol abuse and remind you that there are other sources of pleasure you'll love.

Massage also decreases the levels of stress hormones like cortisol and norepinephrine in the blood.

As I write this chapter I have just returned from a 90-minute massage. All I can say is it was totally amazing! I returned feeling completely relaxed and blissed out. My partner said I looked like I was high. I was high—high on the feelings massage evokes.

If getting naked isn't your thing, consider an energy healing treatment with a trained Reiki practitioner.

Reiki is a Japanese word. **Rei** means *universal transcendental spirit* and **Ki** stands for *life energy*. Hence, the word carries the sense of universal life energy. Many scientific minds, as well as sage healers, have believed throughout the years that the universe is filled with this invisible life energy and that the life and health of all living beings is sustained by it.

Increasing evidence suggests that there does exist a superior *intelligent force* which contains all creation and out of which all life arises. The energy of this force pervades all things and this is the energy that flows through our hands in concentrated form when we treat with Reiki.

Reiki healing is the ancient art of "hands-on healing" and offers a natural and holistic approach to mental, emotional, physical, and spiritual well-being.

You don't have to believe in any religion or be particularly spiritual to benefit from Reiki. It's an inclusive, non-religious form of healing and safe for everyone.

When I was experiencing a huge period of stress, I gained so much immediate benefit from my Reiki treatments that I decided to learn this beautiful healing technique. Recently in Bali, I completed my master level training.

You don't have to be Reiki-trained to live by the principles developed by Reiki founder Dr. Mikao Usui: "Just for today do not worry. Just for today do not anger. Honor your parents, teachers and elders. Earn your living honestly. Show gratitude to everything."

Put more fuel in your tank and give yourself the gift of a therapeutic massage or Reiki treatment.

In the next chapter we'll explore the therapeutic effects of essential oils.

34

THE SMELL OF DESIRE

Recovering alcoholic, Sober Julie once wrote on her blog by the same name, "Today in my 7th year of sobriety, I am looking back remembering how very difficult the early days of recovering from alcoholism or addictions can be. In the early days, there are many discomforts that one experiences…and I had to share how essential oils may help to ease these. Thankfully there are many natural ways to make the process easier."

Aromatherapy, using the scents of plants and flowers, is one of many ancient remedies validated by modern science today. It's the Swiss army knife of all things healing—physically, mentally, spiritually, and emotionally.

Essential oils and aromatherapy may not cure addiction but they can offer great comfort during times of recovery and abstinence from alcohol, including reducing symptoms of stress, anxiety, and depression.

The sense of smell is the most basic and primitive of all our senses and is of vital importance to your well-being. Interestingly, and not surprisingly, it is also one of the most dominant senses that the booze barons exploit to good measure. Even the mere mention of words related to scent can trigger the brain's release of feel-good hormones.

You may think your craving for alcohol dictates what you drink. But your brain can trick you into wanting to quaff sensually evocative drinks that are dangerous for your health. Research confirms the major role that your brain plays, and it can be fooled into secreting hormones that make you crave alcohol.

"A beautiful refreshing ale loaded with passionfruit, melon, and mango from a generous helping of Trans-Tasman hops…a juicy, highly resinous brew exploding with citrus and tropical fruit flavors and aromas," promises Tuatara Brewery of their IPA beers.

Similarly, Panhead beers trigger the scent of desire with the following, "This is an all-American show with Centennial, Citra, and Simcoe overwhelming your nose, kicking you in the taste buds and departing with more bitterness than a Palm Springs divorce. It's a seriously addictive combination."

The same company reeled me in with the following description, which motivated me to try their low-alcohol beer—lychees, yes please. Sounds healthy.

"XPA means Extra Pale, a product of Quickchange's lighter malt base. That delicate color though is undercut by a glorious hit of alpha oils from Mosaic, Galaxy and Citra hops. Sometimes you don't want your mouth flayed raw and your liver worked to a standstill. Sometimes a few luscious notes of mango, guava, lychee and pineapple can be just the thing."

"..with incisive lemon/lime flavors, seductive balance of sweetness and acidity and a lasting finish," promise the winemakers of Gemstone Riesling.

I can feel my mouth watering already. Can you?

As Professor John Prescott, the former director of the Sensory Science

Research Centre at the University of Otago, notes in his book *Taste Matters*, "It's unfortunate that the list of most of those things that our body innately registers as good to ingest—sugar, fat, salt (alcohol)—reads like a set of disease-risk factors. This seems to put our biological drives at odds with the nutritional advice we hear about every day."

Smell is so intrinsic to how we feel that people who lose their ability to smell often report that their enjoyment of taste (and therefore life) is also diminished.

I recall reading how Australian musician the late Michael Hutchence, former lead singer of INXS, lost his sense of smell and developed depression shortly thereafter. He died five years later in what seemed to be suicide, the culmination of what friends called a slow decline in his mental well-being.

Many people have said our sense of smell is the most under-valued and taken for granted of all our senses—until it's gone.

"I can say that losing my sense of smell has been more traumatic than adapting to the disabling effects of the stroke. As the scentless and flavorless days passed, I felt trapped inside my own head, a kind of bodily claustrophobia, disassociated," wrote Elizabeth Zierah about dealing with the aftermath of a stroke at age 30.

The process of smelling is called olfaction and is incredibly complicated, taking place in several areas of the brain including the limbic system which itself has approximately 34 structures and 53 pathways.

The limbic system is linked to sensations of pleasure and pain, and emotions—both positive and negative, including fear and confidence, sadness and joy and other feelings that can either erode or boost happiness and joy.

The simple truth is that even if you are unaware of the power of smell, aroma affects your mood.

The olfactory nerve, the sole conduit from a person's nose to their brain, also happens to be the only cranial nerve that is directly exposed to the environment.

Scientists now believe that all our emotions are the result of neurochemicals such as noradrenaline and serotonin being released into the bloodstream, and mood swings are thought to be a result of these influences, particularly when they are in the extreme.

Given these facts, it's not hard to see how essential oils can help balance and influence your thoughts, feelings, and behaviors.

"Feeling educated about essential oils is such an empowering experience because there are so many different oils you can work with," writes Clinical Aromatherapist Andrea Butje in her book, *The Heart of Aromatherapy: An Easy-to-Use Guide for Essential Oils*.

"They all offer the nourishment of the plant they are distilled from in a single drop, and education helps you understand which oils to reach for at which times. Nature works holistically...and so do we."

As I share in my book, *The Art of Success: How Extraordinary Artists Can Help You Succeed in Business and Life*, Coco Chanel knew the alchemical potency of flowers and plants. She surrounded herself with nature's elixir and amassed a fortune from the essential oils which helped make her perfume Chanel N°5 famous.

The transcendent alchemy of the potions that went into the Chanel N°5 formula was not left to chance. Grieving after her lover Boy Chapel's death, Coco drew upon the essences of jasmine, ylang-ylang, vetiver, and other restorative scents to imbue Coco's Chanel N°5 with hope, healing, and the sensual confidence that love lost would be found again.

AROMATHERAPY FOR EMOTIONAL WELL-BEING

The use of essential oils for emotional well-being is what is often first thought of when someone thinks of the term "aromatherapy".

Although aromatherapy should not be considered a miracle cure for more serious emotional issues, the use of essential oils can assist, sometimes greatly, with certain emotional issues.

For example, lavender is a well-known mild analgesic, useful for healing headaches, wounds, calming the nerves, insomnia, and mild depression.

Rosemary, on the other hand, is a mild stimulant and is used to treat physical and mental fatigue, forgetfulness, and respiratory problems among other ailments.

There are so many different essential oils that can help you. Here are a few essential oils and natural therapeutic remedies to help increase your alertness and refresh and uplift your mind, body, and spirit:

• **Ylang Ylang:** Fights depression and relaxes both the body and soul, thereby driving away anxiety, sadness, and chronic stress. It also has an uplifting effect on mood and induces feelings of joy and hope. It may be an effective treatment for those undergoing nervous breakdowns and acute depression after a shock or an accident.

• **Rosemary:** Instills confidence during periods of self-doubt and keeps motivation levels high when the going gets tough. It is also said to help maintain an open mind and to make you more accepting of new ideas.

• **Cardamom:** Stimulates a dull mind, dispels tensions and worries, and nurtures and supports the brain and nervous system. Many people find it of great support during challenging times. It is an excellent oil for those with an addictive nature.

• **Peppermint:** With its refreshing scent peppermint works like a power boost for your fatigued mind, making you feel sharper and more alert.

• **Basil:** Clears negative thought patterns that may undermine positive change, restores mental energy.

- **Bergamot:** Helps relieve stress and tension, a powerful antidepressant, uplifting and calming—ideal for helping with dependency and anxiety.

- **Black Pepper:** reduces cravings, helps calm withdrawal anxiety, increases serotonin levels.

- **Lavender:** Often referred to as the oil of peace—calming, relaxing and healing. A great aid to help reduce anxiety and insomnia.

- **Lemon:** Improves energy levels, focus, and restores vitality.

- **Jasmine:** Improves mood and strengthens your ability to move forward.

- **Neroli:** Very relaxing and can relieve chronic anxiety, depression, fear, shock and stress and its calming effect can also be beneficial to the digestive tract. A good general tonic.

STRESS-RELIEVING BLENDS

These blends stated below can help during times of stress. When selecting and using oils, be sure to follow all safety precautions and remember that aromatherapy should not be used as a substitute for proper medical treatment.

Blend 1

- Three drops Clary Sage, one drop Lemon, one drop Lavender

Blend 2

- Two drops Romance Chamomile, two drops Lavender, one drop Vetiver

Blend 3

- Three drops Bergamot, one drop Geranium, one drop Frankincense

Blend 4

- Three drops Grapefruit, one drop Jasmine, one drop Ylang Ylang

DIRECTIONS:

1. Select one of the blends shown above.

2. Choose how you'd like to use the blend and follow the directions below:

DIFFUSER BLEND

Multiply your blend by four to obtain a total of 20 drops of your chosen blend. Add your oils to a dark colored glass bottle and mix well by rolling the bottle in between your hands. Add the appropriate number of drops from your created blend to your diffuser by following the manufacturer's instructions.

Bath Oil

Multiply your blend by three to obtain a total of 15 drops of your chosen blend.

Bath Salts

Continue by using the five drops, blend with Bath Salts.

Massage Oil

Multiply your blend by two to obtain a total of 10 drops of your chosen blend.

Air Freshener

Multiply your blend by six to obtain a total of 30 drops of your chosen blend.

There are many ways to empower your mind, body, and soul and reprogram your body's craving for substances—working with essential oils is one of the most effortless and pleasurable.

Investigate the power of aromatherapy. What scents imbue you with confidence? Courage? Strength? Optimism? Sharpen your most potent tools—your heart and your mind. Become a perfumer—experiment with essential oils until you find a winning blend.

Create your own sobriety blends, or have an expert create one for you. Beginning with how you want to feel NOW is a good place to start.

Consider replicating some sensual-smelling alcohol-free recipes. You'll find plenty of suggestions in my book, *Happy Sobriety: Non-Alcoholic, Guilt-Free Drinks You'll Love.*

The right blend of essential oils can also help you sleep.

35

SLEEP

Many people find it difficult to switch off at night, believing a few night-caps will lull their busy minds into compliance and improve their sleep. Others drink late and into the early hours. It's not uncommon to see business men and women or students out on the town still drinking until 3 or 5 am.

Some people think a quick nightcap will help them sleep, but a 2013 review of 27 studies shows that alcohol does a miserable job of improving sleep quality.

According to the findings, alcohol does enable healthy people to fall asleep quicker and sleep more deeply. But this is only a short-term fix. Alcohol disrupts rapid eye movement (REM) sleep. And the more you drink before bed, the more pronounced these effects.

"Alcohol may seem to be helping you to sleep, as it helps induce sleep, but overall it is more disruptive to sleep, particularly in the second half of the night," says researcher Irshaad Ebrahim, the medical director at The London Sleep Centre in the U.K. "Alcohol also suppresses breathing."

No doubt you've heard of tragic cases of people who have left their friends to sleep it off, only to find when they go to check on them in the morning, that they're dead.

Sleep plays a vital role in your health and wellbeing. Getting enough shut-eye helps you maintain your mental and physical health and enhances your quality of life.

Modern science proves conclusively that if you skip out on sleep you're compromising not just your productivity and efficiency, but also your health.

More than a third of American adults are not getting enough sleep on a regular basis, according to a February 2016 study from the Centers for Disease Control and Prevention.

Sleeping less than seven hours a day, they report, can lead to an increased risk of frequent mental distress, impaired thinking, reduced cognitive ability, and increased susceptibility to anxiety and depression.

Lack of sleep also increases the likelihood of obesity, diabetes, high blood pressure, heart disease, and stroke. None of which will aid your quest for happiness and prosperity.

When stress becomes too much, is your quality of sleep affected? The next time you're worrying and feeling anxious around bedtime, try one of these simple hacks to relax and quieten your mind enough to fall asleep:

TAKE time to unwind after a stressful day

Before going to bed, take some time out to unwind from the stresses of the day. Allow at least 30 minutes before bed for a quiet, "preparing to sleep" activity. Enjoying a calming cup of herbal tea, listening to soothing music, reading a novel or book of poems (paperback), an aromatherapy bath with lavender and other scented oils, or even a relaxation or meditation practice.

Clear mental clutter

If the events of the day or other issues are still running through your head before bedtime, start writing them down in a journal for you to revisit later. The simple act of writing down your troubles–and noting how you feel about them in that moment–can help you make sense of the root cause of your problem and free up some space for more important activities like sleeping.

Schedule time to worry

If you want to sleep better, you need to empty your mind of all thoughts, tasks, and stresses. Another way to clear your mental chatter is to "box your worries" by scheduling dedicated "worry time." This is a programmed time that is dedicated to–you guessed it–worrying. A scheduled 30-minute window in your day allows you, and even encourages you, to think constructively through the problem. Many of my clients tell me that when their "worry time" comes around, their issue has disappeared or become less important.

If the worrying issue is still lingering, by granting yourself some time to focus on it, you're forced to either formulate a solution or to let it go.

Be proactive and create a to-do list

Another active way to clear your head and get to bed is with a master to-do list. Write down "things to do" on a list in your diary so that you don't need to keep thinking about them over and over. This is why planning your "tomorrow" the day before is also an effective strategy.

You can sleep well knowing that you have your bases covered. This also minimizes decision fatigue.

Did you know that humans are only capable of keeping seven to nine different things in our working memories at once? When you try to recall all the tasks you need to complete, this uses up valuable mental energy and can prevent you from sleeping soundly.

Creating a list transfers your chores from your mind to the page (paper or digital), freeing up valuable brainpower. You'll be better able to analyze tasks and prioritize, delegate, or even eliminate some of them. It's a win-win success strategy.

Numerous studies reveal that a to-do list can also make you happier. Don't sweat it if you don't manage to cross everything off your list; the act of compiling one can still help you reach your goals, manage your stress levels, and help you relax enough to get some well-earned sleep time.

Disconnect

You can also enhance your sleep by turning off all devices and leaving them outside your bedroom.

"I will not sleep with my phone in my room," Jessie Burton, author of *The Muse*, shared on one of her blogs. After suffering from burnout and severe anxiety, she created a not-to-do list to restore and protect her mental health.

If lack of sleep is keeping you awake at night and making you tired during the day, consider reading and applying the strategies in Arianna Huffington's book, *The Sleep Revolution: Transforming Your Life One Night at a Time*.

Be ruthless about prioritizing your well-being. Remind yourself of the benefits that flow while you sleep, and when you enhance the length and quality of your sleep.

36

BREATHE DEEPLY

In a state of joy and relaxation, you breathe in a deep circular pattern, your heart comes into coherence, and you begin to produce alpha brain waves, giving you access to your own natural tranquillizers, antidepressants, and sleep therapy.

Under stress your breathing is reversed. Instead of breathing slowly and deeply, your breathing tends to become shallower and more rapid. During times of extreme stress, you can forget to breathe at all!

You may even hyperventilate—breathing in an abnormally rapid, deep, or shallow pattern. You will exhale too much carbon dioxide, and as the level of carbon dioxide in the blood drops, the blood vessels narrow, allowing less blood to circulate. If too little blood reaches your brain, you'll become dizzy and may faint.

Calcium in the blood also decreases, causing some muscles and nerves to twitch. The twitching may result in a tingling or stabbing sensation near your mouth or in your chest. These symptoms include a tight feeling in the chest, as though your lungs cannot receive enough air.

This sensation leads to faster and deeper breathing. The heart may begin to pound, and the pulse rate may rise. Experiencing these symptoms will increase anxiety in some people, which can make the condition worse.

If this happens to you, or you have forgotten how to breathe, try this: breathe in deeply for a count of four, and exhale—slowing for a count of eight. Repeat 10 times. Notice how quickly your body and mind relaxes. Try this anywhere, anytime you notice feelings of stress returning, and beat the stress response.

Or tap into a meditation or yoga class for enhanced breathing practice with the added benefit of a mind-body makeover.

Remember to breathe! Breathing deeply can evoke a state of calm and perspective during times of stress, allowing you to cope more effectively and bounce back from setbacks without reaching for a glass.

37

BEAT RESISTANCE

Do you have a death wish?

Freud claimed we all do. The Death Wish, he said, is a destructive force inside human nature that shows its face whenever we consider a challenging, long-term course of action that might do for us, or others, something that's actually good.

Others refer to this as resistance. How many do you recognize as true for you?

- Self-sabotage
- Distraction
- Allowing others to sabotage your success
- Something else that stops you moving forward?

"Speak to your darkest: and most negative interior voices the way a hostage negotiator speaks to a violent psychopath. Calmly, but firmly. Most of all, never back down. You cannot afford to back down: The life you are negotiating to save after all, is your own," writes Elizabeth Gilbert, the author of *Eat. Pray Love*, in her book, *Big Magic*.

The more important taking action becomes to our personal growth and soul's evolution, the more resistance we can feel toward committing to it. This is why, so often, we know we'd be better off not having that extra drink, but we have it anyway.

The following activities, relevant to going sober, most commonly create resistance:

- The launching of any new venture
- Any kind of education and learning of new ways of thinking and being
- The pursuit of any life purpose or calling
- Any act that requires devotion or total commitment
- Taking a stand in the face of setbacks or adversity
- Any acts of courage, including the decision to change for the better some negative habit or toxic pattern or thought or behavior in ourselves

Take heart—resistance is normal! While you may have your work cut out for you, resistance, rather than being a personal failing, is a normal part of the change process. And you can beat it!

THE TUG OF WAR

Have you ever held two magnets in your hands, holding them close but not touching? You'll know then, the energy it takes to keep them apart. Resistance works in the same way. To resist is to struggle, or fight against something you are drawn to be or do. Think of it as a war—a war against your heart. A war against yourself.

A magnet creates an invisible area of magnetism all around it called a magnetic field. Your heart is your body's most powerful magnet. The heart, like the brain, generates a powerful electromagnetic field, McCraty explains in *The Energetic Heart*.

"The heart generates the largest electromagnetic field in the body. The electrical field as measured in an electrocardiogram (ECG) is about 60 times greater in amplitude than the brain waves recorded in an electroencephalogram (EEG)."

Numerous studies by the HeartMath Institute show this powerful electromagnetic field can be detected and measured several feet away from a person's body and between two individuals in close proximity.

So you'll appreciate that it takes a tremendous amount of energy to resist what you know in your heart you really desire.

The feeling of resistance reminds me of a young foal called Venus we were looking after on our rural property. Her owner came to take her to a new home where a young girl was happily waiting to care for her.

But Venus didn't know what the future held. She wanted to stay where she was and with who and what she knew. It was all she would ever know—unless she surrendered and moved to a new, fertile pasture and loving home.

I watched as her owner, unable to coax her to move of her own accord, dragged her from the field. Was it fear and a primal instinctive resistance that she found threatening?

Resistance can be traced to its evolutionary roots in genetics. The cure for humankind is to connect with a "higher realm." To let love, not fear, be your guiding light. This is the place where inspiration, or being in spirit, resides. It's the purpose and passion zone, and the place where magic and manifestation miracles really do happen.

WHY ARE YOU RESISTING?

Now you know that pursuing the best outcomes often meets with the greatest resistance. The things that you feel most scared or apprehensive about are the things that matter most.

Resistance is fueled by fear. It has no strength on its own. Gently accept and acknowledge your fears and then send them on their way and you will conquer resistance.

Perhaps like Venus, you find change threatening. Perhaps like my client Richard, a past story—one of hurt and disappointment—keeps replaying in your head. Or you may be like Katherine who has embarked on a journey of sobriety before and failed. She was worried about what the future held.

Failure is not fatal—plenty of people have fallen off their sobriety wagon. But, they didn't let a fall from grace, hold them back from another alcohol-free ride.

Will you have to be dragged kicking and screaming, rather than walk forward with confidence that you are in safe hands and all will be well? Have you forgotten the consequences of denying your path with heart? By resisting change are you suffering in the process, like Venus who tried to make a great escape and leaped the fence, hurting her leg as she fell?

Are you struggling like she did until she no longer had the strength to resist and surrendered? Are you waiting for someone to make the decisions for you until you have no choice but to change?

Perhaps you can relate to my story. When I stopped struggling and quit boozing because I finally got so sick of feeling shitty, tired and afraid. Maybe you don't want to wait until you're so fed up and stressed that your health is compromised.

"The enemy is a very good teacher," says the Dalai Lama. Whatever your situation, you'll find it helpful to clarify your sources of resistance and learn what needs to change. The following resistance quiz will shed some light so that you are better able to navigate the road ahead.

THE RESISTANCE QUIZ

Increase your awareness and prepare to take some empowered steps by taking the following resistance quiz.

How committed to achieving your best life are you? Do you:

1. Know what you want in your heart, and your gut, but resist taking action
2. Spend time doing anything but the thing which inspires you (drinking, watching television, hanging out with toxic friends etc.)
3. Allow your thoughts to be contaminated by fear, doubt, and other negative emotions like anxiety
4. Sabotage opportunities by breaking promises or not following through
5. Want certainty and absolute guarantees before committing to action
6. Opt for the comfort rut and 'easy fix' rather than embrace a new challenge
7. Do what's practical at the expense of what inspires you
8. Let laziness control you, suffocating your aspirations
9. Procrastinate, dither, make excuses and justifications to explain your lack of progress
10. Have a shopping list of reasons why you can't cut back or stop drinking
11. Consciously try to ignore or repress positive thoughts, feelings, or experiences
12. Take a stand against and actively oppose or block people, things and situations that could help you achieve your dreams
13. Pursue or fight for opportunities that don't excite you
14. Other

OR DO YOU:

1. Know what you want in your heart, and take steps, even small steps to make your dreams a reality
2. Feed your thoughts, and nourish your dreams with love, faith, and clarity
3. Answer the call for change by saying 'yes' to opportunities and following through
4. Act, despite uncertainty, and trust that when you do what you love all else will follow
5. Believe and tap into spiritual supply and providence to manifest your desires
6. Want to make yourself proud and live your best life
7. Proactively exercise good self-care and maintain a healthy balance
8. Regularly do what energizes you
9. Whip laziness into shape by taking inspired action
10. Work with a sense of urgency, knowing if not now, when?
11. Do what you love
12. Surround yourself with a vibe-tribe who inspire and support you
13. Pursue or fight for opportunities that do excite you
14. Other

YOUR ANSWERS to the above will help boost the necessary self-awareness to embrace positive change and design a plan of inspired action.

OVERCOMING RESISTANCE

To find success the following things are important:

- An overriding sense of your purpose for being here—your authentic calling
- A vision and an idea of the right direction for your work and life
- Consistent action and continually taking steps, i.e. doing what lies before you today, tomorrow, next week…
- A willingness to show up every day with your gifts and talents, often in the face of fear and resistance

BEGIN WITH THE END IN MIND

A very powerful strategy to overcome resistance is to begin with the end in mind. Tap into the power of your heart, see your end goal as already accomplished. Allow your body to feel the exact feelings you sense you'll feel when you have achieved your end goal. They may be, love, excitement, joy, satisfaction, or pride.

Draw a timeline. Mark on it the year and date when you would like your business to go live. Feel that goal as already achieved. Then look along that timeline and note all the steps and things you did to achieve your end goal. Note these on your timeline.

A timeline helps you see and feel the end result before you begin. It's a powerful and simple way to free up any perceived or real fears and blockages.

I like to think of all my goals as projects including sobriety. And I always like to visualize what it will feel like when I've actually finished a project. I don't want to wait until the project is finished. I want that feeling of achievement and excitement now! I'm also rewarded with a big juicy dopamine hit!

BUILDING THE HOME OF YOUR DREAMS

I applied this strategy when I visualized building a house on the back of my old villa in Wellington many years ago. At the time, everyone thought achieving my desire was an impossible dream. Even I knew it was audacious—I was a single working mother with no savings.

But I didn't let that stop me from throwing my energy into seeing the house built. To feed my desire and overcome resistance I imagined how beautiful my home could be. I felt the evening sun on my face.

I heard the birdsong in the trees. I saw every aspect of what I wanted—the colors, the expanses of glass. I felt the lovely stone bench tops. I tasted the meals I would cook for friends. I fed my motivation to actually build a house from scratch.

To feed my desire, generate ideas, increase clarity and fuel a sense of possibility I created image boards and gathered clippings of what I wanted to manifest.

I also broke the project into manageable chunks to avoid feeling overwhelmed and also to counteract my fears around cost escalations. I sourced my team—builders, architects, and other pros. In short, I began with the end in mind and broke the project into manageable steps and drew up a project plan.

Don't get me wrong—I am no passionate planner. I am naturally organic and spontaneous. But when the need and the desires arise we are all capable of mastering the skills we need. But first I worked to my preferences and strengths and began creatively.

I like creating projects because they make things seem more manageable. They usually have beginnings and endings, and often tangible concrete results.

Some of my projects have included things like publishing books, building websites, beginning a blog, creating companies and personal brands, generating products, and services, and customers.

As you start to surround yourself with tangible evidence of possibilities and to chart your progress, inspiration, desire, and love build. Suddenly your dreams are no longer dreams but living realities.

Be sure to include completion deadlines—these can flex if need be, but have a date to work towards. Reward yourself each time you complete a milestone; much like builders do when they have the roof shout.

Share your completion deadlines with a supportive cheerleader or nag buddy. This is the reason so many entrepreneurs use business coaches and mentors. Being accountable is motivating.

Unless you start taking action toward sobriety now, unless you're closer to achieving it than you were yesterday or will be tomorrow, your resistance will bury you.

Khalil Gibran said this poignantly when he wrote: "Verily the lust for comfort murders the passion of the soul, and then walks grinning to the funeral."

Cast off from those safe, but dull shores. Break free of the comfort rut and embrace the most comfortable feeling of all. Being sober! You'll discover your authentic self and your heart's desire.

WHAT MAKES YOU HAPPY? DO IT!

Revisit your goals and intentions and remind yourself why achieving them is important to you. Revisit your Sobriety Journal and add more inspiration to feed your heart and fuel your dreams.

Crack on and do what it takes to whip resistance into shape. Do more of what makes you happy and less of what no longer fills you with feelings of love. Do this with a sense of urgency before it is too late.

Trick yourself if need be by imagining you've been told you only have a year to live. Be life—don't just dream it!

"I am a writer," proclaims Elisabeth Gilbert, the best-selling author of *Eat, Pray, Love*, in her book, *Big Magic*. "This proclamation of intent and entitlement is not something you can do just once and then expect miracles; it's something you must do daily, forever.

"I've had to keep defining and defending myself as a writer every single day of my adult life—constantly reminding and re-reminding my soul and the cosmos that I'm very serious about the business of creative living, and that I will never stop creating, no matter what the outcome, and no matter how deep my anxieties and insecurities may be."

38

RIDE THE BUZZ OF THE HELPERS HIGH

Helping others is fundamental to a well-lived life and a core part of many successful therapies. AA, for example, is founded and run by alcoholics who help others. The core underlying principle is that this helps to diminish egocentrism which for many is a root cause of addiction.

Even when you don't want to, it is so easy to focus on your own pain. Focusing on someone else's suffering and feeling you can do something to help feels amazing.

The compelling evidence shows that staying sober by being of service to others feels good and it works.

The helper therapy principle (HTP) is that when helpers help a fellow sufferer they help themselves. The HTP is reflected in the stated purpose of Alcoholics Anonymous (AA): "Our primary purpose is to stay sober and help other alcoholics to achieve sobriety."

The 12th Step integrates spirituality and the principle of service: "Having had a spiritual awakening as the result of these steps, we tried to carry this message to alcoholics, and to practice these principles in all our affairs."

AA also makes focusing less on yourself and more on being of service, abundantly clear, "Our very lives, as ex-problem drinkers, depend upon our constant thought of others and how we may help meet their needs"

Thus, the message is conveyed that sobriety is gained in AA by constant attention to helping other alcoholics. AAH behaviors include acts of good citizenship as a member of a 12-Step program (i.e., putting away chairs at meetings, donating money), formal service positions available in AA (i.e., public outreach, etc.), and transmitting personal experience to another fellow sufferer (i.e., sharing one's story or progress with step work).

The word *constant* indicates that this concern with helping other drinkers must become an enduring daily practice to keep the disease of addiction in remission. "Helping others is the foundation stone of your recovery. A kindly act once in a while isn't enough. You have to act the Good Samaritan every day, if need be."

You don't have to be a member of AA to ride the buzz of the helpers high, random acts of kindness, sharing your personal story of recovery, writing a book like this, or a multitude of other ways you can help someone stay sober, including not rubbishing people, or insisting they have another, when they say they don't drink, all help.

Some people opt to become skilled helpers and train as addiction or trauma counselors, psychologists, and wellness coaches.

I read recently of an 18-year-old teen, Maddi Anderson, whose crippling social anxiety and depression robbed her of the will to go outside. But then she got involved with her mother creating customized packs for people suffering cancer, the loss of a relative, or hard times. She's also started a "Random Acts of Kindness" initiative in the region.

Anderson says she loves bringing cheer to other people. Her love of helping others lifted her depression and she now dedicates her spare time to personally delivering packages to those in need. So, while she's not battling booze, she once battled depression and anxiety—which drives many people to drink. Her inspiring story is further evidence of how turning your focus to help others can bounce back to benefit you.

Here are just a few of the many mood-enhancing, life-affirming benefits of helping others:

- Increases our sense of purpose
- Has an immediate impact on your psyche
- Triggers the release of endorphins, dopamine and other reward-fuelled biochemicals
- Reminds us of the real world, beyond our fixation with ourselves, and fake social media and picture-perfect celebrities
- Reminds us that many people struggle, and this normalizes our own suffering
- Highlights how much is good in our life when we see how others suffer
- Enables us to truly connect with people, and witness how our efforts truly make a difference in others' lives

Try to weave helping others into your daily living in a sustainable, habitual way that goes beyond the quick endorphin highs that result from random acts of kindness.

Consider making a stand for greater alcohol reform and help for those struggling with addiction.

39

MOOD FOOD

As I shared earlier and in my book *Developing a Millionaire Mindset* successful people make their health a priority and regularly tune into their body barometers.

It's tougher to control your drinking if you lack energy, feel stressed, sluggish, lethargic, or unhealthy. Artificially stimulating your mind, body, and soul with alcohol won't cut it in the long term. You know this, right?

But despite the World Cancer Research fund recently reporting that a staggering 40 percent of cancers could be prevented by healthy diet and lifestyle, and the clear link between alcohol abuse and many preventable cancers, many of us don't value our health.

I call this, "Itwonthappentomeistitis."

Alcohol abuse is ballooning. Diabetes is on the rise. Obesity is an epidemic. Cholesterol and blood pressure are going through the roof. And stress, depression, anxiety, and other mental troubles are all trending upward.

Modern nutritionists and health professionals warn of the perils of not only drinking too much alcohol and consuming too much sugar, but also over- and under-eating; not eating fresh, seasonal, organic food; and chewing insufficiently.

In fact, we often take for granted how magnificent and clever our bodies are.

You are what you feed your stomach—which also feeds your mind. For optimum performance, ensure you're putting smart fuel into your body.

As I've said earlier, your gut is also your second brain—a major receptor site of dopamine, a neurotransmitter that helps control the brain's reward and pleasure centers.

Dopamine helps regulate the feel-good emotions we all need to fuel success. It also regulates movement—enabling you to not only see the rewards of your efforts but to also take action towards them.

For feel-good neurons to fire optimally, you need to fuel it with food geared for performance, eat mindfully, and not inhale your meal in a race to the finish.

Benefits of healthy eating practices include:

- Increased clarity of thinking
- Better memory
- Healthy body weight
- Increased positive emotions
- Enhanced mental, emotional, and physical health
- Improved mood
- More energy and stamina
- Increased goal achievement
- Better sleep
- Longevity

Avoid extremes—too much sloth makes one prone to gluttony, too much activity overwhelms, and too many vain pleasures taken to extremes are a cause of failure.

Too much coffee, for example, increases feelings of anxiety. Too much booze can send your stress levels soaring.

When you switch from eating unhealthily to healthily, the difference will be tangibly transformative.

Don't forget to set yourself up for a bouncy day by eating a nourishing breakfast. Too many people skip this important start to the day.

At first glance, **porridge** might not seem like the most exciting breakfast on the planet. But it's great for your health and way better than a greasy fry-up. One bowl of porridge contains more fiber than a slice of wholemeal bread and is rich in minerals including copper, iron and manganese.

It's also been proven to prevent blood sugar spikes, due to the low glycemic index of oats.

LISTED BELOW ARE some helpful energy-enhancing, mood-boosting food tips:

• Eat small but regular meals to sustain energy levels and keep blood sugar levels steady

• Meat and fish contain beneficial amounts of iron, as do green leafy vegetables, dried apricots, lentils and other pulses

• Make sure you get sufficient amounts of B-group vitamins, particularly riboflavin, which converts carbohydrates into energy; vitamin B6 essential for energy metabolism; and vitamin B12, required for forming red blood cells that carry oxygen throughout the body. Useful sources of B-group vitamins include whole grains, chicken, fish, eggs, dairy produce, pulses, shellfish and red meat.

- Help your body absorb more iron by drinking a glass of orange juice once a day with a meal. Vitamin C also helps to boost energy

- Other vital minerals include magnesium, which works with potassium and sodium to ensure the efficient working of muscles, along with zinc, which protects against viral infections that often precede chronic fatigue

Avoid

- Sugary foods, including biscuits, cakes, and chocolate. These also promote short-term energy highs, leading to irritability and lethargy

- Alcohol in large quantities

- Refined carbohydrates in foods like white bread, pasta, and rice. These destabilize energy levels by causing a sharp increase in blood sugar levels.

It's easy to miss meals or reach for crap when you're busy, or stressed, so plan ahead. Your body, mind and spirit will love you back.

AVOID OVER-STIMULATION

Sometimes the best way to feel great is to eat what you don't want, drink what you don't like, and do what you'd rather avoid.

Knock things like coffee, caffeinated drinks and foods, alcohol, and nicotine off your list (or at least limit your intake).

These trigger the production of the stress-related hormone adrenaline —which increases your heart rate, prompts the liver to release more sugar into your bloodstream, and makes the lungs take in more oxygen.

While these things may give you a short-term high, in the long run, the result is fatigue and low energy levels. This, in turn, leads to a vicious cycle of relying on more stimulants to get you through the day.

The impact of excessive coffee and caffeinated drinks has become such a health-hazard, a new disorder, Caffeine Use Disorder, was recently added to the DSM-V—the tool psychologists, psychiatrists, and other mental-health professionals often refer to prior to making their diagnosis.

Are you addicted to caffeine?

If you've experienced these three symptoms within the past year—you may be in trouble:

- You have a persistent desire to give up or cut down on caffeine use, or you've tried to do so unsuccessfully.
- You continue to use caffeine despite knowing it contributes to recurring physical or psychological problems for you (like insomnia, or jitteriness).
- You experience withdrawal symptoms if you don't have your usual amount of caffeine.

Many of my clients notice reduced levels of anxiety, irritability, and depression when they kick the habit. They also report feeling better able to cope with stress, once the coffee habit is culled.

Opt for a natural high. Consider replacing caffeine, alcohol, nicotine and other stimulants with fresh juices, exercise, meditation, or some other activity which makes you feel great and sustains energy. Herbal teas are also healthy, caffeine-free alternatives. Try to drink 6-8 glasses (1.7-2 liters) of water a day to boost energy and flush out toxins.

Less artificial stimulation means more natural life-affirming highs.

JUST ADD WATER

As blood is to your heart, so water is to your body. Our bodies are machines, designed to run on water and minerals. Because we're made up of 72 percent of water, it's vitally important for every bodily function—especially to your liver as we've already discussed.

Insufficient water intake and low consumption of fruit and vegetables can present significant health challenges.

Too much coffee, alcohol, or other diuretics (which increase the amount of water and salt expelled from the body as urine) can also rob your mind and body of energy and vitality.

When you're dehydrated, your thoughts become muddled, anxiety can loom, and you'll feel tired, irritable, unmotivated, and generally lackluster.

In addition to drinking H_2O, many people also find gazing upon or immersing themselves in a body of natural water promotes a positive mindset.

It's no coincidence that most millionaires have houses overlooking water.

I love to bathe in the hot mineral waters at Ngawha Springs in the far north of New Zealand. Local Maori have long known of the therapeutic properties of bathing in its waters. Even if I feel low, I always emerge feeling great, and my energy and health are always instantly restored.

Create more energy and drive by flushing toxins from your body as well as increasing your connection with water. Some simple, but effective strategies include:

- Drinking at least eight glasses of purified water a day
- Reducing alcohol and coffee

- Consuming more fruits and vegetables—as close to raw as possible
- Splash water on your face whenever you're feeling overwhelmed. Cold water steps up circulation, making you feel invigorated
- Swim in the sea or a lake, or bathe in hot mineral water—either in a natural spring or by adding Epsom Salts (a mineral compound of magnesium and sulfate) to your bath.

40

STEP AWAY

Workaholism is an addiction for many passionate people. Others use overwork to medicate their unhappiness in other areas of their life—most commonly dissatisfaction with their relationships.

When you work slavishly, particularly at something you love, your brain releases chemicals called opiates which create feelings of euphoria. No wonder it's hard to step away!

Euphoria stems from the Greek word *euphoría*—the power of enduring easily. But consider what the state of endurance implies. Enduring implies force or strain, or gritting your teeth and bearing it at times. Force or strain with no respite leads to stress, overload, and burnout—robbing you of vital energy and depleting your millionaire mindset.

Many people find when they don't step away from their work they suffer disillusionment, and things that once filled them with passion, including their current writing projects, no longer fills them with joy. Resentment builds and relationships with family, friends, and colleagues can also suffer.

Working addictively offers a short-term fix, but lasting happiness needs variety and nourishment. Being with family or friends, engaging in a hobby, spending time in nature, learning something new, helping others, or just being solitary will help you avoid burnout, nourish your brain, heart, and soul, improve your judgment, and restore harmony.

To be truly happy and successful, you must be able to be at peace when you are working and when you are at rest.

Leonardo da Vinci would often take breaks from his work to refresh his mind and spirit. While others claimed that he took too long to finish things, he knew the importance of replenishing his focus to maintain a clear perspective.

Here we are still talking about him over 500 years later.

"Every now and then go away, have a little relaxation, for when you come back to your work your judgment will be surer. Go some distance away because then the work appears smaller and more of it can be taken in at a glance and a lack of harmony and proportion is more readily seen," he once said.

Leonardo also valued sleep, noting in one of his journals that some of his best insights came when his mind was not working.

Even if you love the work that you do, and think your current obsession is the greatest thing since women were allowed to vote, it's fun to get away from it and have objective-free time to unwind and reset.

One of my author friends shared recently how she was feeling totally overwhelmed and close to burnout. To sustain her life, and her career, she's promising herself a reward for all her long hours—three-months off over winter. She's planning to go on a retreat, somewhere warm, maybe the Bahamas or Mexico.

"The whole point of living life is to enjoy it, right?! I'm coming to grips with that mindset," she wrote to me.

Schedule time out—and be firm with yourself. Stay away from anything that feeds your addiction.

When you return to your work, your focus will be surer, your vision refreshed, and your confidence bolder.

REST

When your stress levels are high and you get depressed, angry, tense, and lethargic, or begin to experience tension headaches, it should be a very simple biofeedback signal that you need to stop, re-evaluate your choices and take some time out.

Sometimes this can be easier said than done. In our overachiever, over-stimulated society, where many people spend more hours every week with their eyes riveted to their iPhone, instead of spending quality time on their own or with family and friends, the whole concept of stopping and resting to restore ourselves seems unusual. But resting to replenish is essential to well-being.

We're pushing ourselves all day long with energy that we don't have. The most common complaint people take to the doctor is fatigue. Research conducted by a company helping people suffering from adrenal fatigue claims that 80% of people don't have as much energy as they'd like to have.

"It's because we're pushing and using caffeine, sugar and energy drinks and nicotine and stress for energy rather than running on our own energy."

Long-term stress and long-term cortisol will literally alter a person's hormonal profile.

Rest allows the adrenal glands to restore, enabling cortisol levels to return to normal. Long-term stress and long-term cortisol overload can lead to adrenal fatigue and burn-out, altering your hormonal profile, changing your personality, and making it more difficult to return to the real, inspired, happy and creative you.

Give yourself permission to take time every day and every week to have fun, rest your mind and rest your body.

GET OUTSIDE

It's hard to feel fantastic when you're suffering from low mood. Very often a lack of outside time is the culprit. You're like a flower—you need at least 20 minutes of sunlight every day just to make your hormones work effectively and enable you to blossom to your fullest potential.

To feel and behave normally you need to be exposed to full-spectrum daylight on a regular basis. Medical research suggests some people need as much as two hours a day of sunlight to avoid Seasonal Affective Disorder.

Combine outside time with exercise like walking and not only will you get the light you need, but you'll also recharge your batteries.

Walking outside can also help you gain a new perspective on a troubling situation. When you for a walk, you increase the electrical activity in your brain, and you breathe negative ions and see three-dimensionally.

All this helps you see with fresh eyes the things which are worrying you. Often you'll find that things are not as bad as they first appear, or discover a relatively simple solution.

Monitor how much time you spend indoors. Bounce away from habits that so many people have, like spending too many hours inside in front of two-dimensional computer monitors and TV screens, and then topping off a 12-hour day at work by trying to read themselves to sleep on their Kindle. These are all two-dimensional visual activities, which seldom spark joy.

Let mother earth, the sea, and the infinite sky boost your mood. Get outside and allow the sun and outside energy to lift your spirits. Schedule regular fresh air time. Improve your breathing, and take a brisk walk to increase your oxygen levels.

41

LAUGH AND PLAY

Laughter, humor, and play are great tonics during stressful times. Taking yourself or your life too seriously only increases stress. When you learn to laugh despite your difficulties, you light up the world.

"When people just look at your face," the Dalai Lama said to the Archbishop Desmond Tutu in *The Book of Joy*, "you are always laughing, always joyful. This is a very positive message. It is much better when there is not too much seriousness. Laughter, joking is much better. Then we can be completely relaxed."

Laughter triggers the release of endorphins, your brain's feel-good chemicals, setting off an emotional reaction which makes you feel better.

"Discovering more joy does not, I'm sorry to say, save us from the inevitability of hardship and heartbreak. In fact, we may cry more easily, but we will laugh more easily, too," says Archbishop Tutu.

"Perhaps we are just more alive. Yet as we discover more joy, we can face suffering in a way that ennobles rather than embitters. We have hardship without becoming hard. We have heartbreak without being broken."

You have to be able to laugh at, with, in spite of, yourself—and whatever situation you find yourself in. Have you ever wondered why?

As I write this, we're thigh deep in mud during our home renovations. It's summer, it's not supposed to rain!

I went in search of scientific articles to validate what I already knew—humor is a fantastic antidote to stress. But I wanted to know what was happening in my brain when I decided to look at something in a more humorous and positive light.

An article posted in Science Direct cited numerous studies validating the benefits of nurturing laughter.

"Without humor, life would undeniably be less exhilarating. Indeed, the ability to comprehend and find a joke funny plays a defining role in the human condition, essentially helping us to communicate ideas, attract partners, boost mood, and even cope in times of trauma and stress," the authors say.

These beneficial manifestations are complemented physiologically, including acting as a natural stress antagonist and possibly enhancing the cardiovascular, immune, and endocrine systems.

Some studies the report says, "have documented increased hemodynamic signal in the mesolimbic dopaminergic reward system, a system known to play a pivotal role in drug reward and motivational behaviors.

"This system encompasses a variety of distinct, but interconnected, dopamine-enriched structures, including the ventral striatum/nucleus accumbens, the ventral tegmental area, and the amygdala." fMRI studies also reveal important clues about the neurological systems involved in regulating reward.

All good to know—and more fuel for reminding myself to create more space to laugh and play.

So instead of wallow in misery, the builders and I stood around and cracked a few jokes and laughed a lot.

"I'm going back to play in the mud," one of them said, whistling as he walked back to work.

Personally, as we all headed straight back into the sludge, I didn't feel the difference in my brain, but I did in my heart. *We love mud,* I affirmed. Okay, I'm lying, but the truth is after joking around it did feel better.

The other thing that helped was playing with my camera for a moment. Using my macro lens and my iPhone I took several stunning photos of a frog surrounded by muddy water. I posted the photo on my blog —http://www.cassandragaisford.com/happy-as-a-frog-in-the-mud-why-laughter-and-play-are-drug-free-antidotes-to-stress/

You may not feel like it, but give laughter a go. Watch a funny movie, stream a stack of whacky comedies, go to a comedy show, or watch a video on YouTube. Hang out with people who know how to have a good time, go to a Laughing Yoga class, or ask someone to tickle you!

Inject some more laughter and playfulness into your life.

Playfulness is bounciness at its best. Cultivate your inner child. Act up a little, goof-off, experiment, relax and detach—if you find yourself in trouble, smile.

Benefits of play include:

• Increasing your productivity

• Boosting your creativity and problem-solving skills

• Reducing stress, anxiety, and depression

• Improving your relationships and connections with others

- Bringing more balance, fun, lightness, and levity into your life

- Diminishing your worries

As play researcher and psychiatrist Stuart Brown says in his book *Play: How it Shapes the Brain, Opens the Imagination, and Invigorates the Soul*, "A lack of play should be treated like malnutrition: it's a health risk to your body and mind."

The Dalai Lama agrees. "I met some scientists in Japan, and they explained that wholehearted laughter—not artificial laughter—is very good for your heart and your health in general."

Some of the many ways I play include: 'wagging' work sometimes and taking my inner child on a playdate to the movies, going for a massage, or indulging in my hobbies and playing with my paints. Listening to music from the 70s is also playful and brings levity. While traveling internationally recently, I watched the Disney children's movie *Frozen*. I haven't laughed so much in years.

I also love reminding myself of the magic of writing and reading. As novelist Caroline Gordon once wrote, "A well-composed book is a magic carpet on which we are wafted to a world that we cannot enter in any other way."

Author Deepak Chopra confirms the power of lightening up, "When we harness the forces of harmony, joy, and love, we create success and good fortune with effortless ease," Chopra says.

Check out my blog for some strategies to reinforce play and create more bounciness in your day—http://bit.ly/29RPQis

42

COLOR YOUR MOOD

Color has a profound effect on us at all levels—physical, mental, emotional, and spiritual.

We live in a world where color dominates our lives, from reading signs on the road to identifying ripe fruit by its color.

Color affects our moods. Blue is calming. Red can make us tense. Green can boost our vitality. We use and react to color every day in our lives without even realizing or appreciating it.

You'll note that the ability of color to influence your purchasing decisions doesn't escape the booze barons, something I discussed in the chapter, *Be Wary of What Catches Your Eye.*

Rather than rely on booze to lift your spirits, decide on the mood you want to be in and choose a color that boosts these feelings. For example, if you want to feel calm, you may choose green or blue. If you want to feel joy, yellows, golds, or oranges may tip the balance in your favor.

Remember that color is individually perceived, so choose what works for you. On some days red may make you feel energized, on others it may fuel feelings of anger or aggression.

You may want to wear your bouncy color in items of clothing, or just to have a small dose of color nearby to prompt these feelings along–for example, it may be some color on your desktop or on a prompt card by your PC or in your wallet.

Wearing color also sparks joy in others. As a shop assistant recently said to me, "You've just made my day with how pink and sparkly you are."

The right color can also empower you and give you the courage and strength of a warrior. During a particularly stressful time in my life, and that of my daughter's, I had to rescue her from the clutches of a former patched gang member. It was like a scene in a movie. I wore white. White lace, in fact. Elegant, chic, peaceful—and regal. He wore black. Dark. Low. Fierce.

Before I arrived to meet him in the hope of retrieving my daughter, I visualized white light all around me. I prayed for help from my angels and guides, and importantly I sent love to this wounded, but dangerous man. Love and the white light won. He surrendered my daughter back to me—something this dominating, controlling man had previously refused to do.

What colors feed your courage? What hues boost your resilience? What color is sobriety to you? Surround yourself with colors that empower you and spark joy and banish those that don't.

43

GO LOW

When life knocks you flat exercise self-compassion and give yourself permission to go low.

It's important to value less-than-positive feelings in equal measure—many times going low is an essential part of your healing process. Remind yourself that grief, loss and the disappointment you feel when you lose someone or something you love, are natural and valid emotions.

Similarly, when you suffer a setback it's natural to be hacked off, hurt or sad.

It's difficult to bounce back when you feel flat. But you must be true to yourself and allow your emotions to be felt and expressed, or risk them doing a sit-in, and being unwilling to budge.

The trick is not to stay low. Be watchful and know when a low mood has the potential to cross the threshold into clinical depression.

Your ability to bounce-back will only stay low if you hold it down and don't take proactive action to help elevate your mood. This may be simply talking to someone, sharing your emotions with a friend or a skilled professional like a counselor, or allowing yourself some time to dress in black.

Sometimes, medical intervention may be required to help you cope with extreme and entrenched cases of low mood.

Practicing some of the other mood enhancing strategies in this book, or recalling a time where you felt similarly stuck and remembering the things that helped you bounce back, may also help you recover your vitality.

If you're worried that you may be clinically depressed don't be too proud to ask for help. You don't have to suffer alone.

All suffering will pass. Any darkness you feel engulfing you right now may just be the experience that will move you into a new authentic expression of your soul. As day follows night, so will light come after a dark period of the soul.

ALWAYS BOUNCE BACK

Resilient people are flexible, they bend with the winter gales and arch with the summer breeze. When the fury of a hurricane knocks them down, they get back up again—and it's the getting back up that elevates your bounce.

When you get back up life will reward you for your efforts. It may not be instant, it may not happen the very same day, but it will happen. That's what you must keep believing in.

What is certain is that unless you put in the energy nothing good will happen at all.

Taking empowered action may result in better health, improved relationships, improved finances, and respect and admiration from people for your courage, tenacity and perseverance.

"You're like a cat with nine lives," a friend once said to me, following my particularly traumatic breakup. "You always land on your feet."

I've been a single mother, receiving no financial support from my daughter's father. I survived a very challenging childhood. I've experienced the most horrific workplace bullying. I've been physically assaulted, intimidated and threatened. And I've also had to rescue my daughter from the fists of a violent man.

I've had to face my fears of public speaking, criticism, failure and standing out. I've had to empower my mind, body and spirit with new tools—many of which I have shared in this book. Meditation, mind power, spiritual-based practices, nutrition, counseling, reading self-empowerment books, like this one—and more.

I've worked hard to cultivate courage, optimism and resilience. In fact, one lady I worked with once said, "You know what your problem is Cassandra? You're too happy."

I knew the bigger problem, the one that lurked inside, was a tendency to be too sad. I decided what I wanted more of...

Happiness.

Feeling sad, staying down—well, it just doesn't spark joy.

I know what it's like to feel so low that you don't think you can go on. I know what it's like to contemplate ending your life. I know a great many people feel the same. And it's these people, the ones with the will to survive who work everyday, as the Dalai Lama urges, to cultivate happiness, optimism, a resilient mindset—and to pay it forward by helping others.

As Robbie Williams once sang, "I get knocked down, but I get back up again. You're never gonna keep me down."

And you can, and will too.

44

REAL RESILIENCE

Ups and downs, highs and lows, troughs and peaks are a rite of passage for all of us.

The fickleness and unpredictability of fluctuating income, the extremities of your emotions, the quick and ready insights you experience, or the acute sensitivity with which you feel almost everything, can make you vulnerable.

But it doesn't have to be this way. By strengthening your inner power, your ability to handle stressful situations, and your skill in persevering after setbacks threaten to topple you, you'll empower and fortify yourself and develop resilient grit.

Grit comes in many shapes and sizes: courageousness, bravery, pluck, mettle, backbone, spirit, steel nerve, resolve, determination, endurance, guts, spunk, tenacity—and the strength of vulnerability. Add the flexibility and determination of resilience and you'll have a winning combination to bounce through life.

Resilience is that indefinable quality that allows some people to be bowled over by life and re-emerge stronger than ever. Rather than letting setbacks overcome them and drain their resolve, they find a way to rise from the ashes.

Psychologists have identified some of the factors that will make you more resilient, among them a positive attitude, optimism, the ability to regulate emotions, and the ability to see failure as a form of helpful feedback.

Life will keep throwing you curveballs— your relationship may turn toxic, job stress may take a toll, life may not take the turn you hoped, a friend or lover may betray you. Or perhaps life threatens to drown you in a deluge of seemingly never-ending hassles: family dramas, environmental mayhem, world affairs, or some other distraction.

As Buddhists say, life is suffering—it's how you react to a setback that counts. We choose our attitude via our thoughts. "With our thoughts, we make the world," Buddha once said.

Importantly, I hope your thoughts will turn to hope—not drinking alcohol—to alleviate your stress. The hope that things will get better. The hope that whatever is getting you down will pass. The hope that having reached the bottom, the rollercoaster of life will track upward again.

Many brilliant minds believe in the magic and resilient power of optimism. Leonardo da Vinci once wrote, "One's thoughts turn towards hope."

The magic of hope is grounded firmly in spiritual and religious practices but also in science. Like the ancient Greeks and Romans, da Vinci, and even 18th-century physicians, recognized the physiological effects of mind-power and hope on the body.

Successful medical outcomes, even when the intervention is a placebo, further evidence the impact of maintaining a positive expectation.

Dr. Joe Dispenza powerfully illustrates this fact in his fabulous book *You Are the Placebo: Making Your Mind Matter*.

If like me, and Joe Dispenza, you've manifested miracles in your own life by maintaining a positive expectation, you'll know the power of hope.

Thoughts *do* become things. Scientists Gregg Braden and Bruce Lipton, author of *The Biology of Belief,* have evidenced this.

But hope can only flourish when you believe that what you do can make a difference, that you recognize that you have choices and that your actions can create a future which differs from your present situation. Hope also requires faith.

When you empower your belief in your ability to gain some control over your circumstances and your drinking you are no longer entirely at the mercy of forces outside yourself. You're back in the driving seat.

Many of the strategies I've shared with you in this book will help you develop more empowerment in many areas of your life and with it more staying power, passion, perseverance, and grit.

Testing your knowledge, focusing on the benefits of sobriety, acknowledging wounds that may need healing, understanding the neurology of addiction, and how more mindfulness can help you avoid excessive alcohol consumption, are just some of the sobriety techniques you've learned in *The Sobriety Experiment.*

Avoiding being sucked in by sugar and sweet-talking salesmen and slick one-sided marketing campaigns, are some of the other strategies you've mastered. Importantly, you've learned to value and trust your own experience.

Keeping your thoughts positive, surrounding yourself with a vibe tribe of supporters, getting rid of toxicity (friends, family, or stinkin' thinkin'), meditating, exercise, reprogramming your subconscious beliefs, and other empowering strategies, will help you keep alcohol where it should be—within your control.

But, as someone said to me recently, "Life's hard enough without having to do all this 'feel good' stuff." That, dear reader, comes down to choice. Your choice.

Personally, I don't want to live, nor end my life, as the author F. Scott Fitzgerald did—a poor drunk who felt like a failure and only found success when he was dead.

I don't want to lie in my grave like Amy Winehouse, a dead, tortured "success" at 27—all because she had refused help to overcome her demons and change her mindset. What a sad and tragic waste of talent and potential.

It's not easy to overcome many of the things that hold you back. But you can do it—if you're willing to be strong and fight for your well-being, happiness, and audacious dreams. Within many of us lies an innate seam of strength, which, when mined skilfully, will produce an endless source of pure gold.

As Buddha once said, "It is better to conquer yourself than to win a thousand battles. Then the victory is yours. It cannot be taken from you, not by angels or by demons, heaven or hell."

If fear, wounds of the past, victim thinking, destructive health behaviors, or anything else detrimental to living your best life has a grip on you, prioritize breaking free.
Seeking help doesn't have to cost a fortune. You may heal your life with writing, work with a coach or therapist, or self-help your way to success.

When you seize the reins of control and take responsibility, you will empower your life—and your prosperity.

Let experience be your guide, as it was Leonardo's. Give your brain a well-needed break. Let go of 'why' and embrace how you feel or how you want to feel. Honor the messages from your intuition and follow your path with heart.

45

HOW TO PARTY SOBER

Happily, changing attitudes to alcohol means it's suddenly super cool to be teetotal. Think no hangover, no waking up next to a stranger with a total lack of recall, bye-bye blackouts, vomiting in a bowl, being sick as a dog or generally feeling lousy the next day.

Imagine waking every morning feeling clearheaded, fresh, on-fire and jumping for joy, eager to kick off your day.

In the early days of sobriety partying sober can seem challenging—and often is. Pressure to drink can come in ever increasing waves. It's not uncommon for people to feel bullied, manipulated to drink, or to find yourself roped into a booze-fuelled all-nighter—all despite your iron-clad best intentions to adhere to your sobriety oath.

"I do feel pressure to drink around friends," said one of the respondents of my sobriety questionnaire. "I believe I could go without alcohol, but my lifestyle over the years has been built on social situations where my friends and I drink. There are many bars in Chicago and they tend to be where friends meet up."

85.71 percent of respondents to the Sobriety Questionnaires aid they feel they must drink to get ahead or be accepted at work. Wow! No wonder so many people are disengaged.

Lack of confidence and self-esteem also rated highly, and a whopping hundred percent said improving their happiness without alcohol seemed out of their control—they'd love to stop drinking but they didn't know how.

Hopefully after reading this book, you now know how to be happier without alcohol.

When it comes to socializing, as I mentioned earlier, a flurry of alcohol-free venues and socializing opportunities are sprouting globally which of course makes it easier to abstain.

However, the odds are extremely high that you'll find yourself in social situations which may test your self-control.

Elle Magazine recently ran an article highlighting how to party sober. Their advice is to head for places that make sobriety fun.

Actually, you can make sobriety fun any place, any time—it all starts and ends in your mind. Of course you may need to amp up and apply all your coping skills—many of which I've shared in this book.

Don't tell yourself it will be hard, and don't buy into the fear you won't cope if you don't drink. Feel your way through the discomfort. You know the saying, "when you do the thing you fear, the death of fear is certain."

The same goes for anxiety, or whatever else may cause you to scull a vodka cruiser or opt for a night of binge drinking just to fit in.

Believe me, when I say, you can party sober. I gave up drinking before Christmas 2017, did the whole family get-together sober, and then spent 2-weeks alcohol-free in a booze-soaked resort in the Pacific Islands. Easy-peasy. Plus I saved buckets of money too!

Below are a few tips to help you party sober:

1. **Treat sobriety like a scientific experiment in human behavior**—study how booze affects people around you. This doesn't mean you have to judge or place yourself in a morally superior mindset. Just observe. Slurring words, spilled drinks, inappropriate sexual moves, aggression—observing the natural and predictable path alcohol weaves through people's behavior is truly sobering.
2. **Excuse yourself early**—either in total, or in part. Sometimes I disappear for a while, gain more energy and come back to join the party, or leave early. I either make an acceptable excuse or don't say anything at all. I manage Christmas parties and family get-togethers really well this way. If people are partying at my place I simply go to bed. Time has shown me that people either don't mind, don't notice, or don't remember your absence.
3. **Arm yourself with your go-to-sobriety drink**. I often order cocktails but ask the bar staff to take out the alcohol. Or, I pour my sparking water into a sexy glass—no one knows and no one cares. You don't have to make a fuss about it.
4. **Remind yourself why you're not drinking and be selective with whom you share your news with.** Not everyone is as accepting as others. I can't be bothered justifying my choices or engaging in some insane dialogue. Again, experience has shown me you can't always predict people's reactions. Some people feel threatened when you don't drink, or feel you are moralizing—even though you're not. You're just not drinking. Full stop.
5. **Exercise prior to partying, meditate, or amp up your yoga to release a heady mix of endorphins** and natural opiates. Your naturally high will surpass and outlast synthetics every time!
6. **Socialize with sober people or stay in!**

"I'M NOT DRINKING," AND OTHER REPLIES

People will inevitably ask you why you're not drinking. Many will genuinely be impressed. Others less so. Many people can be uber sensitive when you start to scale back.

Happily, there is a growing acceptance of not drinking, and even better a great reverence for people who do life sober.

In 2018 Elle Magazine reported that the average volume of alcohol consumed per capita in Australia hit a 55-year low, dropping 9.37 litres in 2016-17. At the same time, the number of people under 25 who are choosing to abstain from alcohol is increasing.

It's a worldwide trend and proof of the importance people are placing on their wellbeing.

Below is a smorgasbord of a few responses to select from if you ever feel lost for words when it comes to explaining your sobriety:

"I'm not drinking—no, I'm not pregnant. I'm just not into alcohol." (yes people actually ask that!)

"No, I don't have a problem drinking—I have a problem stopping. I love it too much."

"I'm on a break."

"I'm allergic to ethanol."

"It's my New Years resolution—not to ingest poison."

"Hit me with vitamin C—make mine an orange juice."

Consider adopting Deepak Chopra's empowering lines, "I gave up alcohol. I enjoyed it far too much, to the point where I frequently get intoxicated. Everything in my life changed for the better when I stopped. It was the right decision."

Or, more easily still, avoid all the conversations about why, how and when and arm yourself with decoy drinks—they look like alcohol, but they're not alcohol.

You'll find a few of my favorite recipes from *Mind Over Mojitos: How Moderating Your Drinking Can Change Your Life: Easy Alcohol-Free Recipes for Happier Hours & a Joy Filled Life,* in the excerpt at the end of this book.

I invite you to visit my YouTube channel and watch my video, *How To Party Sober.*

FREE WORKBOOK!

The Passion Journal: The Effortless Path to Manifesting Your Love, Life, and Career Goals

Thank you for your interest in my new book.
To show my appreciation, I'm excited to be giving you another book for FREE!

Download the free *Passion Journal Workbook* here>>https://dl.bookfunnel.com/aepj97k2n1

I hope you enjoy it—it's dedicated to helping you live and work with passion, resilience and joy.

You'll also be subscribed to my newsletter and receive free giveaways, insights into my writing life, new release advance alerts and inspirational tips to help you live and work with passion, joy, and prosperity. Opt out at anytime.

CONCLUSION

CONCLUSION

CONCLUSION

Throughout *The Sobriety Experiment* you've discovered ways to find happiness, overcome adversity, build resilience, and increase joy by intensifying your desire, and increasing your ability to cope with stress, setbacks and disappointment.

And you've discovered ways to feed your soul and achieve your highest potential—following your passion, jumping with joy and bouncing high…and much more.

Positive health behaviors including journaling, meditation, regular exercise, good diet, relaxation exercises, and rest are a few of the many techniques we've covered. You've also created ways to cultivate positive addictions that result in natural healthy highs.

SUMMARY OF HOLISTIC STRATEGIES

Listed below are some helpful reminders of some of the many holistic coping strategies you can call upon during times of need and to boost your mood:

Behavioral

- Reducing or eliminating alcohol (of course!)
- Balanced lifestyle
- Support groups/Counseling
- Sharing with friends and family
- Humor
- New interests/activities
- Hobbies
- Socializing
- Entertaining
- Taking time out
- Music/dancing/singing/creative expression
- Meditating

CONCLUSION

- Yoga
- Being proactive and taking control of situations
- Change careers
- Making time to do nothing at all

Physical

- Learning to listen to your body
- Adequate exercise
- Physical touch/massage
- Muscle relaxation
- Sleep
- Relaxation breathing
- Healthy diet, i.e. reducing stimulants, increasing water, and eating organic non-processed foods
- Yoga
- Massage

Cognitive / Perceptual (thinking)

- Critical thinking regarding the truth of alcohol
- Analysis of why you drink
- Rational thinking techniques to help change the way you interpret stressful situations
- Positive thinking/cultivating optimism
- Self-assertion training
- Personal development
- Building self-esteem
- Priority clarification
- Reflection
- Mindfulness
- Acceptance/forgiveness
- Hypnosis
- CBT/REBT

- Trusting your gut

Emotional

- Releasing emotions and expressing feelings (laugh, talk, cry, write in a journal, paint, REBT etc.)
- Learning how to "switch off"
- Taking time out
- Solitude and space
- Intimacy
- Counseling and support
- Challenging your emotional reactions to situations
- Passion/Joy
- Going low
- Music
- Mood food
- Color
- Art therapy

Social

- Scheduling time to spend with important people in your life
- Making plans with friends, family and loved ones in advance
- Sharing your experiences of stress with certain people in your life, especially letting them know the ways that stress has been affecting you, so they understand
- Practicing assertive communication within your significant relationships to decrease conflicts, while also continuing to find ways to show people around you that they are important

Spiritual

- Prayer and meditation—scheduling regular time
- Helping others (talking, writing, supporting)

CONCLUSION

- Reiki and other energy healing techniques
- Talking with a spiritual confidant or leader to explain any spiritual issues or doubts that you may have encountered
- Forgiveness (of self or others)
- Compassion/loving kindness
- Continuing to read and learn about your faith, belief or value system
- Connecting with others who share your beliefs
- Gratitude

A FEW LAST WORDS

Having read *The Sobriety Experiment* I hope you're feeling better informed about a topic that for most is challenging, confusing, painful and sensitive—your relationship to alcohol

It's my sincerest desire that any insights or gems you have taken away will result in a more rewarding, healthier and successful life for you and those who matter most to you.

Like me, I hope you too can see a world where sobriety is normalized not stigmatized.

I hope what you have found in this book is a way to discover freedom, find happiness and change your life by easing up on the booze, or lose the habit entirely.

My deepest desire is that in the process, you'll make this year, and those that follow, the best years yet.

The power to live a significant and sober life lies within you.

Count your blessings and remember to be happy and thankful for even the simplest, and often the most valuable, things. These may include:

- Enjoying good health and mobility
- Being loved and loving in return
- Tapping into your infinite potential
- The ability to say, think, do, and create what you truly feel
- The ability to enchant and inspire others with your commitment to sobriety
- Healing the world—one alcohol-free day at a time
- Inspiring others with your courage
- Feeling happy with yourself
- Fulfillment
- Living authentically
- Being audacious

. . . Or something else.

What matters most is not how you overcome obstacles to success. What matters is how meaningful the end result is for you.

Take care of yourself and your heart, and nourish your mind, body and soul.

If you continue to approach alcohol mindfully, exercise self-care and adopt a spirit of playfulness through challenging times, then this unpredictable and often crazy life will manifest in favorable outcomes—for you, for those you love, and those drawn to you because of your resilience, joy, beauty, power, and magic of who you truly are.

Let the beauty you love be the life that you live.

Thank you for going on this journey with me. I look forward to staying in touch.

You'll find plenty of ongoing support and cheerleading in our Facebook community https://www.facebook.com/Sobrietyexperiment/

TO YOUR HAPPINESS AND JOY, **and with love,**

If you know of someone else who could benefit from this book please do let them know that it's available in print and eBook.

Sign up for my newsletter to be the first to know when this and other new books are released, and receive practical tips to live your best life—http://eepurl.com/bEArfT

But before we part I hope you enjoy the following bonus gift.

BONUS: ALCOHOL-FREE DRINKS YOU'LL LOVE

Enjoy this carefully curated selection of alcohol-free alternatives from my book, *Mind Over Mojitos: How Moderating Your Drinking Can Change Your Life*

Available in eBook and paperback

MIND OVER MOJITOS

How Moderating Your Drinking Can Change Your Life

Easy Alcohol-Free Recipes for Happier Hours & a Joy Filled Life

Bestselling author of Stress Less. Love Life More

EXCERPT: MIND OVER MOJITOS: HOW MODERATING YOUR DRINKING CAN CHANGE YOUR LIFE

PRAISE FOR MIND YOUR MOJITOS

"Anyone who needs to cut back their drinking, be kept on track or inspired will find genuine help in this honest, insightful book."

~ CS Sloan, counselor

"More motivating inspiration from Cassandra. Be honest with yourself ... do you drink too much? Do you want to take back the control that alcohol has over you? Cassandra shows you how you can do this without missing out on the fun. Complete abstinence does not have to be the answer, neither does drinking water in boring tumblers at social functions have to be subject to questioning peers.

As the daughter of an alcoholic father, I am well aware of my own predisposition. When he fought for control, he would drink orange juice on ice, in a highball glass with a splash of soda and a wedge of orange. It looked just like a Screwdriver and no-one ever questioned it.

With Cassandra's advice and delicious mocktail recipes, you too can release the grip of alcohol and regain your life."

~ Niki Firth, 5-Star Review

"Geared toward problem drinkers struggling to cut back or quit drinking as well as those who want to be reinspired during recovery, this book helps those looking for alternatives to alcohol to take pleasure in booze-free alternatives... For readers who sincerely want to stop drinking the recipes in this book will pave the way."

~ L. Wells, Director

"Great Writer. Great Recipes. Pleasantly surprised by the quality of writing and the inventiveness of the recipes."

~ 5-star Review

ABOUT THESE RECIPES

Organized into two volumes, Spring/Summer, and Fall/Winter, this book is a series of carefully curated fun and healthy alcohol alternatives. *Mind Over Mojitos* guides you through a variety of different mock-tail recipes and booze-free alternatives that will make your tastebuds sing and send your dopamine levels soaring.

I've chosen a range of wonderfully refreshing drinks, particularly during the summertime, which are great for picnics or barbeques or just enjoying around the home. Many contain seasonal fruits and berries, are thirst-quenching and also pack some vitamins. Perfect for people who don't like drinking or are not of legal drinking age.

There are two kinds of wintery yet festive drinks to guzzle during the cooler seasons: sparkly and fun mixes that utilize winter fruit, and those that are warm and cozy.

Enjoy this selection, or channel your own mixologist and create your own.

Don't forget, if you ever find yourself in a bar and at a loss for what to drink, or you want to fit in, simply ask for a mocktail (which is what I

ABOUT THESE RECIPES

did when I got the bar staff to create the Virgin Island Fox recipe in this book). Or order a look-alike drink in a fancy glass by saying, "Make mine alcohol-free."

Voila! You'll blend in without having to give everyone a lengthy spiel or justifying why you're not drinking alcohol.

Be prepared—plan your booze-free alternative ahead of time and you'll never default to drinking alcohol simply because there was nothing else.

If you create something tasty please share in the dedicated Facebook group where you'll find plenty of thirsty booze-free devotees—https://www.facebook.com/Sobrietyexperiment/

Drinking a non-alcoholic drink should be a fun, sensual and pleasurable experience. Before we dive deeper into some luscious recipes lets remind ourselves of why we need to lose the booze, and then look at the importance of giving good glass. And yes, we will have fun!

GIVING GOOD GLASS

Remember it's all in the glass—be sure to pour your drinks into something nice. Drinking a non-alcoholic drink should be a pleasurable experience, and presentation and pleasure go hand-in-hand.

Check out this list below and learn more about the scientific and psychological reasons that it's important to be choosy about your glass.

- The elegance of certain glasses (can give individuals a perception of a finer drinking experience
- The shape of your glass can affect how much and how quickly you drink
- Different glasses bring out the aromas and flavors
- Tall, tapered shapes capture the carbonation and color; glasses with wider bases allows room for swirling to release aromas, which then get trapped at the narrow top. A rounded bottom makes it easy to cup in your hand, simultaneously warming your drink.
- A martini glass's cone shape prevents your ingredients from separating. The long stem also ensures your hands won't

affect the temperature of the drink. As a bonus, the martini glass is sexy no matter who's holding it!
- Champagne coupes, the champagne flutes of our grandparents' generation look elegant, plus the stem keeps your drink cool
- The highball glass is ideal for carbonated mocktails. It's best to keep less surface liquid exposed to air—the more exposed, the quicker the carbonation will evaporate, leaving you with a flat drink.
- Lowball glasses are ideal for high-intensity drinks served on the rocks because they average two to four ounces. Nice since drinking a two-ounce mocktail in a 10-ounce highball may feel a little weak.
- Tulip or white wine glass. Small, slender, tulip-shaped glassware, help slow down any rise in temperature from the chilled beverages, while the stem of the glass allows you to hold your drink without your hands heating it up—keeping your drink cooler for longer.
- Warmer drinks should be served in larger, bowl-shaped glasses to increase surface area and allow for more aroma release.
- Tulip champagne flutes. The narrow, tulip-shaped flute is a familiar drinking vessel at weddings and toast-worthy occasions for holding your celebratory bubbly. The carbonation is the major reason behind the shape. The glass helps retain Champagne's trademark carbonation, and the bowl is also designed to visually highlight the rising bubbles. Perfect for non-alcoholic champagne mixes and carbonated drinks with fizz.
- Stemless glass. With their clean design and easy-to-clean shape (no worries about shattering a delicate stem here!), stemless glasses are best for drinks served at room temp since your hands holding the glass can unintentionally heat up cooler drinks.

Size matters! Small can be beautiful. A tiny crystal long stemmed-glass is one of my favorite glasses to enjoy a wee sip of beer or wine on special occasions. Remember sobriety is not about abstinence but about being in control of your drinking.

But, with so many tasty alternatives to booze, you'll soon find, as I did, that you'll kick the drink habit easily.

Are you ready to discover easy recipes for happier hours of joy- filled sober living? Part One starts with spring and summer, alcohol- free alternatives to enjoy. Recipes for the cooler months follows in Part Two.

First up, my personal favorite—Virgin Island Fox!

PART I

NON-ALCOHOLIC DRINKS FOR SPRING & SUMMER

1

VIRGIN ISLAND FOX

A mocktail version of a classic created for me by the hip-cool folk at Charlotte's Kitchen in Pahia, The Bay of Islands, New Zealand—my spiritual home. An elegant and restrained cocktail with subtle richness balanced with lovely zest.

Ingredients

- 1 tsp orange marmalade
- 90mls grapefruit juice
- 30mls lime juice
- 15 mls sugar syrup
- Ice

Method

- Add all ingredients except the ice into a mixer
- Single strain over ice into a wine glass
- Garnish – grapefruit

2

PASSION FRUIT BUBBLY

Guilt-free sparkle when passion fruit is in season and mixed with sparkling wine for a festive drink.

INGREDIENTS

- 1/2 Lemon, juice of
- 1 small bunch of mint
- 2 cups caster sugar
- 1/2 tsp Salt
- 1 cup of ice
- 1 bottle sparkling wine or soda water
- 2 cups water
- 1 tsp citric acid
- 1 cup of passion fruit pulp (fresh or tinned)

Method

- Place all the ingredients in a saucepan and stir over a medium heat until the sugar is dissolved
- Bring to the boil, take of the heat and allow to cool
- Taste to see if the cordial needs some extra lemon juice
- Serve I part cordial to 3 parts bubbly over lots of ice and garnish with fresh mint
- Keep any leftover cordial in a clean and airtight container, refrigerated for up to 4 weeks
- Makes about 750ml of cordial

3

PASSION FRUIT POWER PUNCH

Perfect for a hot day and easy to mix. Displays aromas of bright fruit and hints of citrus. Rich texture and a sparkling twist. Finishes just like an Indian Summer—long and lovely.

INGREDIENTS

- 1 cup of passion fruit pulp (fresh or tinned)
- I good handful of mint leaves (plus extras to serve)
- I squeezed lime (1 lime per 4 drinks)
- I cup of sparkling water per drink

METHOD

Combine passion fruit, lime juice and mint over ice and then top with sparkling water. Serve with extra mint in the glass.

4

BLUEBERRY AND MAPLE MOJITO

Stunning and stimulating! Exotic in style, clean and crisp, zesty on the palate with aromas of mint and limes. A complete winner and sure to impress even the most discerning drinker.

Ingredients

- 8-10 mint leaves, plus more for garnish
- 1 tsp fresh lime juice
- 1 tbsp. good-quality maple syrup
- 1/3 cup organic blueberry juice-no added sugar
- 1/2 cup soda
- Frozen blueberries, for garnish

Method

. . .

Add the mint leaves to a glass (size depends on how much you want). Muddle well until the mint releases its flavor.

Add the lime juice, maple syrup, blueberry juice and soda to the glass and stir until all the ingredients are well-combined.

Serves 1, prep time 5 minutes

5

VIRGIN MOJITO

Easy to mix and refreshing to drink on a simmering hot day. Fresh, bright and crisp. Feel the love in this powerful, tight and elegant perennial favorite. Wow!

INGREDIENTS

- 1/3 cup Apple juice
- 1/3 cup Sparkling water
- 1 whole lime, sliced and quartered
- 3 mint leaves
- 1 teaspoon sugar

METHOD

- Muddle the lime, sugar and mint leaves until they are just releasing the juice

- Place ice in a glass, add muddled mixture and pour in apple juice
- Top with sparkling water and stir
- Garnish with a slice of lime and mint leaf and serve

SOURCE:

https://www.soberjulie.com/2016/06/mojito-recipe/

DID YOU ENJOY THIS EXCERPT?

Grab The Ultimate Guide to Alcohol-Free Drinking

Easily cut back or quit drinking alcohol entirely without becoming a hermit, being ostracized, or cutting back on an enjoyable social life.

Mind Over Mojitos: How Moderating Your Drinking Can Change Your Life—Available in eBook and paperback

EXCERPT: HOW TO FIND YOUR JOY AND PURPOSE

PRAISE FOR HOW TO FIND YOUR JOY AND PURPOSE

"This is really, really good! A wonderful and inspiring book. LOVE it! It's concise, personal, and practical. I can think of so many people who could benefit from this book."

~ **Heather Dodge, Founder Kaleidoscope Solutions**

"How to Find Your Joy and Purpose is a practical guide with thought-provoking realistic tools that guided me on a journey of discovery, learning me. It is easy reading, practical, and from the heart. It is written for me and speaks to me—which is how any self-help/improvement book should be. I loved the book!"

~ **Joanna Baldwin**

"My takeaway is that the power is within me to navigate through the dark periods and emerge, empowered, and capable of managing my emotions, moods, and those dips in life. And I can do this without need to access outside of myself, which is an amazing gift. Broken down in manageable steps, it's achievable! :) *How to Find Your Joy and*

Purpose was very thorough. A reflection of Cassandra's extensive experience and Hannah's recent, very fresh experience in re-finding her joy. Loved it."

~ **Jamie S.**

"A great self-help healing book aimed at empowerment and positivity while not running away from real life and some of the harsh realities that we face."

~ **Advance Review.**

AUTHORS NOTE

"WE WROTE THIS BOOK BECAUSE WE NEEDED TO READ IT."

We're feeling joyful as we collaborate, as mother and daughter, on our first book together, *How to Find Your Joy and Purpose: Four Easy Steps to Discover A Job You Want And Live the Life You Love.* This is a particularly significant project for us, as you'll discover.

We're writing at a time of great personal upheaval and turmoil. Over an abruptly short period we realized that we had lost our joy. We were burned out and stressed out. And it seemed as though the world had become more toxic, selfish, and meaner. We had been following our passions, but life didn't seem to be flowing.

Wasn't it supposed to get easier?

Follow your bliss, we were told, and shared with others. What we didn't heed was the need to keep our vibrations high and prioritize self-care.

Everything got better for us when we began to make peace with the fact that it might never get easier. The world can be crazy-busy.

WE CAN BE CRAZY-BUSY.

Life is a great teacher, sometimes brutally so, but the lessons are enduring ones.

Whether you are burned out, stressed out, blissed-out, or checked out, the question is always the same: How do you find your joy and purpose and keep it without crashing or sacrificing your mental health?

This book is a list of things that have helped us. We wrote to heal ourselves, and in the process of recovery we discovered how extraordinarily powerful everyday joy is.

We learned how simple, quick, and effective joy can be in healing so many of the things facing humanity: depression, anxiety, stress, lack of meaning and purpose, toxic careers and unhappiness at work, shocking rates of suicide and addiction, acute loneliness, and more.

We wrote *How to Find Your Joy and Purpose* primarily for anyone trying to create and sustain a meaningful, healthy, and prosperous life. Whether you are a homemaker, retiree, entrepreneur, artist, employee, activist, career-changer, or looking for a lift, this book is for you.

There are no hard and speedy rules, of course—life is an art, not a science. Your route may vary. Pack what you need and leave the rest.

Hang on to hope, follow your joy, keep going, and take care of your beautiful self—mentally, emotionally, physically, and spiritually.

We'll do the same.

INTRODUCTION

"We need joy as we need air. We need love as we need water. We need each other as we need the earth we share."
Maya Angelou

Joy is the truth. The whole truth. And always our truth. Without joy, we lack vitality. Without vitality, we have lethargy.

Finding a job you want and living a life you love is impossible without joy, purpose, passion, enthusiasm, zest, inspiration, and the deep satisfaction that comes from doing something that delivers some zing.

Yet, it's staggeringly, and dishearteningly, true that many people don't know what fills them with joy, or how they can channel it into an enriching life and rewarding career. Some research suggests that only 10% of people are living and working with joy.

Many people feel trapped and frustrated. People like Tom, an estate planning attorney in the US who wrote to Cassandra, "I have spent 29 years as an attorney, mostly unhappy, but it's hard to get out. I still do not know my passion. I have some ideas, but I am not sure which 1 or

INTRODUCTION

2 will cause me to jump out of bed at 5:30 a.m., drink a lot of coffee and eat a few biscuits and begin my mission."

If you're like many people who don't know what they feel joyful, passionate, or purposeful about or what gives your life meaning and purpose, this book will help provide the answers.

If you believe it's not realistic to work and live with joy, this book will help change your mindset.

If you're recovering from burnout, washout, or timeout, *How to Find Your Joy and Purpose* comes to your rescue.

Together we'll help you get your mojo back, challenge your current beliefs, and increase your sense of possibility. By tapping into a combination of practical strategies, Law of Attraction principles, and the spiritual powers of manifestation, you'll reawaken dreams, boost your self-awareness, empower your life, and challenge what you thought was possible.

We'll do this in an inspired, yet structured way, by strengthening your creative thinking skills, boosting your self-awareness and helping you identify your non-negotiable ingredients for career success and happiness.

Little steps will lead naturally to more significant leaps, giving you the courage and confidence to follow your joy and purpose and fly free towards career happiness and life fulfillment. All while keeping your sanity!

What you're about to read isn't another self-help book; it's a self-empowerment book. It offers ways to increase your self-knowledge. From that knowledge comes the power to create a life worth living.

How to Find Your Joy and Purpose will help you:

- Explore and clarify your joys, passion, interests, and life purpose

INTRODUCTION

- Build a strong foundation for happiness and success
- Value your gifts, and talents and confirm your natural knacks and work-related strengths
- Direct your energies positively toward your preferred future
- Strengthen your creative thinking skills, and ability to identify possible roles you would enjoy, including self-employment and enriching hobbies
- Have the courage to follow your dreams and super-charge the confidence needed to make an inspired change
- Find your point of brilliance

Let's look briefly at what each chapter in this book will cover:

Step One, "The Call For Joy," will help you explore the meaning of joy and discover the benefits of following it, and the consequences of ignoring your happiness. You'll identify any blocking beliefs and intensify joy-building beliefs to boost your chances of success.

Step Two, "Discover Your Joy," will help you to identify your sources of bliss and joy criteria. What you'll discover may be a complete surprise and open up a realm of opportunities you've never considered.

Step Three, "Joy at Work," will assist you in identifying career options and exploring ways to develop your career in light of your joy and life purpose.

Step Four, "Live Your Joy," looks at joy beyond the world of work and ways to achieve healthy balance and fulfillment. You'll also identify strategies to overcome obstacles and maximize your success.

How to Find Your Joy and Purpose concludes by showing you how to identify your point of brilliance.

INTRODUCTION

THIS BOOK IS MAGICAL

This book proves less really is more. Sometimes all it takes to radically transform your life is one word, one sentence, one powerful but simple strategy to ignite inspiration and reawaken a sense of possibility.

We have successfully used the knowledge we're sharing with you in this book professionally with our clients and personally during numerous reinventions—including recovering from a recent trauma.

We stand by every one of the four steps and the 50+ strategies you will learn. They are grounded in strong evidence-based, scientific, and spiritual principles. We have successfully used them to create turnaround, after turnaround in every area of our life.

How to Find Your Joy and Purpose is the culmination of all that we have experienced, applied, and taught others for decades. We don't practice what we preach; we preach what we have practiced—because it gets results.

WHY DID WE WRITE THIS BOOK?

As we shared in the Authors' Note, after experiencing a period of extreme stress and burnout, we both crashed. For Hannah Joy, neglecting self-care, over-working, and discovering a historical trauma that had lain buried in the subconscious for over 23 years exploded to the surface in a violent storm.

Her life was busy, busy, busy. Too busy. She was running her business full-time, studying with other coaches, attending numerous workshops on personal development—and leading others. Plus, she was partway through a full-time tertiary course to qualify as a counselor.

Add to that the trauma of discovering that her partner of four years had been cheating on her, it's no wonder she flipped out. Like many people, she turned to alcohol to help her cope.

INTRODUCTION

Following binge-drinking 3/4 of a bottle of Jack Daniel's Tennessee whiskey in one session, she was lucky she didn't die. Instead, she suffered alcohol-induced psychosis and instead of being taken somewhere safe to sober up she was admitted into psychiatric care and medicated.

We'll share more of Hannah's story in a book Hannah is writing, but suffice to say we quickly discovered how truly broken and antiquated the mental health system is. Pharmaceuticals may offer a bridge to healing but seldom cures—particularly when the real issue is sexual assault trauma and alcohol harm.

We were both significantly progressed on our spiritual paths, and valued a holistic approach—something at odds with The System.

While struggling from the outside to help her daughter (then 'owned' by The State), Cassandra struggled to reach her. She couldn't even bring her home.

Cassandra began to think, What would our life be like if we just leaned toward joy? This question led us to do what Cassandra calls a *da-Vinci* and *to* conduct our own experiment.

As part of Hannah's journey to recovery, Cassandra asked her to write a chapter of this book—something that would help Hannah with whatever she was going through at the time.

And we began to measure our success based on how Hannah's feelings of hopelessness and disempowerment and fear changed.

At the same time, Cassandra wrote chapters that would help her. If you've ever supported anyone though a mental health crisis, or saved them from acting out suicidal thoughts, or loved someone who is suffering (often brutally so), you'll know you suffer too.

Hannah and I went on a quest for joy and purpose. We began looking for joy in trauma, seeking purpose in suffering, and going out of our

INTRODUCTION

way to find joy in all situations—especially the more challenging areas of our life.

We began questioning addictive over-working, mindlessly drinking, blurring boundaries, and escaping healing by numbing and distraction. Instead, we opted to test-drive new hobbies and laughing at our worry-minded thinking. Hannah has a new passion for crochet, and Cassandra has taken up jewelry making!

Whenever we'd notice ourselves getting stuck in a negative story, we'd challenge ourselves to be the heroine of our own story and fast-froward to a new scene. Or we'd try to rescript the story and see it with the high-vibe perspective of joy.

We'd say to ourselves, "What if we just chose joy? What if we just did this for fun? What if we just allowed." Asking ourselves these questions, and others you'll find in this book, in any given moment immediately catapulted us back into a place of joy.

HOW TO USE THIS BOOK

This book is a concise guide to making the most of your life. The vision was simple: a few short, easy to digest tips for time-challenged people who were looking for inspiration and practical strategies to encourage positive change.

From our own experience, we knew that people didn't need a large wad of words to feel inspired, gain clarity, and be stimulated to take action.

In this era of information obesity, the need for simple, life-affirming messages is even more critical. If you are looking for inspiration and practical tips, in short, sweet sound bites, this guide is for you.

Similarly, if you are a grazer, or someone more methodical, this guide will also work for you. Pick a page at random, or work through the steps sequentially. We encourage you to experiment, be open-minded, and try new things. We promise you will achieve outstanding results.

Clive, a 62-year-old man who had suffered work-related burnout, did! He thought that creating a journal, *Tip 14* in this guide, was childish—something other stressed executives in his men's support group would refuse.

HOW TO USE THIS BOOK

But once he'd taken up the challenge, he told me enthusiastically, "They loved it!" They are using their journals to visualize, gain clarity, and create their preferred futures. Clive used it to help manifest his new purpose-driven coaching business.

Let experience be your guide. Give your brain a well-needed break. Let go of 'why,' and embrace how you *feel* or how you want to feel. Honor the messages from your intuition and follow your path with heart.

Laura, who at one stage seemed rudderless career-wise, did just that. She was guided to *Tip 21: Who Inspires You?* Following that, her motivation to live and work like those she looked up to sparked a determination to start her own business. It was that simple. And now she's done it!

HOW TO USE THIS BOOK—YOUR VIRTUAL COACH

To benefit from this book, think of it as your 'virtual' coach—answer the questions and complete the additional exercises included in each chapter.

Questions are great thought provokers. Your answers to these questions will help you gently challenge current assumptions and gain greater clarity about your goals and desires.

All the strategies are designed to facilitate greater insight and to help you integrate new learnings. Resist the urge to process information in your head. We learn best by doing. Research has repeatedly proven that the act of writing deepens your knowledge and understanding.

For example, a study conducted by Dr. David K. Pugalee found that journal writing was an effective instructional tool and aided learning. His research found that writing helped people organize and describe internal thoughts and thus improve their problem-solving skills.

Henriette Klauser, Ph.D., also provides compelling evidence in her book, *Write It Down and Make It Happen*, that writing helps you clarify what you want and enables you to make it happen.

Writing down your insights is the area where people like motivational guru Tony Robbins, say that the winners part from the losers because the losers always find a reason not to write things down. Harsh, but perhaps true!

KEEPING A JOY JOURNAL

A joy journal is also a great place to store sources of inspiration to support you through the career planning and change process. For some tips to help you create your inspirational joy journal, go to Cassandra's media page on her website and watch her television interview and interview with other experts here:

http://www.cassandragaisford.com/media

SETTING YOU UP FOR SUCCESS

"Aren't you setting people up for failure?" a disillusioned career coach once challenged Cassandra.

Thirty-five years of cumulative professional experience as a career coach and holistic therapist, helping people work with joy and purpose and still pay the bills, answers that question. Cassandra is setting people up for success. We're not saying it will happen instantly, but if you follow the advice in this book, it will happen.

We promise.

We've proven repeatedly, both personally and professionally, that thinking differently and creatively, rationally and practically, while also harnessing the power of your heart, and applying the principles of manifestation, really works. In this book, we'll show you why—and how.

HOW TO USE THIS BOOK

A large part of our philosophy and the reason behind our success with clients is our fervent belief that to achieve anything worthy of life you need to follow your joy. And we're in good company.

As trauma survivor and media giant Oprah Winfrey once said, "I define joy as a sustained sense of well-being and internal peace—a connection to others."

JOY'S PAY CHEQUE

By discovering your joy and purpose, you will tap into a vast source of potential energy and prosperity. Pursuing your joy can be profitable on many levels:

- When you do what you love, your true talent will reveal itself; joy can't be faked
- You'll be more enthusiastic about your pursuits
- You'll have more energy to overcome obstacles
- You will be more determined to make things happen
- You will enjoy your work
- Your work will become a vehicle for self-expression
- Joy will give you a competitive edge
- You'll enjoy your life and magnetize positive experiences toward you
- Your find eternal peace

Without joy, you don't have a connection to what truly matters, and without connection you are alone.

Let the higher vibrations of joy, peace, love, desire, purpose, and passion lift you higher. Allow this higher energy to lift fear, ambivalence, apathy, and negativity.

Don't waste another day feeling uninspired. Don't be the person who spends a life of regret, or waits until they retire before they follow their joy. Don't be the person too afraid to make a change for the better, or who wishes they could lead a significant life. Make the change now before it's too late.

Reach For Your Dreams

Joy, fulfillment, passion, purpose, peace, and love—call it what you will, our deepest desire is that this book encourages you to reach for your dreams, to never settle, to believe in the highest aspirations you have for yourself.

You have so many gifts, so many talents that the world so desperately needs. We need people like you who care about what they do, who want to live and work with joy and purpose.

And what we can promise you is this—whatever your circumstances, it's never too late to re-create yourself and your life.

Let's get started!

STEP 1: THE CALL FOR JOY

Read through the following tips numbered 1-12 and consider your responses to each strategy. You may want to keep notes about your answers in a dedicated book or journal.

Tips 1-12 ask you to consider what you believe joy is and to identify what joy means to you. What role do you think joy should have in your life? Do you have any joy-blocking beliefs? What are your joy-building beliefs?

What are the consequences of ignoring your joy? How do you think not pursuing your dreams might affect you? How has it affected other people you know? What are your goals, hopes, and dreams for your future? What will having more joy in your life do for you?

1

WHAT IS JOY?

> "The two most inspiring life forces are anger and joy – I could write six zillion songs about these two feelings alone."
> Alanis Morissette

Joy is energy.
Joy is a feeling.
Joy is about emotion.
Joy is one of the highest vibrations we can experience.
Joy is about delight and rapture.
Joy is about jubilation, elation, euphoria, and exultation.
Joy is about eagerness and preoccupation.
Joy is about excitement, animation, and delight.
Joy is about triumph, conscious cultivation, and choice.
Joy is peace and transcendence.
Joy is being wholehearted.
Joy is love.

CASSANDRA GAISFORD

Joy is many things. What is joy to you?

2

JOY FOR ALL

> "'Where is my soul?' That is perhaps the only question worth answering. Each of us answers in his or her own way."
> Piero Ferrucci

Every human being is capable of joy. Different people are joyful in different ways and about different things.

Many people think that being joyful only means being loud and extraverted.

This isn't true at all. Many joyful people are contained, or quiet or reserved. Joyful people come in all shapes, sizes, and ages. You can pursue your joy at any age and stage of your life. You can even choose to be joyful in the face of great difficulty.

Where is your soul? How does joy show up for you?

3

WHAT CAN JOY DO?

> "Joy is something different from happiness. When I use the word happiness, in a sense I mean satisfaction. Sometimes we have a painful experience, but that experience, as you've said with birth, can bring great satisfaction and joyfulness."
> His Holiness The Dalai Lama

Joy energizes people.
Joy inspires people.
Joy helps people lead happier lives.
Joy is an indispensable part of feeling alive.
Joy helps us overcome difficulties.
Joy liberates us. It frees us to be ourselves.
Joy opens up fresh horizons.
Joy is fabulous for our health.

When we are pursuing something we are enthusiastic about our energy, drive and determination are infinite. Our courage and resilience soar and we are able to stretch to anything, accommodate any setback, and bounce forward again.

People immobilized by fear and passivity snap like twigs.
Joy is the light of balance for those of us seeking a way out of the darkness of depression and suffering. Joy gives us a zing in our soul, a reason for living and the confidence, tenacity, and drive to pursue our dreams.

Record all the reasons why you want more joy in your life. What would you do if you were 10 times joyful?

What are all the benefits that will flow?

4

REALITY CHECK ON JOY

"Everyone seeks happiness, joyfulness, but from outside—from money, from power, from big car, from big house. Most people never pay much attention to the ultimate source of a happy life, which is inside, not outside."
His Holiness, The Dalai Lama

Joy does not always come easily. Life is challenging—sometimes overwhelmingly so. Like anything worthwhile, finding and following your joy often involves great commitment, courage, and sacrifice.

Joyful people are prepared to give up things they once enjoyed or people they may have endured to live a more peaceful life. They're prepared to wave bye-bye to addictions that keep them boringly distracted, disconnected, or toxically numbed. They commit daily to waving farewell to deep diving into narcissism, drama, and negativity.

They affirm with joy 'yes' to letting go of pain, fear, and judgment. 'Yes' to embracing unconditional love, vulnerability, taking risks and coping with the possibility of failure. "Yes!Yes!Yes! To embracing their essence and being who they truly are.

Joyful people aren't always chasing 'happy.' Contribution, compassion, and caring—for self and others—are more important virtues.

The compensation for being 'real' is a bigger, richer, more authentically fulfilling life.

What are you prepared to trade-off to be more joyful? What are you prepared to change in your life? What or who would help you? What or who would stop you?

5

COMPARISON ROBS JOY

"Comparison is the thief of joy."
Theodore Roosevelt

Constantly thinking what others are doing, stalking others on social media, and berating yourself for feeling inadequate in comparison drains your energy and robs your joy. Yet it can be addictive.

Like any addiction again it's a harmful habit if taken to extremes, comparison can be self-sabotaging and a form of self-abuse. It's also a hard pattern to stop. But stop you must if your joy is to be returned to you.

We're curious, social beings. We are drawn to others, we like to know what people are up to, and we like to follow successful people.

But we don't see everyone's entire life. We only see one glance—and often it's a carefully curated one.

We don't befriend ourselves enough and acknowledge our difficult journey, and how we have triumphed over trauma, or how far we've come. Some of what we have experienced others may never have experienced—much less survived.

Instead of comparing ourselves to others negatively, to reclaim joy we need to think about where we are now and compare this to where we have been—yesterday, last week, last month, last year. This is especially important when we are recovering for illness or a setback of any kind. Traumatic experiences or mental health challenges can make us especially vulnerable.

Use aspirational comparisons. Compare yourself to people similar to you or who have been in the same spot and are now flourishing. Think of someone you aspire to be like. Oprah? Drew Barrymore? Your mother? Or a dear friend?

Surround yourself with your mentors. People who are inspiring and smile in the face of adversity are like vitamins for our souls.

Look back at a time you felt joy and compare yourself to that person. But be careful you don't hold onto the old you and forget to feed the new emerging you.

DID YOU ENJOY THIS EXCERPT?

How to Find Your Joy and Purpose: Four Easy Steps to Discover A Job You Want And Live the Life You Love.

AVAILABLE FOR NOW in audiobook, paperback, hardback and eBook.

ALSO BY CASSANDRA GAISFORD

Transformational Super Kids:

The Little Princess
The Little Princess Can Fly
I Have to Grow
The Boy Who Cried

Mid-Life Career Rescue:

The Call for Change
What Makes You Happy
Employ Yourself
Job Search Strategies That Work
3 Book Box Set: The Call for Change, What Makes You Happy, Employ Yourself
4 Book Box Set: The Call for Change, What Makes You Happy, Employ Yourself, Job Search Strategies That Work

Career Change:

ALSO BY CASSANDRA GAISFORD

Career Change 2020 5 Book-Bundle Box Set

Master Life Coach:

Leonardo da Vinci: Life Coach
Coco Chanel: Life Coach

The Art of Living:

How to Find Your Passion and Purpose
How to Find Your Passion and Purpose Companion Workbook
Career Rescue: The Art and Science of Reinventing Your Career and Life
Boost Your Self-Esteem and Confidence
Anxiety Rescue
No! Why 'No' is the New 'Yes'
How to Find Your Joy and Purpose
How to Find Your Joy and Purpose Companion Workbook

The Art of Success:

Leonardo da Vinci
Coco Chanel

Journaling Prompts Series:

The Passion Journal
The Passion-Driven Business Planning Journal
How to Find Your Passion and Purpose 2 Book-Bundle Box Set

Health & Happiness:

The Happy, Healthy Artist
Stress Less. Love Life More

ALSO BY CASSANDRA GAISFORD

Bounce: Overcoming Adversity, Building Resilience and Finding Joy
Bounce Companion Workbook

Mindful Sobriety:

Mind Your Drink: The Surprising Joy of Sobriety
Mind Over Mojitos: How Moderating Your Drinking Can Change Your Life: Easy Recipes for Happier Hours & a Joy-Filled Life
Your Beautiful Brain: Control Alcohol and Love Life More

Happy Sobriety:

Happy Sobriety: Non-Alcoholic Guilt-Free Drinks You'll Love
The Sobriety Journal
Happy Sobriety Two Book Bundle-Box Set: Alcohol and Guilt-Free Drinks You'll Love & The Sobriety Journal

Money Manifestation:

Financial Rescue: The Total Money Makeover: Create Wealth, Reduce Debt & Gain Freedom

The Prosperous Author:

Developing a Millionaire Mindset
Productivity Hacks: Do Less & Make More
Two Book Bundle-Box Set (Books 1-2)

Miracle Mindset:

Change Your Mindset: Millionaire Mindset Makeover: The Power of Purpose, Passion, & Perseverance

Non-Fiction:

ALSO BY CASSANDRA GAISFORD

Where is Salvator Mundi?

More of Cassandra's practical and inspiring workbooks on a range of career and life-enhancing topics are on her website (www.cassandragaisford.com) and her author page at all good online bookstores.

FURTHER RESOURCES

DOCUMENTARIES AND MOVIES

***Making Good Men**,* Hollywood actor Manu Bennett (Azog the Defiler in the *Hobbit*) and former All Black Legend, Norm Hewitt share their personal stories of alcohol and how their lives and careers were nearly destroyed. A powerful story of tragedy, redemption, reconciliation and restoration. The documentary is no longer available on-demand, however if you would like to purchase a DVD copy email: fiona@teamokura.com.

http://www.teamokura.com/making-good-men/

The Truth About Alcohol, join British emergency room doctor Javid Abdelmoneim and other experts as they explore the benefits, risks and science of drinking. If you're determined to drink, you also discover ways to lessen the impact of alcohol.

https://www.netflix.com/nz/title/80185861

Death in the West, topics tobacco, cigarette, television, adverse

FURTHER RESOURCES

effects, anti-smoking advocacy, brand image, carcinogen, emphysema, lung cancer, and the industry response. A 1983 investigative report about the documentary "Death in the West" that was produced for British television and later suppressed by Philip Morris.

https://archive.org/details/tobacco_doo23e00

SUPPORT GROUPS

You'll find plenty of inspirational people who've devoted themselves to living joyfully alcohol-free. Here are just a few:

The Sobriety Experiment. Our dedicated Facebook community. We see a world where sobriety is normalized not stigmatized—you'll find plenty of support here.

https://www.facebook.com/Sobrietyexperiment

Hello Sunday Morning was founded in 2009 when Chris Raine undertook a year-long experiment to change his relationship with alcohol. A nightclub promoter at the time, Chris blogged about the challenges and successes of this experiment when he woke up hangover-free. Join Chris and his movement towards a better drinking culture

https://www.hellosundaymorning.org/

No Beers, Who Cares encourages and supports a mindful approach to alcohol abstinence.

https://nobeerswhocares.com/pages/about

Sobriety Aotearoa proves support and fellowship to help you maintain sobriety

https://www.facebook.com/groups/sobrietyaotearoa/

Soberly. Founder Libby W. is passionate about encouraging women to have a positive and meaningful life that is not based around alcohol. You'll find plenty of encouragement here—https://www.soberlyempire.com/

SURF THE NET

The New Zealand Health Promotions Agency provides an excellent guide to quickly gauge how much you're drinking—or intend to drink. The downloaded PDF can be found here—https://www.alcohol.org.nz/sites/default/files/images/1.0%20AL%20437%20Guide%20to%20Standard%20Drinks_FA_May2015_WEB.pdf

A good summary about the role of different parts of your brain and how alcohol affects optimal functioning can be found here—http://sciencenetlinks.com/student-teacher-sheets/alcohol-and-your-brain/.

Mathew Johnstone has a wide range of books and resources on mental wellness and mindfulness: www.matthewjohnstone.com.au

www.whatthebleep.com—a powerful and inspiring site emphasizing quantum physics and the transformational power of thought.

www.heartmath.org—comprehensive information and tools help you access your intuitive insight and heart-based knowledge. Validated and supported by science-based research. Check out the additional information about your heart-brain.

Experience the transformative power of hypnosis. One of my favorite hypnosis sites is the UK-based Uncommon Knowledge. On their website http://www.hypnosisdownloads.com you'll find a range of self-hypnosis mp3 audios to help you quit drinking.

Celebrity hypnotherapist and author Marissa Peer is another favorite source of subconscious reprogramming and liberation—www.marisapeer.com.

What beliefs are holding you back? Check out Peer's Youtube clip "How To Teach Your Mind That Everything Is Available To You" here —https://www.youtube.com/watch?v=IKeaAbM2kJg

Tim Ferriss recommends a couple of apps for those wanting some help getting started with meditation—Headspace (www.headspace.com) or Calm (www.calm.com).

National Geographic: The Science of Stress: Portrait of a killer

https://www.youtube.com/watch?v=ZyBsy5SQxqU

Effects of Stress on Your Body

https://www.youtube.com/watch?v=1p6EeYwp1O4

Mindfulness training

Wellington-based Peter Fernando offers an introductory guided meditation which you can take further. He also meets with individuals and groups in Wellington for philosophical talks on mindfulness and Buddhism. Very enjoyable and great for the soul.

http://www.monthofmindfulness.info

Guided meditations

www.calm.com

Free app with guided meditations

http://eocinstitute.org/meditation/emotional-benefits-of-meditation/

Includes a comprehensive list of the benefits of meditation.

FURTHER RESOURCES

Johann Hari, a long-time suffer of depression, says research into the medicalisation of trauma and mental health led him to unearth the liberating facts that he says drug companies conceal—learn more about how you can heal yourself and the great placebo cover-up. https://www.theguardian.com/media/2018/jan/07/johann-hari-depression-brain-lost-connections-book-interview

BOOKS

Marc Lewis, a former addict and now a leading neuroscientist and lecturer blends first-hand experience of addiction with leading science in his book, T*he Biology of Desire: why addiction is not a disease*

Duff McKagan, the former bass guitarist of Guns N' Roses and one of the world's greatest rock musicians devised his own program of alcohol recovery. Read the inspiring story of a man who partied so hard he nearly died, *It's so Easy and Other Lies: Duff McKagan, The Autobiography.*

Russel Brand is a comedian and an addict. After being addicted to drugs, sex, fame, money and power, his book *Recovery: Freedom From Our Addictions* shares his journey, reinterprets The Twelve Step recovery process and champions the call for abstinence.

Drink: The Intimate Relationship Between Women and Alcohol—journalist and recovering alcoholic Anne Dowsett Johnson urges us all to wake up to the wilful blindness to the damages of drinking in our culture, and explores disturbing trends and false promises peddled by alcohol barons.

A great book with a strong and clear message—getting sober is not a loss is Ross Perry's *The Sober Entrepreneur: Change Your Family Tree.*

FURTHER RESOURCES

The Unexpected Joy of Being Sober: Discovering a happy, healthy, wealthy alcohol-free life by Catherine Gary contains a great overview of the sobriety movement and many reminders of the life-changing magic of sobriety. Yes, you can have fun, dance, be popular, look like a lunatic and not be drunk!

Fortify your superconscious power with Dr. Joe Dispenza— *Becoming Supernatural: How Common People Are Doing the Uncommon*

Power up with a new personality—read *Breaking the Habit of Being Yourself: How to Lose Your Mind and Create a New One* by Dr. Joe Dispenza.

Unleash the power of your mind by reading *You Are the Placebo: Making Your Mind Matter,* by Dr. Joe Dispenza.

The Upward Spiral: Using Neuroscience to Reverse the Course of Depression, Dr Alex Korb.

How to Survive and Thrive in Any Life Crisis, Dr. Al Siebert

Thrive: The Third Metric to Redefining Success and Creating a Happier Life, Arianna Huffington

(This book has great content throughout and some excellent resources listed in the back.)

The Power of Now: A Guide to Spiritual Enlightenment, Eckhart Tolle

The Book of Joy, The Dalai Lama and Archbishop Desmond Tutu

The Sleep Revolution: Transforming Your Life One Night at a Time, Arianna Huffington

Quiet the Mind: An Illustrated Guide on How to Meditate, Mathew Johnstone

Comfortable with Uncertainty: 108 Teachings on Cultivating Fearlessness and Compassion, Pema Chodron

Power vs. Force: The Hidden Determinants of Human Behavior, David R. Hawkins

Learn how to live an inspired life with Tarot cards and other oracles. Read Jessa Crispin's book, *The Creative Tarot: A Modern Guide to an Inspired Life.*

Check out all of Collette-Baron-Reid's books, including: *Uncharted: The Journey Through Uncertainty to Infinite Possibility* and *Messages from Spirit: The Extraordinary Power of Oracles, Omens, and Signs.*

PLEASE LEAVE A REVIEW

Word of mouth is the most powerful marketing force in the universe. If you found this book useful, I'd appreciate you rating this book and leaving a review. You don't have to say much—just a few words about how the book helped you learn something new or made you feel.

"Your books are a fantastic resource and until now I never even thought to write a review. Going forward I will be reviewing more books. So many great ones out there and I want to support the amazing people that write them."

Great reviews help people find good books that change lives.

Thank you so much! I appreciate you!

PS: If you enjoyed this, or any of my books, could you do me a huge favor and leave a review and help others by spreading the word about them and sharing links, or reviews on Facebook, Twitter, Instagram and other social networks.

STAY IN TOUCH

FOLLOW ME AND CONTINUE TO BE INSPIRED

www.cassandragaisford.com
www.twitter.com/cassandraNZ
www.instagram.com/cassandragaisford
www.facebook.com/cassandra.gaisford
http://www.youtube.com/cassandragaisfordnz
https://www.pinterest.com/cassandraNZ
www.linkedin.com/in/cassandragaisford

I invite you to join the sobriety experiment. Share your stories and experiences, we'd love to hear from you! To join, please visit our dedicated Facebook group— https://www.facebook.com/Sobrietyexperiment.

And please, do check out some of my videos where I share strategies and tips to drink less and love life more—http://www.youtube.com/cassandragaisfordnz

If you create a tasty non-alcoholic recipe or drink please share it with use—you'll find plenty of thirsty booze-free devotees.

STAY IN TOUCH

BLOG

Be inspired by regular posts to help you follow your bliss, slay self-doubt, and sustain healthy habits. You'll find a variety of articles and tips about people pursuing their passion and strategies to help you pursue yours—personally and professionally.
http://www.cassandragaisford.com

PRESENTATIONS

For information about products and workshops navigate to: www.cassandragaisford.com/contact/speaking

To ask Cassandra to come and speak at your workplace or conference, contact: cassandra@cassandragaisford.com

ABOUT THE AUTHOR

CASSANDRA GAISFORD is best known as *The Queen of Uplifting Inspiration.*

A former holistic therapist, award-winning artist, and #1 bestselling author. A corporate escapee, she now lives and works from her idyllic lifestyle property overlooking the Bay of Islands in New Zealand.

Cassandra's unique blend of business experience and qualifications (BCA, Dip Psych.), creative skills, and wellness and holistic training (Dip Counseling, Reiki Master Teacher) blends pragmatism and commercial savvy with rare and unique insight and out-of-the-box-thinking for anyone wanting to achieve an extraordinary life.

COPYRIGHT

Copyright © 2020 Cassandra Gaisford
Published by Blue Giraffe Publishing 2020

Blue Giraffe Publishing is a division of Worklife Solutions Ltd.

Cover Design by Cassandra Gaisford

All rights reserved. No part of this publication may be reproduced, distributed, or transmitted in any form or by any means, including photocopying, recording, or other electronic or mechanical methods, without the prior written permission of the author or publisher, except in the case of brief quotations embodied in reviews and certain other non-commercial uses permitted by copyright law.

Neither the publisher nor the author are engaged in rendering professional advice or services to the individual reader. The ideas, procedures, and suggestions contained in this book are not intended as a substitute for psychotherapy, counseling, or consulting with your physician.

COPYRIGHT

The intent of the author is only to offer information of a general nature to help you in your quest for emotional, physical, and spiritual well-being.

Any use of information in this book is at the reader's discretion and risk. Neither the author nor the publisher can be held responsible for any loss, claim or damage arising out of the use, or misuse, of the suggestions made, the failure to take medical advice or for any material on third party websites.

ISBN PRINT: 978-1-99-002007-0

ISBN EBOOK: 978-1-99-002005-6

First Edition

www.ingramcontent.com/pod-product-compliance
Lightning Source LLC
Chambersburg PA
CBHW020514080526
44583CB00013B/591

Praise for *Sincerely, Addison's Sister*

She lived with an addict, she loved an addict, and she lost an addict, but Jessica Akhrass found sense in senseless loss. She found a purpose. Five long years of visceral introspective reflection have brought before you, the reader, a gateway in Sincerely, Addison's Sister. *Walk through it and live in vivid detail the journey a courageous young woman takes. With God at her side, she stands in the gap. This prayerful sister in Christ makes the difference. Ralph Waldo Emerson once said, "It's not the destination, it's the journey." Will you go on the journey? I did. I thank you, Addison's Sister.*

---R. R. Stephens MSC, RTC
Clinical Therapist
St. Augustine, Florida

Sincerely, Addison's Sister, a Memoir *is an awesome book. As I read it, it took me down memory lane: the first phone call from Jessica, the first meeting (and trying to get her into the building), passing this impactful legislation, and just walking alongside Jessica throughout it all. The story brought out many emotions as I read it: sadness of the lives we lose to drugs, hurt for the men and women who are addicted and their families, and pride in Jessica, her mom, and all the others who helped fight this battle and wanted to address something so horrific and make life better for others. It also was convicting to me as a legislator about how important it is that I be compassionate, patient, and resourceful for the people who call me with the problems they are facing. In the busyness of the legislature, I won't forget—for Addison.*

---Tennessee Senator Becky Massey

The descriptions of Jessica's experience regarding her loss and pain are raw, honest, and compelling. [Her story] is very difficult to ignore, and the book is hard to put down because she is a truthful and passionate storyteller.

---Judge Chuck Cerny, Sessions Court, Knox County, Tennessee

Jessica's book demonstrates how anger can be transmuted as fuel for justice. Jessica's brother tragically succumbed to today's drug epidemic, and she transformed to become a resilient sister committed to changing prescription laws. Jessica was able to generate strength from a deep spiritual and mental perspective. The author shares a personal story that relates to millions of families impacted by drugs. This book is inspiring, and it takes readers on an emotional journey of sadness, anger, and redemption. This is an important book, and Jessica's story should be shared with everyone. I highly recommend this riveting tome.

---Dr. James Arthur Williams, author of *From Thug to Scholar*

Jessica, I have just finished your incredibly powerful book. Wow! You never cease to amaze me. The love you have for Addison and the way you shared your deepest emotions and journey of grief but allowed God to use you in a mighty way are gifts that will spread hope to others. Your faith and the love for your family is evident throughout the words you have so beautifully written. For anyone who has lost a loved one to this horrific disease, reading this book will provide comfort in knowing that you are never alone and that God will never leave you and will answer prayers if you are willing to surrender. With great pain comes great joy. Your willingness to step out and engage with others to break down stigma and shame will be comforting to all who read Sincerely, Addison's Sister. *You ARE a hero and one of the strongest people I know.*

---Karen Pershing, MPH, CPS II
Executive Director of Metro Drug Coalition